FUNDING A REVOLUTION

GOVERNMENT SUPPORT FOR COMPUTING RESEARCH

Committee on Innovations in Computing and Communications:
Lessons from History

Computer Science and Telecommunications Board

Commission on Physical Sciences, Mathematics, and Applications

National Research Council

NATIONAL ACADEMY PRESS
Washington, D.C. 1999

Support for this project was provided by the National Science Foundation under grant EIA-9529482. Additional support was provided by the Association for Computing Machinery and the Institute of Electrical and Electronics Engineers' Computer Society. Any opinions, findings, conclusions, or recommendations expressed in this material are those of the authors and do not necessarily reflect the views of the sponsors.

Library of Congress Catalog Card Number 98-88131
International Standard Book Number 0-309-06278-0

Additional copies of this report are available from:
National Academy Press (http://www.nap.edu)
2101 Constitution Ave., NW, Box 285
Washington, D.C. 20055
800-624-6242
202-334-3313 (in the Washington metropolitan area)

iii

Preface

Computing technology is widely touted as fast moving. Generations of products and their underlying electronics are introduced at intervals of 18 to 24 months, and the number and variety of computer- and communications-based goods and services are growing. Technology and industry experts believe that the double-digit rates of improvement experienced in the last couple of decades can be sustained for computer-based technologies over at least another decade if appropriate investments are made, but it is not clear what those investments should be and on what they depend. Similarly, there is little understanding of how to relate a seemingly strong and steady flow of new technology to the slower and more diffuse processes of assimilating new technology into the economy.

As described in *Evolving the High-Performance Computing and Communications Initiative to Support the Nation's Information Infrastructure,* also known as the Brooks-Sutherland report,[1] part of the reason for the tremendous advances in information technology since World War II has been the extraordinarily productive interplay of federally funded university research, federally and privately funded industrial research, and entrepreneurial companies founded and staffed by people who moved back and forth between universities and industry. To a degree that appears

---

[1]Computer Science and Telecommunications Board (CSTB), National Research Council. 1995. *Evolving the High Performance Computing and Communications Initiative to Support the Nation's Information Infrastructure.* National Academy Press, Washington, D.C.

uncommon in all but a few other disciplines, there has been a mix of people and ideas that highlights the limitations of the linear model of innovation, which posits that innovation proceeds sequentially from laboratory research to product development to manufacturing and sales. The dynamic nature of the process is evidenced by the fact that many of today's leading computer technology firms did not exist 20 years ago; many innovative firms that did exist have failed as businesses, but their innovations have endured or become the bases for subsequent developments; many familiar products and businesses can be traced back to federally funded research, often conducted at universities; and the ebb and flow of individual firms is fueled by the movement of people among universities, government laboratories, and private companies. Understanding this interplay and the ways the private sector has leveraged publicly funded activities is important for sustaining success in this arena. Understanding the changes in these elements—such as downward pressures on research support in industry and government—and the potential implications of such change is important for directing federal research and development efforts.

THE COMMITTEE AND ITS CHARGE

To better understand these issues, the National Science Foundation (NSF), along with the Association for Computing Machinery and the Institute of Electrical and Electronics Engineers, asked the Computer Science and Telecommunications Board (CSTB) of the National Research Council to initiate a study of lessons to be learned from the history of innovation in computing and communications technology. The committee was charged to expand on the analysis in the Brooks-Sutherland report to understand the way federal research funding affects the economy and creates new industries. The study was to address questions such as the following:

• How did the U.S. computing and communications industries achieve developmental fertility? On what have they built, and on what does their continuation depend?
• What are the interactions among players in academia, government, and industry? What is special or unique about these players and interactions compared to other technologies? Where are the frictions—where have the interactions foundered, and why?
• How can success be calibrated? How often are there unexpected successes and how well are they tracked? What are notable instances of failure, what were the underlying factors, and what has been learned? How well can we assess causality, as opposed to associations?

• What are the key lags, to what are they attributable, and how constant are they? How long does it take for an advance to show up as a commercial product—and how long does it take from commercial introduction to market acceptance?

To conduct this study, CSTB assembled a committee of 13 members and one special advisor with experience in both computing and communications technology and relevant social sciences. Members included (1) individuals involved in developing key computer and communications technologies who had experience in academic research, government research and development, and industrial research, development, and commercialization and (2) economists, historians, sociologists, and others with insight into the history of technology and the analysis of economic impacts of technology. This was a project in which experience, judgment, and expert interpretation were needed to produce balanced presentations of events and formulation of lessons. The study was strengthened by involving social science experts in relevant forms of data gathering, analysis, and interpretation.

The committee met six times between July 1996 and June 1998 to plan its course of action, meet with relevant experts, deliberate over its findings, draft its final report, and respond to reviewer comments. In order to combine a broad understanding of the major trends in computing and communications with more in-depth knowledge of particular fields and innovations, the committee took a two-pronged approach to the study. First, it examined the broad history of computing and communications, extending from early attempts to design and build computers in the post-World War II era to the present. The goal was not to document each innovation in computing and communications, but rather to identify the key trends in each historical era and identify the primary government activities that contributed to the industries' development. Data were gathered on federal and industrial funding levels for research and development in computing technology, as well as investments in research infrastructure and human resources.

Second, the committee developed case studies of five specific areas: relational databases, the development of the Internet and the World Wide Web, theoretical computer science, artificial intelligence, and virtual reality. These areas were selected because of the expertise of individual committee members and because they were believed to represent a broad range of federal roles in the innovation process. The case studies were not intended to be exhaustive histories of the topics investigated, but rather to provide illustrative examples that could inform the committee's attempt to discern lessons regarding the role of federal research funding in computing. As a result, they differ significantly in length, structure, and tone.

Nevertheless, the committee derived overarching themes from seemingly discrete events regarding the relationship between public and private investment, the roles of federal research funding in stimulating innovation, and characteristics of effective government support for research.

Additional information for the study was gathered through a series of interviews with key leaders in federal science and technology policy making and in computing research: Claude Barfield (American Enterprise Institute), Gordon Bell (formerly with the National Science Foundation), George Brown (U.S. House of Representatives), Mel Ciment (National Science Foundation), Fernando Corbato (Massachusetts Institute of Technology), Tice DeYoung (National Aeronautics and Space Administration), Howard Frank (Defense Advanced Research Projects Agency), Juris Hartmanis (National Science Foundation), Charles Holland (Air Force Office of Scientific Research), Anita K. Jones (Department of Defense), John Lehmann (National Science Foundation), John Machado (Naval Electronic Systems Command), Steven Squires (Corporation for National Research Initiatives), John Toole (National Coordination Office for Computing, Information, and Communications), Bruce Waxman (University Research Foundation), Gilbert Weigand (Department of Energy), and Patrick Winston (Massachusetts Institute of Technology). These interviews provided considerable guidance on policy debates surrounding federal funding of research and served to inform the committee's evolving set of conclusions. The interviews revealed a broad consensus regarding the importance of the federal government in funding research in computing and communications. Regardless of their political affiliations and different roles in the research enterprise, the experts interviewed for this study confirmed the value of federal funding in computing research, especially federal support for university research.

This report attempts to summarize, as concisely as possible, the main conclusions of the study while providing needed justification and support. As such, this report is not a comprehensive history of computing, nor is it a complete accounting of federal involvement in computing. Rather, it provides an overview of the innovation process in computing technology based on a select set of seemingly representative examples and buttressed by more comprehensive data. The lessons derived regarding the federal role in computing and communications will, it is hoped, provide relevant guidance for continued efforts in these fields.

ACKNOWLEDGMENTS

This report represents the cumulative and cooperative efforts of many people. The study committee, itself a blend of technologists, historians, and social scientists, worked tirelessly to overcome differences in cultural perspectives and predilections to form a more unified view of the history of computing and the government's role in supporting it. Committee members' contributions to the case studies and their deliberations formed the backbone of this project. Special thanks are due to David Mindell, assistant professor in the Science, Technology, and Society (STS) program at the Massachusetts Institute of Technology (MIT), who as a consultant to this project assisted in all aspects of its development—helping to define the study and its scope, participating in committee discussions, and drafting sections of the final document. Jed Gordon, an undergraduate in the STS program at MIT, played a key role in collecting and analyzing data on the contributions of various government organizations to computing research and in writing brief histories of specific federal research programs, such as Project Whirlwind and Project MAC. He also analyzed federal statistics on research funding in computing and educational support of computer science students. Hui Zeng, a graduate student in computer science at George Mason University, assisted in compiling and analyzing information about federal funding of computing research and development of human resources. Laura Ost, editor-consultant, helped to turn the original manuscript into a readable text.

Beyond those directly affiliated with the project were many others who contributed valuable information to the report. Jennifer Sue Bond, John Jankowski, Margaret Machen, Ronald Meeks, and Raymond Wolf at NSF were instrumental in providing a wide range of data on federal and industrial support for computing and communications. John Lehmann at NSF opened his historical files to the committee, making available a wealth of information about NSF programs in computing and communications. David Gries at Cornell University provided historical data from the Taulbee surveys, tracking the growth of academic computer science activities. Francis Narin and Anthony Breitzman at CHI Research, Inc., generated special tabulations of patent and citation data in computing. John Warwick, a computer science student at Carnegie Mellon University, built a Web crawler to gather data on U.S. patents in artificial intelligence. Margaret Taylor of Carnegie Mellon University's Department of Engineering and Public Policy helped to design the search and to sort and analyze the data.

The committee is also grateful to those who took time to meet with its members and provide relevant briefings: John Alic (then with the Johns Hopkins University School of Advanced International Studies), Paul Ceruzzi (National Air and Space Museum), Kenneth Flamm (Brookings Institution), John Hennessy (Stanford University), Robert Kahn (Corporation for National Research Initiatives), Nils Nilsen (Stanford University), Paul Romer (Stanford University), Ivan Sutherland (Sun Microsystems, Inc.), and William Wulf (National Academy of Engineering). Their input pro-

Acknowledgment of Reviewers

This report was reviewed by individuals chosen for their diverse perspectives and technical expertise, in accordance with procedures approved by the National Research Council's (NRC's) Report Review Committee. The purpose of this independent review is to provide candid and critical comments that will assist the authors and the NRC in making the published report as sound as possible and to ensure that the report meets institutional standards for objectivity, evidence, and responsiveness to the study charge. The contents of the review comments and draft manuscript remain confidential to protect the integrity of the deliberative process. We wish to thank the following individuals for their participation in the review of this report:

Robert Aaron, AT&T Bell Laboratories (retired),
John Armstrong, IBM Corporation (retired),
William Aspray, Computing Research Associates,
Daniel Bobrow, Xerox Palo Alto Research Center,
Lewis N. Branscomb, Harvard University,
Donald Chamberlin, IBM Almaden Research Center,
Lynn Conway, University of Michigan,
Stephen Cook, University of Toronto,
John L. Hennessy, Stanford University,
Richard Herman, University of Maryland,
Robert Lucky, Bellcore,
Arthur Norberg, University of Minnesota,

Fernando Pereira, AT&T Laboratories Research,
Alex Roland, Duke University,
Richard Rosenbloom, Harvard University,
Herbert Simon, Carnegie Mellon University,
Ivan Sutherland, Sun Microsystems, Inc.,
John Swets, BBN Corporation, and
Keith Uncapher, Corporation for Networking Research Initiatives.

Although the individuals listed above provided many constructive comments and suggestions, responsibility for the final content of this report rests solely with the study committee and the NRC.

Contents

Boxes, Figures, and Tables

FIGURES

TABLES

FUNDING A REVOLUTION

Executive Summary

At a time when the U.S. style of competitive market capitalism attracts the world's attention—even its envy—and U.S. computer firms dominate the global marketplace, it is difficult to recall and acknowledge that the federal government has played a major role in launching and giving momentum to the computer revolution, which now takes pride of place among the nation's recent technological achievements. Federal funding not only financed development of most of the nation's early digital computers, but also has continued to enable breakthroughs in areas as wide ranging as computer time-sharing, the Internet, artificial intelligence, and virtual reality as the industry has matured. Federal investment also has supported the building of physical infrastructure needed for leading-edge research and the education of undergraduate and graduate students who now work in industry and at academic research centers.

The computer revolution is not simply a technical change; it is a sociotechnical revolution comparable to an industrial revolution. The British Industrial Revolution of the late 18th century not only brought with it steam and factories, but also ushered in a modern era characterized by the rise of industrial cities, a politically powerful urban middle class, and a new working class. So, too, the sociotechnical aspects of the computer revolution are now becoming clear. Millions of workers are flocking to computing-related industries. Firms producing microprocessors and software are challenging the economic power of firms manufacturing automobiles and producing oil. Detroit is no longer the symbolic center of the U.S. industrial empire; Silicon Valley now conjures up visions

1

of enormous entrepreneurial vigor. Men in boardrooms and gray flannel suits are giving way to the casually dressed young founders of start-up computer and Internet companies. Many of these entrepreneurs had their early hands-on computer experience as graduate students conducting federally funded university research.

As the computer revolution continues and private companies increasingly fund innovative activities, the federal government continues to play a major role, especially by funding research. Given the successful history of federal involvement, several questions arise: Are there lessons to be drawn from past successes that can inform future policy making in this area? What future roles might the government play in sustaining the information revolution and helping to initiate other technological developments? This report reviews the history of innovation in computing (and related communications technologies) to elucidate the role the federal government has played by funding computing research and to identify factors that have contributed to the nation's success in this field.[1] It draws on a series of case studies that trace the lineage of innovations in particular subdisciplines of computing and on a more general historical review of the industry since World War II. The lessons derived from this examination are intended to guide ongoing efforts to shape federal policy in this field (Box ES.1).

GOVERNMENT-INDUSTRY-UNIVERSITY INTERACTION

Innovation in computing stems from a complementary relationship among government, industry, and universities. In this complex arrangement, government agencies and private companies fund research that is conducted primarily in university and industry research laboratories and is incorporated into myriad new products, processes, and services. While the contributions of industry to the computing revolution are manifest in the range of new products, processes, and services offered, those of the federal government are harder to discern. Nevertheless, federal funding of major computing initiatives has often contributed substantially to the development and deployment of commercial technologies. Commercial developments, similarly, have contributed to government endeavors.

The federal government has played a critical role in supporting the research that underlies computer-based products and services. From less than $10 million in 1960, federal funding for research in computer science climbed to almost $1 billion in 1995. Federal expenditures on research in electrical engineering (which includes semiconductor and communications technologies—necessary underpinnings for computing) have fluctuated between $800 million and $1 billion since the 1970s. Such funding has constituted a significant fraction of all research funds in the comput-

BOX ES.1
Why a Historical Approach?

Science and technology policy issues are usually approached in an analytical and quantitative way that projects the future from the present by extrapolating from quantitative data. A historical approach, as used in this report, provides a different perspective. History offers empirical evidence of the success and failure of past policies and allows patterns to be discovered that can inform future decisions. It allows analogies to be drawn between events that occurred decades apart but that may be applicable in the future. Furthermore, historical narrative can accommodate messy complexity more easily than can a tightly structured analytical essay, and it allows reflection on long-term process development and evolution. The case studies in this report present finely nuanced accounts that convey the ambiguities and contradictions common to real-life experiences.

Of course, history is limited in its ability to serve as a guide to the future. History cannot suggest what would have happened if circumstances had changed in the past. For example, history can show the influence of federal funding on historical innovations in computing, but it cannot suggest what directions might have been taken without federal support. In addition, teasing out lessons from history that can inform the future is a difficult task. Past outcomes are often tied to specific circumstances. The success or failure of specific research programs, for example, may be influenced as much by the particular people involved as by the amount of funding available. The case studies presented in this report attempt to overcome some of the limitations of history as a guide by examining events that occurred at various points in time and identifying lessons that many, if not all, of the cases offer. In this way, they can contribute to judgments about basic policies that are effective in different contexts.

---

ing field (Figure ES.1). The vast majority of this funding has been awarded to industry and university researchers, where it has supported innovative work in computing and, to a larger extent, communications (see Chapter 3 for detailed information on spending patterns).

Federal research funding plays an important role in supporting university efforts in computing. Federal support has constituted roughly 70 percent of total university research funding in computer science and electrical engineering since 1976. This funding has had several effects. First, it has promoted advances in fields such as computer graphics, artificial intelligence, and computer architecture: algorithms for rendering three-dimensional graphics images, expert systems for assisting in drug design, and time-shared computing systems all derive from federally funded university research. Beyond these direct contributions to the technology base, federal funding for universities has had other benefits as well. It has played a critical role in educating students in the computing field. In computer science departments at universities such as the Massachusetts

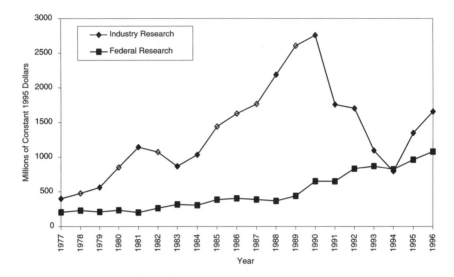

FIGURE ES.1 Federal and industry funding for computing research, 1977-1996. Industry research, as shown, consists of company-funded research in the computing and office equipment industry; it does not include company-funded research in other computing-related industries such as communications equipment, semiconductors, or computing and communications services. Government-funded research, as shown, consists of total federal funding for research in computer science. Industry research data for 1978, 1980, 1982, 1985-1987, and 1989 were estimated from data on total research and development expenditures and from the ratio of expenditures for research to expenditures for research and development in years for which actual data were available.
SOURCE: Federal research funding from NSF (1998b), Table 25; industry research funding compiled from the 1979-1998 editions of the annual National Science Foundation report *Research and Development in Industry*.

Institute of Technology (MIT), Stanford University, the University of California at Berkeley (UC-Berkeley), and Carnegie Mellon University, over half of all graduate students receive financial support from the federal government, mostly in the form of research assistantships. In addition, most of the funding used by academic computer science and electrical engineering departments to purchase research equipment comes from federal agencies. By placing computing equipment in engineering schools and universities, the government has made possible hands-on learning experiences for countless young engineers and scientists and has enabled university researchers to continue their work.

The effects of federal support for computing research are difficult to quantify but pervasive. Patent data, although a limited indicator of innovation, provide strong evidence of the links between government-supported research and innovation in computing. More than half of the papers cited in computing patent applications acknowledge government funding (see Chapter 3).[2] More specific evidence of the value of federally funded research derives from a close examination of particular innovations. Each of the major areas examined in the five case studies presented in Part II of this report—relational databases, the Internet, theoretical computer science, artificial intelligence, and virtual reality—benefited from federal research funding (Box ES.2). Such funding provided a means for sustaining research in universities and industry and complemented research expenditures by industry.

LESSONS FROM HISTORY

Why has federal support been so effective in stimulating innovation in computing? Although much has depended on the unique characteristics of individual research programs and their participants, several common factors have played an important part. Primary among them is that federal support for research has tended to *complement*, rather than preempt, industry investments in research. Effective federal research has concentrated on work that industry has limited incentive to pursue: long-term, fundamental research; large system-building efforts that require the talents of diverse communities of scientists and engineers; and work that might displace existing, entrenched technologies. Furthermore, successful federal programs have tended to be organized in ways that accommodate the uncertainties in scientific and technological research. Support for computing research has come from a diversity of funding agencies; program managers have formulated projects broadly where possible, modifying them in response to preliminary results; and projects have fostered productive collaboration between universities and industry. The lessons below expand on these factors. The first three lessons address the complementary nature of government- and industry-sponsored research; the final four highlight elements of the organizational structure and management of effective federally funded research programs. Greater elaboration of these lessons is provided in Chapter 5 of this report.

1. Government supports long-range, fundamental research that industry cannot sustain.

Federally funded programs have been successful in supporting long-term research into fundamental aspects of computing, such as computer graphics and artificial intelligence, whose practical benefits often take years to demonstrate. Work on speech recognition, for example, which

BOX ES.2
Case Studies of Innovation in Computing

The case studies contained in Chapters 6 though 10 of this report provide detailed accounts of innovation in particular areas of computing: relational databases,
the Internet, theoretical computer science, artificial intelligence, and virtual reality.
Representing a range of technologies and time frames, the cases demonstrate significant interaction among industry, universities, and government in developing and
commercializing new computing technology. The lessons learned from these cases
highlight the variation and similarities in the interactions, as well as key elements of
the innovation process. The following brief summary of the case studies includes
limited examples of the results of federal investments in research. Readers are
directed to the full case studies for a more complete description of federal involvement in these areas.

Relational Databases

Development of relational database technology—now a billion-dollar industry
dominated by U.S. companies such as Informix, Sybase, IBM, and Oracle—relied on
the complementary efforts of industry and government-sponsored academics. Although originating within IBM, relational database technology was not rapidly commercialized because it competed with IBM's existing database products. The National Science Foundation (NSF) funded the Ingres project at the University of
California at Berkeley, which refined and promulgated the technology, thus spreading expertise and rekindling market interest in relational databases. Many of the
companies now producing relational databases have on their staffs—or were founded
by—participants in Ingres.

Internet

Development of the Internet grew largely out of government-sponsored research,
development, and deployment programs. Building on research conducted by Paul
Baran and Donald Davies, the Defense Advanced Research Projects Agency
(DARPA, during certain periods called ARPA) funded the development of a packet-
switched network, the ARPANET, by industry and academia. It subsequently supported creation of the protocols used for interconnecting networks across the Internet. To further its goals of supporting research and educational infrastructure, NSF
funded development of networks for research and educational uses and, in effect,
laid the groundwork for today's Internet. The World Wide Web and browser technology currently used to navigate the Internet were devised by Timothy Berners-Lee
at CERN and Marc Andreesen, then a student at the NSF-sponsored National Center
for Supercomputing Applications at the University of Illinois at Urbana-Champaign.

Theoretical Computer Science

Typically viewed as the province of academia, theoretical computer science has
benefited from the efforts of both industry and university researchers. Although some
advances—such as number theory and cryptology—have translated directly into
practice, many others (such as finite state machines and complexity theory) have
entered engineering practice and education more subtly, influencing the way researchers and product developers approach and think about problems. Progress in
theory has both informed practice and been driven by practical developments that
have challenged or outpaced existing concepts.

Artificial Intelligence

Work in artificial intelligence broadly addresses capabilities for enabling machines (computers) to exhibit characteristics of human intelligence, such as understanding language, learning, and problem solving. Support for research in artificial intelligence (AI) over the past three decades has come largely from government agencies, such as DARPA, NSF, and the Office of Naval Research (ONR). Firms that initiated AI research programs in the 1960s scaled back their programs once they realized that commercial applications lay many years in the future. Continued federal investments allowed a number of advances in areas such as expert systems, speech recognition, and image processing. For example, speech recognition systems, which had been the focus of DARPA funding in the early 1970s, finally entered the marketplace in the mid-1990s. Many other AI technologies have been commercialized and embedded into a range of new products.

Virtual Reality

Research in virtual reality attempts to develop technologies for creating computer-generated environments that are indistinguishable from real ones. Innovation in virtual reality stems from the convergence of advances in numerous interrelated fields, such as computer graphics, psychology, computer networking, robotics, and computer hardware. It has been both pushed by technological advances in these underlying areas and pulled by creative attempts to devise particular applications, such as flight simulators, entertainment, virtual surgery, engineering design, and tools for molecular modeling. Much of the underlying research has been conducted by universities, with federal support from agencies such as DARPA, NSF, and the National Aeronautics and Space Administration, but industry has played an important role in commercializing technologies and identifying key research needs. Interdisciplinary research efforts have been the norm in this field, as exemplified by the collaborative research effort between the computer graphics laboratory at the University of North Carolina at Chapel Hill and Hewlett-Packard.

was begun in the early 1970s (some started even earlier), took until 1997 to generate a successful product for enabling personal computers to recognize continuous speech. Similarly, fundamental algorithms for shading three-dimensional graphics images, which were developed with defense funding in the 1960s, entered consumer products only in the 1990s, though they were available in higher-performance machines much earlier. These algorithms are now used in a range of products in the health care, entertainment, and defense industries.

Industry does fund some long-range work, but the benefits of fundamental research are generally too distant and too uncertain to receive significant industry support. Moreover, the results of such work are generally so broad that it is difficult for any one firm to capture them for its own benefit and also prevent competitors from doing so (see Chapter 2). Not surprisingly, companies that have tended to support the most fundamental research have been those, like AT&T Corporation and IBM

Corporation, that are large and have enjoyed a dominant position in their respective markets. As the computing industry has become more competitive, even these firms have begun to link their research more closely with corporate objectives and product development activities. Companies that have become more dominant, such as Microsoft Corporation and Intel Corporation, have increased their support for fundamental research.

2. Government supports large system-building efforts that have advanced technology and created large communities of researchers.

In addition to funding long-term fundamental research, federal programs have been effective in supporting the construction of large systems that have both motivated research and demonstrated the feasibility of new technological approaches. The Defense Advanced Research Projects Agency's (DARPA's) decision to construct a packet-switched network (called the ARPANET) to link computers at its many contractor sites prompted considerable research on networking protocols and the design of packet switches and routers. It also led to the development of structures for managing large networks, such as the domain name system, and development of useful applications, such as e-mail. Moreover, by constructing a successful system, DARPA demonstrated the value of large-scale packet-switched networks, motivating subsequent deployment of other networks, like the National Science Foundation's NSFNET, which formed the basis of the Internet.

Efforts to build large systems demonstrate that, especially in computing, innovation does not flow simply and directly from research, through development, to deployment. Development often precedes research, and research rationalizes, or explains, technology developed earlier through experimentation. Hence attempts to build large systems can identify new problems that need to be solved. Electronic telecommunications systems were in use long before Claude Shannon developed modern communications theory in the late 1940s, and the engineers who developed the first packet switches for routing messages through the ARPANET advanced empirically beyond theory. Building large systems generated questions for research, and the answers, in turn, facilitated more development.

Much of the success of major system-building efforts derives from their ability to bring together large groups of researchers from academia and industry who develop a common vocabulary, share ideas, and create a critical mass of people who subsequently extend the technology. Examples include the ARPANET and the development of the Air Force's Semi-Automatic Ground Environment (SAGE) project in the 1950s. Involving researchers from MIT, IBM, and other research laboratories, the SAGE project sparked innovations ranging from real-time computing to core memories that found widespread acceptance throughout the computer industry. Many of the pioneers in computing learned through hands-on experimentation with SAGE in the 1950s and early 1960s.[3] They subsequently staffed the companies and laboratories of the nascent computing and communications revolution. The impact of SAGE was felt over the course of several decades.

3. Federal research funding has expanded on earlier industrial research.

In several cases, federal research funding has been important in advancing a technology to the point of commercialization after it was first explored in an industrial research laboratory. For example, IBM pioneered the concept of relational databases but did not commercialize the technology because of its perceived potential to compete with more-established IBM products. National Science Foundation (NSF)-sponsored research at UC-Berkeley allowed continued exploration of this concept and brought the technology to the point that it could be commercialized by several start-up companies—and more-established database companies (including IBM). This pattern was also evident in the development of reduced instruction set computing (RISC). Though developed at IBM, RISC was not commercialized until DARPA funded additional research at UC-Berkeley and Stanford University as part of its Very Large Scale Integrated Circuit (VLSI) program of the late 1970s and early 1980s. A variety of companies subsequently brought RISC-based products to the marketplace, including IBM, the Hewlett-Packard Company, the newly formed Sun Microsystems, Inc., and another start-up, MIPS Computer Systems. For both relational databases and VLSI, federal funding helped create a community of researchers who validated and improved on the initial work. They rapidly diffused the technology throughout the community, leading to greater competition and more rapid commercialization.

4. Computing research has benefited from diverse sources of government support.

Research in computing has been supported by multiple federal agencies, including the Department of Defense (DOD)—most notably the Defense Advanced Research Projects Agency and the military services—the National Science Foundation, National Aeronautics and Space Administration (NASA), Department of Energy (DOE), and National Institutes of Health (NIH). Each has its own mission and means of supporting research. DARPA has tended to concentrate large research grants in so-called centers of excellence, many of which over time have matured into some of the country's leading academic computer departments. The

Office of Naval Research (ONR) and NSF, in contrast, have supported individual researchers at a more diverse set of institutions. They have awarded numerous peer-review grants to individual researchers, especially in universities. NSF has also been active in supporting educational and research needs more broadly, awarding graduate student fellowships and providing funding for research equipment and infrastructure. Each of these organizations employs a different set of mechanisms to support research, from fundamental research to mission-oriented research and development projects, to procurement of hardware and software.

Such diversity offers many benefits. It not only provides researchers with many potential sources of support, but also helps ensure exploration of a diverse set of research topics and consideration of a range of applications. DARPA, NASA, and NIH have all supported work in expert systems, for example, but because the systems have had different applications—decision aids for pilots, tools for determining the structure of molecules on other planets, and medical diagnostics—each agency has supported different groups of researchers who tried different approaches.

Perhaps more importantly, no single approach to investing in research is by itself a sufficient means of stimulating innovation; each plays a role in the larger system of innovation. Different approaches work in concert, ensuring continued support for research areas as they pass through subsequent stages of development. Organizations such as NSF and ONR often funded seed work in areas that DARPA, with its larger contract awards, later magnified and expanded. DARPA's Project MAC, which gave momentum to time-shared computing in the 1960s, for example, built on earlier NSF-sponsored work on MIT's Compatible Time-Sharing System. Conversely, NSF has provided continued support for projects that DARPA pioneered but was unwilling to sustain after the major research challenges were resolved. For example, NSF funds the Metal Oxide Semiconductor Implementation Service (MOSIS)—a system developed at Xerox PARC and institutionalized by DARPA that provides university researchers with access to fast-turnaround semiconductor manufacturing services. Once established, this program no longer matched DARPA's mission to develop leading-edge technologies, but it did match NSF's mission to support university education and research infrastructure. Similarly, NSF built on DARPA's pioneering research on packet-switched networks to construct the NSFNET, a precursor to today's Internet.

5. Strong program managers and flexible management structures have enhanced the effectiveness of computing research.

Research in computing, as in other fields, is a highly unpredictable endeavor. The results of research are not evident at the start, and their most important contributions often differ from those originally envisioned. Few expected that the Navy's attempt to build a programmable aircraft simulator in the late 1940s would result in the development of the first real-time digital computer (the Whirlwind); nor could DARPA program managers have anticipated that their early experiments on packet switching would evolve into the Internet and later the World Wide Web.

The potential for unanticipated outcomes of research has two implications for federal policy. First, it suggests that measuring the results of federally funded research programs is extremely difficult. Projects that appear to have failed often make significant contributions to later technology development or achieve other objectives not originally envisioned. Furthermore, research creates many intangible products, such as knowledge and educated researchers whose value is hard to quantify. Second, it implies that federal mechanisms for funding and managing research need to recognize the uncertainties inherent in computing research and to build in sufficient flexibility to accommodate mid-course changes and respond to unanticipated results.

A key element in agencies' ability to maintain flexibility in the past has been their program managers, who have responsibility for initiating, funding, and overseeing research programs. The funding and management styles of program managers at DARPA during the 1960s and 1970s, for example, reflected an ability to marry visions for technological progress with strong technical expertise and an understanding of the uncertainties of the research process. Many of these program managers and office directors were recruited from academic and industry research laboratories for limited tours of duty. They tended to lay down broad guidelines for new research areas and to draw specific project proposals from principal investigators, or researchers, in academic computer centers. This style of funding and management resulted in the government stimulating innovation with a light touch, allowing researchers room to pursue new avenues of inquiry. In turn, it helped attract top-notch program managers to federal agencies. With close ties to the field and its leading researchers, they were trusted by—and trusted in—the research community.[4]

This funding style resulted in great advances in areas as diverse as computer graphics, artificial intelligence, networking, and computer architectures. Although mechanisms are clearly needed to ensure accountability and oversight in government-sponsored research, history demonstrates the benefits of instilling these values in program managers and providing them adequate support to pursue promising research directions.

6. Collaboration between industry and university researchers has facili-tated the commercialization of computing research and maintained its relevance.

Innovation in computing requires the combined talents of university and industry researchers. Bringing them together has helped ensure that industry taps into new academic research and that university researchers understand the challenges facing industry. Such collaboration also helps facilitate the commercialization of technology developed in a university setting. All of the areas described in this report's case studies—relational databases, the Internet, theoretical computer science, artificial intelligence, and virtual reality—involved university and industry participants. Other projects examined, such as SAGE, Project MAC, and very large scale inte-grated circuits, demonstrate the same phenomenon.

Collaboration between industry and universities can take many forms. Some projects combine researchers from both sectors on the same project team. Other projects involve a transition from academic research labora-tories to industry (via either the licensing of key patents or the creation of new start-up companies) once the technology matures sufficiently. As the case studies demonstrate, effective linkages between industry and universities tended to emerge from projects, rather than being thrust upon them. Project teams assembled to build large systems included the range of skills needed for a particular project. University researchers often sought out productive avenues for transferring research results to indus-try, whether linking with existing companies or starting new ones. Such techniques have often been more effective than explicit attempts to en-courage collaboration, many of which have foundered due to the often conflicting time horizons of university and industry researchers.

7. Organizational innovation and adaptation are necessary elements of federal research support.

Over time, new government organizations have formed to support computing research, and organizations have continually evolved in order to better match their structure to the needs of the research and policy-making communities. In response to proposals by Vannevar Bush and others that the country needed an organization to fund basic research, especially in the universities, for example, Congress established the Na-tional Science Foundation in 1950. A few years earlier, the Navy founded the Office of Naval Research to draw on science and engineering resources in the universities. In the early 1950s during an intense phase of the Cold War, the military services became the preeminent funders of computing and communications. The Soviet Union's launching of Sputnik in 1957 raised fears in Congress and the country that the Soviets had forged ahead of the United States in advanced technology. In response, the U.S. Department of Defense, pressured by the Eisenhower administration, established the Advanced Research Projects Agency (ARPA, now DARPA) to fund technological projects with military implications. In 1962 DARPA created the Information Processing Techniques Office (IPTO), whose initial research agenda gave priority to further development of computers for command-and-control systems.

With the passage of time, new organizations have emerged, and old ones have often been reformed or reinvented to respond to new national imperatives and counter bureaucratic trends. DARPA's IPTO has transformed itself several times to bring greater coherence to its research efforts and to respond to technological developments. NSF in 1967 established the Office of Computing Activities and in 1986 formed the Computer and Information Sciences and Engineering (CISE) Directorate to couple and coordinate support for research, education, and infrastructure in computer science. In the 1980s NSF, which customarily has focused on basic research in universities, also began to encourage joint academic-industrial research centers through its Engineering Research Centers program. With the relative increase in industrial support of research and development in recent years, federal agencies such as NSF have rationalized their funding policies to complement short-term industrial R&D. Federal funding of long-term, high-risk initiatives continues to have a high priority.

As this history suggests, federal funding agencies will need to continue to adjust their strategies and tactics as national needs and imperatives change. The Cold War imperative shaped technological history during much of the last half-century. International competitiveness served as a driver of government funding of computing and communications during the late 1980s and early 1990s. With the end of the Cold War and the globalization of industry, the U.S. computing industries need to maintain their high rates of innovation, and federal structures for managing computing research may need to change to ensure that they are appropriate for this new environment.

CONCLUSION

As this report demonstrates, the federal government has played a significant role in the development of the computing industry. Although difficult to quantify precisely, the returns from federal investments in computing and communications have been tremendous. Many of the leading concepts being exploited today—from virtual reality to the Internet—derive from research funded by federal agencies. As the industry has grown, the role of the government has evolved, but it has remained essential in supporting long-term research and efforts to build large systems. The computing industry has advanced at an astonishing rate, driven by competition and commercial reward. Research—funded by the government and privately—has made that remarkable progress possible.

Policymakers attempting to develop sound science and technology policies and promote the continued vitality of the computing industry can find useful guidance in history. The explorations of Meriwether Lewis and William Clark suggest an analogy. They drew on numerous stories told by others, including native Americans and fur traders, who had tentatively explored the lands west of the Mississippi. From these histories they imaginatively created with broad brush strokes a picture of the frontier and prepared for the host of contingencies that they might encounter. So, too, can the stories contained in the case studies in this report provide illustrations to help policymakers address the challenges they face as computing enters the next millennium.

NOTES

1.   A variety of other federal policies have shaped the computer industry and influenced computing research. These include enforcement of antitrust laws, patent policy and intellectual property protection more generally, and assistance in developing technical standards. The granting of a monopoly to AT&T in the telephone industry exerted great influence on research in communications. DOE has also stimulated advances in high-performance computing through procurement of supercomputers. This report focuses on federal research funding, not because these other factors are not important, but because of the range of public policy issues currently surrounding federal research investments (see Chapter 1).

2.   This estimate is based on an analysis of patent citations in the computing field conducted specifically for this project by Francis Narin and Anthony F. Breitzman at CHI Research, Inc., Haddon Heights, N.J.

3.   The lessons implicit in the SAGE project can be compared to the learning experiences associated with the construction of the Erie Canal early in the 19th century. Engineers then referred to the Erie as the leading engineering school in the United States.

4.   The degree of trust between office or program managers and the research community was facilitated by the many common bonds they shared. In the 1960s and 1970s, Licklider, Sutherland, and Roberts, for example, all had ties to MIT.

Part I

The Federal Role in
Computing Research

1

Introduction

The latter part of the 20th century has witnessed a revolution in computing and related communications technology. As earlier eras witnessed transformations wrought by steam power, internal combustion engines, and electricity, the 1990s have seen the development, elaboration, and diffusion of a general-purpose technology that is transforming society. Computing technology has infiltrated all corners of society, from the workplace and the laboratory to the classroom and the home, changing the way people conduct business, govern, learn, and entertain themselves.

The computer revolution is predicated on 50 years of effort by industry, universities, and government. Together, these entities have created an innovation system that has vastly improved the capabilities of computer-related technologies, from semiconductors to computers, and from software to data communications networks. Real-time, online operating systems, graphical user interfaces, the mouse, the Internet, high-performance computers, and microprocessors are all offspring of the productive interaction among government, universities, and industry in the innovation process. Understanding the interplay among industry, government, and universities in developing new computing technology is an important step in framing both public and private policies that will shape future research activities. As the nation attempts to maintain its leadership in computing, business leaders, policymakers, and university researchers will need to understand the sources of their past success.

This report examines the history of innovation in the field of computing and related communications technologies with emphasis on the role of the federal government in supporting computing research.[1] It provides an overview of the federal government's investments in the nation's research infrastructure for computing and, through a series of historical case studies, illustrates the ways in which these investments have influenced the field. As such, the report is not a comprehensive history of computing, but rather an attempt to provide insight into the role of federal research funding in the innovation process for computing. It is hoped that the lessons learned from this report will provide guidance to policymakers attempting to plot the course of federal research investments over the next several decades.

USING HISTORY AS A GUIDE

Historical analysis is one means of informing debates over the role of the federal government in computing research. History provides empirical evidence of the success and failure of different policies over time, and it offers evidence from which patterns can be seen and conclusions drawn about the funding process in particular and innovation in general. Examining changes in government support for technology over many decades helps eliminate spurious events resulting from short-lived fads, political and technical fashions, and individual anomalies. It allows recognition of the often long time lags between initial funding of research and its subsequent incorporation into commercial products. Similarly, it puts into perspective the frequently long lag times between the implementation of policies and the realization of their major and lasting effects.

Case studies are a standard tool of historical analysis, allowing one to move more deeply into the mix of events, people, and organizations associated with the funding of computer research. Case studies provide an intimacy with history akin to that experienced by persons who lived it. They present the messy details of real-life experiences not available in abstract, quantitative analysis. At the same time, case studies are limited in their analytical capabilities. To some extent, the conclusions learned from case studies are conditioned by the particular cases examined (see Box 1.1 for an example). As economist Richard Nelson noted after conducting case studies of seven major U.S. industries to derive lessons for federal policy, broad analogies are difficult to identify and outcomes often are tied closely to special circumstances of the industry, a specific technical problem, or the policy approach taken. "It is very hard to tease out from the historical record clear cut lessons that are applicable to future policy decisions," he concluded. Nevertheless, he noted that it is possible to make judgments about the kinds of policies that are feasible and effective in different contexts (Nelson, 1982, p. 454).

This report uses a series of case studies, supplemented by a historical

BOX 1.1
Drawing Conclusions from Case Studies

The selection of case studies can greatly influence the nature of the conclusions drawn from them. For example, examination of the development of voice telephony networks would suggest lessons different from those to be found in case studies of data networking. A case study of telephony might suggest that computing research would witness a decline in government funding and the rise of other types of government support, as well as industry support for research and development. It would demonstrate the role of the federal patent system in providing companies and individual inventors a means for protecting their innovations long enough to recover research and development funds, stimulating further expenditures. It would suggest the possibility of government support for—and industrial inclination toward—mergers, monopolies, and regulation. Considering the negative attitude today toward government regulation of private enterprises, the likelihood of a return to regulated monopoly seems unlikely. Yet, contrary to conventional wisdom, private enterprise has in the past favored government regulation under certain circumstances. During the first quarter of this century, for example, state governments supported the spread of telephone service through the granting of natural monopolies coupled with government regulation.[1] Possession of a natural monopoly allowed AT&T to levy a supplemental charge on customers that provided funds for research at Bell Laboratories.

---

[1]A classic example from the electric power industry involves the Commonwealth Edison Company of Chicago asking the State of Illinois to grant it a natural monopoly in a large region surrounding Chicago. In exchange, in 1914 Commonwealth Edison readily accepted state regulation of price and service. Previously, the City of Chicago had regulated Commonwealth Edison and limited the company's area of supply to the city limits. Other urban utilities followed a similar policy. This resulted in a cascading effect. The natural monopoly allowed the utilities to avoid competition resulting from duplication of service.

overview of federal involvement in computing, to derive lessons regarding innovation in computing technology. The cases in this report build on earlier work by the Computer Science and Telecommunications Board (CSTB, 1995a) that identified the role of federal research funding in stimulating innovation in several areas of computing and communications (Figure 1.1). The case studies are not intended to be definitive surveys of the various subjects; nor are they necessarily fully representative of the interactions of federal research funding with other elements of the nation's innovation system. Instead, they are narratives that illustrate the kinds of influences federal research funding has exerted on the innovation system and that highlight the interactions among government, universities, and industry. The cases represent a diversity of examples, differing in the time periods they cover, the technologies they address, and the type of

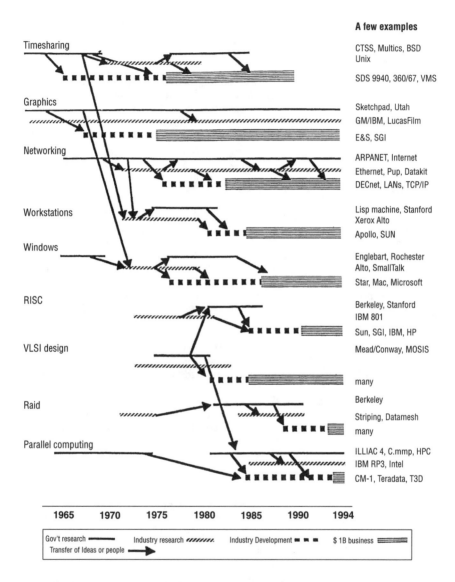

FIGURE 1.1 Illustrations of the role of government-sponsored computing research and development in the creation of innovative ideas and industries. RAID, redundant arrays of inexpensive disks; RISC, reduced instruction set computing. SOURCE: CSTB (1995a), Figure 1.2, p. 20.

government involvement. They range from limited discussions of particular projects and programs (such as relational databases and the Internet) to broader discussions of federal support for various fields of inquiry (such as artificial intelligence and virtual reality).

Applying historical lessons to future policy making is a difficult exercise, one historians justifiably are reluctant to do. A stock answer is that history does not repeat itself, but this response is misleading. From everyday observation, professional historians and others know that comparable, recurring events are embedded in long-term trends and enduring factors. The impressive ability of statisticians to predict the level of automobile accidents on national holidays, the accurate predictions of trends in economics and demography, and the long-term forecasts of particular cyclical effects of climate changes on agricultural production and energy consumption provide examples of the durability of trends and the persistence of circumstances. French historian Fernand Braudel in his study, *The Mediterranean and the Mediterranean World in the Age of Philip II*, writes persuasively of the influence of the physical environment upon society and the resulting slow but perceptible rhythms of social behavior: "a history in which all change is slow, a history of constant repetition, ever-recurring cycles" (Braudel, 1972, pp. 21-22).

Historians use two processes to apply the past to the future: projection and analogy. Projection, in a sense, moves the past into the future in a continuous, linear way. It assumes that conditions prevalent in the past will continue to exist largely unchanged in the future and that yesterday's lessons apply equally well to tomorrow's problems. Analogies, on the other hand, presume a discontinuity between present and future. They assume that the future will not be like the recent past, but may in fact resemble the more distant past when circumstances differed. Analogies raise interesting and unorthodox questions that can inform policy making and business strategy (see Box 1.2 for an illustration of analogy in scientific thought), but the art of drawing analogies requires a sensitive touch in choosing what is comparable. Analogies can be dramatically misleading if events and trends in the past are wrongly assumed to have arisen from conditions and contexts that will repeat themselves in the future. History is replete with examples of poorly applied analogies that resulted in poor decisions.[2] Thus, great care must be taken in extrapolating from the past to the future, and it must be recognized that reasoning through analogy may prove erroneous in detail, even if it allows anticipation of events and outcomes.

Clearly, the future of computing will differ from the history of computing because both the technology and environmental factors have changed. Attempts by companies to align their research activities more closely with product development processes have influenced the role they

BOX 1.2
Analogy in Technological Innovation

Analogies are often used in the process of technological innovation. Inventors use analogy to help them conceptualize new ideas. Edison conceived of the quadruplex telegraph, perhaps the most elegant and complex of his inventions, "almost entirely on the basis of an analogy with a water system including pumps, pipes, valves, and water wheels."[1] Later, continuing to reason by analogy, he conceived of the interaction of existing illuminating-gas distribution systems and the illuminating, incandescent-light system he intended to invent. The analogy stimulated him to invent a system, not simply an incandescent lamp (Friedel et al., 1986, pp. 63-64). Lee de Forest, inventor of the triode vacuum tube, also inclined to analogy. Observing under a microscope the flow of minute particles between electrodes in his wireless receiver, he imagined, "Tiny ferryboats they were, each laden with its little electric charge, unloading their etheric cargo at the opposite electrode and retracing their journeyings or, caught by a cohesive force, building up little bridges, or trees with branches of quaint and beautiful patterns" (de Forest, 1950, p. 119). Spurred on by analogous thinking, he resolved to invent a flaming hot-gas (ionized), or incandescent-particle, receiver, a search that culminated in his invention of a gas-filled, three-element electronic tube (Hughes, 1990; Aitken, 1985).

The emerging history of computer networks also reveals instances of invention by analogy.[2] J.C.R Licklider, whose vision of the future of computing inspired the problem choices and research and development activities of numerous of his contemporaries, opened his 1960 seminal paper, "Man-Computer Symbiosis" (Licklider, 1960), with a metaphor:

> The fig tree is pollinated only by the insect *Blastophaga grossorum.* The larva of the insect lives in the ovary of the fig tree, and there it gets its food. The tree and the insect are thus heavily interdependent: the tree cannot reproduce without the insect; the insect cannot eat without the tree; together, they constitute not only a viable but a productive and thriving partnership. This cooperative "living together in intimate association, or even close union, of two dissimilar organisms" is called symbiosis.[3]

Man-computer symbiosis, he adds, is a subclass of man-machine systems. Other human-machine systems use machines as extensions of humans. Still others deploy humans to extend machines—to perform functions, for instance, that cannot yet be automated. By contrast, man-computer symbiosis depends on an interactive partnership of man and machine.

MIT professor John McCarthy, an early contributor to computer time-sharing, suggested by analogy the potential of commercialized time-sharing and computing utilities. In a 1961 lecture he predicted:

> If computers of the kind I have advocated [time-sharing] become the computers of the future then computing may someday be organized as a public utility just as the telephone system is a public utility. . . . The computer utility could become the basis of a new and important industry. (Fano, 1979, p. 43)

After a successful demonstration of the ARPANET in 1972, other computer engineers and scientists saw the analogy. They no longer considered ARPANET a research site for testing computer communications but a communications utility comparable to the telephone system. "It was remarkable how quickly all of the sites really began to want to view the network as a utility rather than as a research project," Alexander McKenzie, an ARPANET pioneer, pointed out.[4]

An analogy drawn between a conventional office and a future electronic one provided a metaphoric bridge for ingenious computer scientists and engineers at Xerox PARC (Palo Alto Research Center). In the 1970s they invented the "Electronic Office," which they embodied in the Alto computer system. Not long afterward the PARC group began to use visual analogies to introduce icons into the displays of personal workstations.

---

[1]Edison, Theodore M. 1969. "Diversity Unlimited: The Creative Work of Thomas A. Edison," a condensation of a paper given before the MIT Club of Northern New Jersey, January 24.

[2]The discussion of the use of metaphors by ARPANET/Internet pioneers is based on a chapter on the ARPANET in Hughes (1998).

[3]Licklider quoting the definition for "symbiosis" in *Webster's New International Dictionary* (Springfield, Mass.: Merriam Company, 1958), p. 2555.

[4]Alexander McKenzie as quoted in an interview conducted by Judy O'Neill, Charles Babbage Institute, University of Minnesota, Minneapolis, March 17, 1990.

---

may play in the innovation process. As the computing industry has grown and the technology has diffused more widely throughout society, government has continued to represent a proportionally smaller portion of the industry. The lessons contained in this report attempt to discern crosscutting, pervasive themes and patterns regarding federal support for computer-related research. As such, the report attempts to identify fundamental, enduring trends and relationships that will survive change. It is hoped that they will both help historians better understand development of a dynamic industry and provide technologists with a deeper appreciation of the heritage of their trade, as well as assist policymakers in making more informed judgments about federal support for computing.

THE COMPUTING REVOLUTION

The United States is clearly a leader in the computing revolution. Computing technology has diffused throughout the U.S. economy with far-reaching effects. Over 36 percent of households in the United States owned a personal computer in 1995, a number far exceeding that of other major regions of the world (Table 1.1). Spurred by advances in comput-

TABLE 1.1 Worldwide Deployment of Computers in 1995

	World	United States	Europe	Japan	Rest of World
Population (millions)	5,700	264	477	125	4,834
Number of computers (millions)	257	96	54	18	89
Percentage of world's computers	100	37	21	7	35
Percentage of region's population with a computer	4.5	36.5	11.3	14.5	1.8

SOURCE: Petska-Juliussen and Juliussen (1996).

ing power and data communications, government, industry, and home users moved onto the Internet in record numbers to exchange electronic mail, buy and sell goods and services, gather and disseminate information, and browse the World Wide Web. Recent surveys indicate that some 58 million adults in the United States and Canada are now online (Nielsen Media Research, 1997). Computers have become ubiquitous, with microprocessors running desktop and laptop computers, quietly controlling the operation of aircraft and automobile engines, and adding functionality to common household devices, such as telephones, thermostats, and coffeemakers.

Effects on the Economy

The effects of this revolution on the economy are pervasive. Although productivity gains from computing have remained difficult to measure quantitatively,[3] the qualitative effects are manifest. Many industries, from banking to insurance to airline reservations, could not operate at current levels of activity without computing and communications systems. Computer-based devices, such as automated teller machines, have dramatically altered the ways banks operate, and they enable banks to offer a range of new services to customers. Electronic commerce is changing the way customers and vendors buy and sell goods. As individuals and businesses become more familiar with the technology and industry churns out more innovative information-technology products, it is clear that the influence will be felt in ways that cannot yet have been foreseen.

U.S. firms have led the computer revolution. Companies such as International Business Machines (IBM), Intel, and Microsoft dominate global markets for computing devices and software. Others, such as Cisco

Systems and Lucent Technologies, are leaders in the data communications field. Computer-related manufacturing represents a significant fraction of the nation's economy. Sales of computers, telecommunications equipment (including data networking equipment), software, and semiconductors by U.S. firms topped $280 billion in 1996 (Table 1.2), a figure that has grown at an average rate of almost 10 percent a year since 1960. Taking into account the changing prices of information-processing equipment of equivalent performance, annual expenditures on information-processing equipment grew at an average pace of 9.7 percent per year in real terms from 1970 to 1994. The corresponding figure for investments in computers and peripheral equipment (monitors, disk drives, and so forth) increased at a rate of 27.5 percent per year (Sichel, 1997, Table 4.1). Employment in these manufacturing industries stood at over 1 million in 1996, representing 6 percent of the total U.S. manufacturing workforce.

Related service industries have also blossomed. Computer and data processing firms generated close to $150 billion in revenues in 1996, with revenues from domestic telecommunications services climbing from $10 billion to $320 billion between 1960 and 1996.[4] Employment in U.S. communications services and computer and data-processing-services companies topped 2.4 million in 1996 (U.S. Department of Labor, 1997, Table B-12). The U.S. Department of Labor predicts that demand for information technology workers in all sectors of the economy will grow by 95,000 jobs annually between 1994 and 2005, with systems analysts posting the largest gains and the service sector absorbing most of these workers.[5]

TABLE 1.2 Sales and Employment in the Information Technology Industry, 1996

Industry Sector	Sales Revenues (in billions of dollars)	Employment
IT Manufacturing		
Computing and office equipment	111	254,700
Communications equipment	65	263,000
Software[a]	36	215,900
Semiconductors	68	257,000
IT Services		
Computing and data processing	144	1,037,300
Communications services	322	1,404,000

[a]Includes prepackaged software only, standard industrial classification (SIC) code.
SOURCE: Sales revenues for multiple industries from Bureau of the Census (1997). Employment data from U.S. Department of Labor (1997), Table B-12.

Technological Roots

The computing revolution is predicated on a series of technological advances made since the end of World War II. Between 1945 and 1995, the power of computing devices increased at an exponential rate. Whereas the earliest large-scale electronic computing machine in the United States, the Electronic Numerical Integrator and Computer (ENIAC), operated at a speed of 5,000 operations per second, the standard desktop computer in 1995 operated at nearly 100 million instructions per second, and the fastest supercomputers operated at 1 trillion operations per second. Driving much of this improvement were advances in integrated circuit technology. Following the invention of the integrated circuit, as described in patents filed by Jack Kilby in February 1959 and Robert Noyce in July 1959, the number of circuits fabricated on a single silicon chip has doubled every 18 to 24 months—a phenomenon known as Moore's law.[6] Such advances enable similar advances in the processing speed of computers and in storage capacity (or memory) that, over time, have a significant, cumulative effect. Between 1971 and 1995, the speed of a standard, general-purpose microprocessor increased more than 7,000-fold, from 60,000 to 440 million instructions per second, and the storage capacity of a dynamic random access memory chip swelled from 4,000 to 256 million bits (Table 1.3). Concomitant reductions in the price-performance ratios of computers, integrated circuits, and related devices have facilitated their diffusion.[7]

Other technological advances have allowed computing systems to take better advantage of the growing capability of microelectronic de-

TABLE 1.3 Historical Improvement in Microprocessors and Memories

Year	Microprocessor	Speed (MIPS)	Transistors	Memory (bits of DRAM)
1971	4004	0.06	2,300	1 K
1972				4 K
1974	8080	0.60	6,000	
1975				16 K
1978	8086	0.80	29,000	
1980				64 K
1982	80286	2.70	134,000	256 K
1985	386	6.00	275,000	1 M
1988				4 M
1991	486	13.00	1,185,000	16 M
1993	Pentium	100.00	3,106,000	
1995	Pentium Pro	440.00	5,500,000	64 M

NOTE: MIPS, millions of instructions per second; K, kilobit (1,000 bits); M, megabits (1 million bits); DRAM, dynamic random access memory.
SOURCE: Data from Intel (1996); OTA (1991).

vices. Improvements in the density, cost, and performance of magnetic disk storage devices, for example, have kept pace with advances in integrated circuits, allowing computers (from small personal computers to large mainframes) to have rapid access to appropriately large amounts of stored information at reasonable cost. Additionally, advances in system architecture have facilitated the transition from mainframe computers to time-shared minicomputers, personal microcomputers, and laptops connected by local and wide area networks. Other architectural innovations, such as reduced instruction set computing and parallel processing, have increased overall processing speeds, especially in high- and mid-range machines. New programming languages and data structures have facilitated development of applications as well as the storage and retrieval of information. Improvements in data communications have further enhanced the capability and utility of computers. Development of packet-switched networks, the Internet for instance, have allowed for more rapid communication of information among an expanding number of computers. Such innovation has increased the effectiveness of computing systems in a variety of personal, business, and government activities.

SOURCES OF U.S. SUCCESS

That the United States should be the leading country in computing and communications was not preordained. Early in the industry's formation, the United Kingdom was a serious competitor. The United Kingdom was the home of the Difference Engine and later the Analytical Engine, both of which were programmable mechanical devices designed and partially constructed by Charles Babbage and Ada, Countess of Lovelace, in the 19th century. Basic theoretical work defining a universal computer was the contribution of Alan Turing in Cambridge just before the start of World War II. The English defense industry—with Alan Turing's participation—conceived and constructed vacuum tube computers able to break the German military code. Both machines and their accomplishments were kept secret, much like the efforts and successes of the National Security Agency in this country. After the war, English universities constructed research computers and developed computer concepts that later found significant use in U.S. products. Other European countries, Germany and France in particular, also made efforts to gain a foothold in this new technology.

How then did the United States become a leader in computing? The answer is manifold, and a number of external factors clearly played a role. The state of Europe, England in particular, at the end of World War II played a decisive role, as rebuilding a country and industry is a more difficult task than shifting from a war economy to a consumer economy.

The movement of people among universities, industry, and government laboratories at the end of World War II in the United Kingdom and the United States also contributed by spreading the experience gained during the war, especially regarding electronics and computing. American students and scholars who were studying in England as Fulbright Scholars in the 1950s learned of the computer developments that had occurred during the war and that were continuing to advance.

Industrial prowess also played a role. After World War II, U.S. firms moved quickly to build an industrial base for computing. IBM and Remington Rand recognized quite early that electronic computers were a threat to their conventional electromechanical punched-card business and launched early endeavors into computing (Box 1.3). Over time, fierce competition and expectations of rapid market growth brought billions in venture money to the industry's inventors and caused a flowering of small high-tech innovators. Rapid expansion of the U.S. marketplace for computing equipment created buyers for new computing equipment. The rapid post-World War II expansion of civilian-oriented industries and financial sources created new demands for data and data processing. Insurance companies and banks were at the forefront of installing early computers in their operations. New companies, such as Engineering Research Associates, Datamatic, and Eckert-Mauchly, as well as established companies in the data processing field, such as IBM and Sperry Rand, saw an opportunity for new products and new markets. The combination of new companies and established ones was a powerful force. It generated fierce competition and provided substantial capital funds.

These factors helped the nation gain an early lead in computing that it has maintained. While firms from other nations have made inroads into computing technology—from memory chips to supercomputers—U.S. firms have continued to dominate both domestic and international markets in most product categories. This success reflects the strength of the nation's innovation system in computing technology, which has continually developed, marketed, and supported new products, processes, and services.

Research and Technological Innovation

Innovation is generally defined as the process of developing and putting into practice new products, processes, or services. It draws upon a range of activities, including research, product development, manufacturing, and marketing. Although often viewed as a linear, sequential process, innovation is usually more complicated, with many interactions among the different activities and considerable feedback. It can be motivated by new research advances or by recognition of a new market need.[8]

BOX 1.3
Early Industrial Efforts in Computing

IBM and Remington Rand were two early industrial pioneers in computing. Both were engaged in electromechanical punched-card machines at the close of World War II, with IBM holding 90 percent of the domestic market and Remington Rand having most of the rest. Between them, they also had most of the much smaller foreign market. IBM chose to build its electronic computer business internally, whereas Remington Rand purchased two small computer companies that had gotten their start primarily through government encouragement and funding. The first of these small companies was Engineering Research Associates (ERA), which was established in January 1946 with the active support of military leaders and a promise of lucrative government contracts. Initially ERA's only business was to design and build top-secret, electronic, code-breaking equipment—a task that could no longer be accomplished adequately in the Navy once the war ended and technically trained people were free to seek better opportunities elsewhere. By 1947 ERA had begun to design general-purpose, electronic, stored-program computers because it was concluded that they would be more cost-effective than the special-purpose equipment ERA had designed previously. The first of these computers, code-named Atlas, was delivered to the government in Washington, D.C., in December 1950.

The second of these small companies was the Eckert-Mauchly Computer Corporation (EMCC), which was founded in June 1946 by the chief designers of ENIAC. The business of EMCC was to design and manufacture computers (of the von Neumann rather than ENIAC design) and to sell them in the commercial market to displace punched-card equipment in installations having very large data processing requirements.

Short of money, despite a contract with the Census Bureau for its first large-scale computer, EMCC accepted an offer to be acquired by Remington Rand in 1950. Just over 1 year later in March 1951, the company's first Univac was accepted by the Census Bureau. One year later, Remington Rand acquired ERA, which needed additional funding to enter the commercial market with the computers it had previously sold only to the government. Thus, by 1952 the number two supplier of punched-card equipment had become the leading supplier of large-scale electronic computers.

The decision of IBM to build its electronic capability internally was based on the belief that it had a leadership position in applying electronic computing capability in commercial equipment. Using electronic circuits developed in its Endicott Laboratory as the country was entering World War II, IBM in 1946 introduced its 603 Electronic Multiplier, the first commercial product to incorporate electronic arithmetic circuits. Two years later in the fall of 1948, shipments of the IBM 604 began. Containing over 1,400 vacuum tubes, its electronic circuits performed addition, subtraction, multiplication, and division, and could execute up to 60 plugboard-controlled program steps between reading data from a card and punching out the result. Beginning in 1949, the IBM CPC (card-programmed electronic calculator) was shipped to customers. It combined the electronics of the 604 with other equipment to permit the user to enter both data and program commands on cards. Architecturally similar to the ENIAC, but much smaller, the IBM CPC was sometimes referred to as "a poor man's ENIAC."

Thus, IBM was first in the marketplace with electronic accounting and computing

continued on next page

BOX 1.3 continued

equipment. Over 5,000 IBM 604s and 700 CPCs were shipped to customers during the first half of the 1950s when Remington Rand delivered only 14 UNIVACs. IBM had also begun work on large stored-program computers to compete with those of Remington Rand and of other companies drawn into the field by large government research, development, and procurement contracts. This growing competition forced IBM to make a major policy change in 1950. Previously it had avoided government research and development contracts in electronics because it did not want to lose proprietary rights to its developments. Finally recognizing that its own technical and financial resources were insufficient to compete with the countrywide effort the government was orchestrating, it began to seek government research and development contracts in electronic computing. The first such project was the development of NORC (a supercomputer for the Navy), the design and construction of which was authorized early in 1951 and completed late in 1954. But without doubt, IBM's most important government contract put it in close collaboration with the Massachusetts Institute of Technology's Lincoln Laboratory (beginning in 1952) to design and manufacture computers for the Semi-Automatic Ground Environment (SAGE) air-defense system (see Chapter 4).

Thus began an era of vigorous competition that pitted IBM against Remington Rand, RCA, General Electric, NCR, Honeywell, Raytheon, Philco, and many others. These companies vied with each other to lead in computer-related technologies lest they fall behind in the marketplace. They sought government research contracts, collaborated with government laboratories and agencies, and worked with people in universities. Technical people published articles on their work in professional society journals and spoke at professional meetings where they could also talk informally with people from other laboratories. Although proprietary and classified information was carefully guarded by most participants, the information that could be exchanged was invaluable in moving forward the government's overall research and development effort. Government funding of computer research, development, and procurement had dramatically stimulated the rapid growth of the computer industry.

SOURCE: Summarized from Pugh (1995).

Government, universities, and industry all play a role in the innovation process.

Research is a vital part of innovation in computing. In dollar terms, research is just a small part of the innovation process, representing less than one-fifth of the cost of developing and introducing new products in the United States, with preparation of product specifications, prototype development, tooling and equipment, manufacturing start-up, and marketing start-up comprising the remainder (Mansfield, 1988, p. 1770).[9] Indeed, computer manufacturers allocated an average of just 20 percent of their research and development budgets to research between 1976 and 1995, with the balance supporting product development.[10] Even in the largest computer manufacturers, such as IBM, research costs are only about 1 to 2 percent of total operating expenses.[11] Nevertheless, research plays a critical role in the innovation process, providing a base of scientific and technological knowledge that can be used to develop new products, processes, and services. This knowledge is used at many points in the innovation process—generating ideas for new products, processes, or services; solving particular problems in product development or manufacturing; or improving existing products, for example.

Both industry and government fund research activities, with the research itself generally conducted by workers in industry or university laboratories. The computer industry has supported several large and highly productive research facilities, such as IBM's T.J. Watson Research Center, American Telephone and Telegraph's (AT&T) Bell Laboratories, and the Xerox Palo Alto Research Center (PARC). In 1996, computer manufacturers invested about $1.7 billion in research (out of $8.1 billion in total R&D), most of which supported research in their own facilities.[12] Federal research expenditures in computer science totaled roughly $960 million in 1995, approximately $350 million of which supported university research, the remainder supporting work in industry and government laboratories (see Chapter 3 for a more complete discussion of federal investments in computer-related research).

Traditionally, research expenditures have been characterized as either basic or applied. The term "basic research" is used to describe work that is exploratory in nature, addressing fundamental scientific questions for which ready answers are lacking; the term "applied research" describes activities aimed at exploring phenomena necessary for determining the means by which a recognized need may be met. These terms, at best, distinguish between the motivations of researchers and the manner in which inquiries are conducted, and they are limited in their ability to describe the nature of scientific and technological research. Recent work has suggested that the definition of basic research be expanded to include explicitly both basic scientific research and basic technological research (Branscomb et al., 1997). This definition recognizes the value of exploratory research into basic technological phenomena that can be used in a variety of products. Examples include research on the blue laser, exploration of biosensors, and much of the fundamental work in computer engineering.[13]

Federal Policy Toward Research Funding

Federal funding for research in computing technologies has been based on the rationale first enunciated by Vannevar Bush in his 1945 report to then-President Truman, *Science, The Endless Frontier* (Bush, 1945a). Drawing from the nation's experience in World War II, Bush argued that government funding of research was necessary to meet the nation's needs in defense, health, and the economy in general. Industry, he argued, had little incentive to support such work, but would pursue more applied research geared toward developing new products, processes, and services. This policy set in place new government activities that over the last 50 years have brought new agencies into existence, such as the National Science Foundation, and made the U.S. research system the envy of the world.

Cold War policies of the United States aimed at military and political containment of the Soviet Union and other communist adversaries provided additional impetus for computing research. Defense agencies, such as the Office of Naval Research, Army Research Office, Air Force Office of Scientific Research, and Defense Advanced Research Projects Agency, invested in computing research with long-term effects on military capabilities (and, indirectly, civilian capabilities). They, and other federal agencies, such as the National Security Agency (NSA), Department of Energy (DOE), National Aeronautics and Space Administration (NASA), and National Institutes of Health (NIH), have funded research in computing related to their own missions: maintaining national security, developing new energy sources and nuclear weapons, exploring space, and improving human health. Although these agencies have funded projects linked to their own needs, they have also, to varying degrees, created technical knowledge or specific products that have been adopted by the commercial marketplace (Alic et al., 1992).

Many mechanisms have been used to support federal contributions to computing research. Until the mid-1980s, most federal support took the form of research grants or contracts. This included federal contracts for product development or procurement that, in turn, demanded significant research. In each of these arrangements, the government acts as the customer for research services, specifying a period of performance and program objectives. After 1985, a growing number of programs were established that involved partnerships among government, universities, and industry. Such programs tended to pool public and private monies to support research in a variety of organizations in industry, universities, and government. In computing, such programs have included (1) SEMATECH, a consortium of semiconductor manufacturers who, with their own and federal funding, support research and development of semiconductor manufacturing equipment (see Chapter 4);[14] (2) Semiconductor Research Corporation, which pools industry and some federal funding to support university research in semiconductor technology; (3) Engineering Research Centers that require collaborative work between universities and industry on engineering problems of interest to industry (with some federal funding); (4) cooperative research and development agreements (CRADAs)

between government laboratories and industry; and (5) extramural cooperative research programs sponsored by the National Institute of Standards
and Technology (NIST), such as the Advanced Technology Program.[15]
All of these mechanisms are considered in this report.

Other Mechanisms for Federal Support of Innovation

Federal research support has been an important element of the
nation's innovation process, but other government activities have also
had a significant impact on innovation in computing. Federal procurement and standardization efforts, for instance, have also been highly influential. In a number of areas, ranging from semiconductors to supercomputers, government's specialized needs for computing technologies
created a market for high-performance devices and systems and under-
wrote the deployment of prototypes and core elements of new technologies in computing. Federal procurement of integrated circuits (IC) for the
Apollo spacecraft and the Department of Defense (DOD) Minuteman intercontinental ballistic missile program, for example, was a major impetus for early investments in IC manufacturing capability. The needs of
DOE and its predecessors for high-performance computers for nuclear
weapon development and testing drove early markets for supercomputers.
In software, the federal government helped drive the marketplace toward
the American National Standards Institute's version of COBOL by establishing it as a federal data processing standard. It also supported efforts
to set a standard for message-passing interfaces in parallel computing
and supported the High Performance FORTRAN forum to extend the
FORTRAN programming language to parallel computers (OTA, 1995).

Antitrust actions have also had a significant impact. For example, the
antitrust suit brought against IBM in 1952 and settled in 1956 required the
company (among other things) to sell as well as rent its equipment, to
help others get into the business of servicing IBM equipment, and to
license at reasonable rates all of its current and future patents on informa-
tion-processing equipment, including electronic computers. The settlement of the IBM suit and a similar settlement reached with AT&T one day
earlier (together with a suit then pending against RCA) were described by
the chief of the Justice Department's antitrust division as "part of one
program to open up the electronics field." The manner in which these
suits were settled facilitated the entry of other companies into the computer industry (Pugh, 1995, pp. 254-255). Similarly, the Modified Final
Judgment of Judge Greene created competition in the long-lines industry,
which, together with Computer Inquiries I, II, and III of the Federal Communications Commission, ensures the lowest prices for lease and resale of

long-lines carriage in the world. Such actions were arguably as important as research in advancing the telecommunications industry and the Internet.

ISSUES RELATED TO FEDERAL SUPPORT OF RESEARCH

Despite the wide range of influences on innovation in computing, federal research funding deserves particular attention, both because of the leverage it exerts over the entire innovation process and because of the policy issues currently under debate. Throughout the 1990s, changes in the policy environment and in the industry itself have raised new questions about the role of the federal government in funding computing research. The end of the Cold War and increasing calls for fiscal stringency in government spending have renewed debates over federal funding of research in the United States, as well as in other industrially advanced nations. To some extent, these debates are not new: the second half of the 20th century has seen numerous reviews of federal policies, programs, and institutions affecting research and education in science and engineering. The debates of the 1990s differ in that they represent the first time in which fundamental questions are being raised about the infrastructural commitments and organizational principles that have guided federal support for research.

Few challenge the appropriateness of government developing or sponsoring new technologies for its specialized needs, especially regarding national defense, but the arguments for government support for commercially relevant technology are less clear and their effects more controversial. Although many believe that fundamental, knowledge-expanding research, whose benefits are openly available through publication, is an appropriate course for government, support is not without question. These questions do not arise just out of budgetary considerations. Even as federal budget deficits have given way to promises of surpluses in the late 1990s, and proposals have been made for increasing federal research spending,[16] Congress initiated a study to determine the proper role of government in supporting science and engineering.[17] Such studies attempt to determine how federal monies can be most productively spent and, more generally, what role the federal government should play in supporting research and innovative activities.

Computing research poses an especially difficult challenge in this regard. First, advocates of computing research must counter the claim that computing technology has matured and that the industry is less dependent on fundamental research than it was in the past. Why should the government continue to support computing research that will yield only incremental improvements in the technology? Answering this question requires an appreciation of the evolution of computing technology over the past five decades and an understanding of the role research has played in prompting—and responding to—new advances and developments. It requires an analysis of the ways in which pathbreaking innovations have dramatically altered the landscape of computing over time so that policymakers can appreciate the evolution of the industry as a whole.

Second, advocates of computing research must demonstrate why the federal government should continue to support research when a healthy industry exists that could develop its own technology. Why would companies in such a highly competitive and profitable industry not fund computing research and develop new technologies on their own? Clearly, the computer industry does fund research and does develop new technologies on its own. Answering the question more fully requires a better understanding of the interplay among industry, government, and universities in creating and applying new information technologies. Federal policymakers must determine what role government plays in supporting such work and how federal efforts supplement, rather than duplicate or displace, those of industry. Similarly, policymakers must understand how federal needs differ from those of the commercial marketplace and how federal needs can drive industrial innovation.

Furthermore, policymakers and federal research managers are under increasing pressure to enhance the effectiveness of government research programs. The desire to streamline federal government operations has led to renewed efforts to improve federal programs and their management, as manifested by passage of the Government Performance and Results Act of 1993. This act requires federal agencies to account for program results through integrating strategic planning, budgeting, and performance measurement.[18] For agencies that support scientific and technical research, the act implies that methods be developed for measuring the results of federal research investments. Doing so requires an understanding of the many different ways research influences the innovation process, the time delays involved, and the uncertainties inherent in innovation. Such a task would benefit from an examination of past federal research programs to identify examples of successful federal research programs and to provide guidance on the kinds of metrics, if any, that could be applied to federally funded research.

These are the kinds of issues this report hopes to inform. The lessons contained in Chapter 5 attempt to answer questions about the role of federally funded research in the innovation process, the cycle of innovation, and the results of federal investments. They discuss the effects federally funded research had on industry and society as a whole and identify characteristics of effective federal research programs. With this kind of historical background, policymakers can be better informed to face the challenges ahead.

ORGANIZATION OF THIS REPORT

The remainder of this report examines the history of computing and communications to derive lessons for public policy. Chapter 2 provides the economic rationale for federal support of fundamental research. It identifies the economic properties of research and discusses market failures in the support of research that justify a government role. Chapter 3 presents an overview of the federal role in creating the research infrastructure that supports the U.S. computing and communications industries. It reviews federal investments in research, education, and research equipment over the past several decades. Chapter 4 reviews the changing organizational context of computing research in the United States, with an emphasis on federal funding agencies. It describes the changing political, technical, and organizational context in which innovation has occurred and contains mini-case studies of particularly important innovations—such as time-shared computing and very large scale integrated circuits—identifying the federal role in each. Chapter 5 contains a summary of the lessons learned from this study. It identifies general lessons about the role of federal funding in the innovation process and about the structure of successful research programs. It is hoped that such lessons will be useful to policymakers, researchers, and research managers. Part II of this report, Chapters 6 through 10, contains the case studies that form the backbone of this report. The cases represent a sampling of important technologies that have had an enduring influence on the computing and communications industry and society: relational databases, the Internet, theoretical computer science, artificial intelligence, and virtual reality. Although by no means comprehensive, they cover a wide range of technologies, degrees of success, and interactions among government, universities, and industry.

NOTES

1. This report uses the term "computing research" in a broad sense, to include work in semiconductors, software, and data communications, in addition to computer science and engineering. It does not include all research in telecommunications (such as voice communications), which has a very different history characterized by regulated monopolies for telephone services.

2. Many historians offer as a classic case of a dangerously misleading analogy the assumption that conditions in southeast Asia in the 1950s were comparable to those in Europe in 1939. This analogy led some policymakers in the United States to assume that, if the country immediately and directly confronted North Vietnam, it would result in a compromise like that offered Hitler at Munich and another large-scale war would be averted. For a discussion of poor presidential decisions resulting from the misapplication of analogies, see May (1972).

3. The so-called productivity paradox was first noted by economist Robert Solow (hence it is often referred to as the Solow Paradox). Explanations have ranged from measurement problems to lag times to the difficulties inherent in integrating computing into the workplace. Nevertheless, recent research suggests a correlation between higher levels of information technology capital and increased productivity in large companies, especially in companies that use information technology to enhance customer service. See Brynjolfsson and Hitt (1996). For a discussion of the difficulties in measuring productivity gains associated with information technology, see CSTB (1995b).

4. Revenues cited for the telecommunications services industry include both voice and data communications over a range of media—wireline and wireless. Data are from Bureau of the Census (1997).

5. Employment of systems analysts and computer scientists and engineers is projected to increase 158 and 142 percent, respectively, in the service industries between 1994 and 2005, versus 26 and 37 percent, respectively, in manufacturing industries. The number of computer programmers in service industries is expected to grow 37 percent, versus a 26 percent decline in manufacturing. See U.S. Department of Commerce (1997).

6. Moore's law is named after Gordon Moore, who first noted the relationship and predicted its continuation in 1964. It is the result of two underlying processes: continuous reductions in the size of individual circuits etched onto computer chips through advances in lithography and other manufacturing processes, and increases in the overall size of the integrated circuit (or chip) resulting from improvements in processing of silicon wafers and reductions in contaminants. See Bashe et al. (1986), pp. 56-58.

7. Between 1960 and 1995, the average unit price of computers sold in the United States declined from $330,000 to $3,700, helping to propel growth in annual sales from 1,790 units to over 21 million units. See ITI (1997). The price-performance ratio of the typical computer during that time period also declined by a factor of 100. The U.S. Department of Commerce's (Bureau of Economic Analysis) hedonic price index for computer equipment for 1970-1994 implies that the price-performance ratio was 1.9 percent of its 1970 level in 1994, an average annual rate of decrease of 15.3 percent. Estimating a slower rate of decline in the 1960s of approximately 7.0 percent per year, the price performance ratio in 1994/1995 would have stood at approximately 1/100 of its 1960 level. See Sichel (1997) Table 4-1.

8. For a more complete overview of the innovation process, see OTA (1995).

9. This figure has remained remarkably constant over the past several decades. A 1967 report from the Department of Commerce that relied on data from the previous 10 years found that product conception and design accounted for 15 to 30 percent of the cost of new product introduction; manufacturing preparation, manufacturing start-up, and marketing start-up made up the balance. See U.S. Department of Commerce (1967), p. 8.

10. This estimate was calculated from data contained in the biennial report, National Science Foundation, *Research and Development in Industry*. Other data from the National Science Foundation show that 40 percent of all research and development expenditures in the United States supported research in 1995; the

remaining 60 percent supported development. See National Science Board (1996), pp. 4-5.

11.   This figure assumes that about 20 percent of IBM's total R&D expenditures support research. R&D was about 7 percent of IBM's operating expenses (the sum of the cost of goods sold, R&D, and general, administrative, and sales costs) in 1997. See IBM (1997).

12.   This figure includes research expenditures for firms in the office and computing-equipment industry only. It does not include expenditures by firms in data communications, prepackaged software, or semiconductors. See NSF (1998a), Table A-24.

13.   The National Science Foundation, which is the source of most of the research funding data in this chapter, defines research as "systematic study directed toward fuller knowledge or understanding of the subject studied." It defines development as "systematic use of the knowledge gained from research, directed toward the production of useful materials, devices, systems, or methods, including design and development of prototypes and processes. It excludes quality control, routine product testing, and production." See NSF (1997a).

14.   In 1997, after 10 years of roughly even funding from industry and government, SEMATECH became fully self-supported, using only industry funding for its programs.

15.   NIST's Advanced Technology Program (ATP), for example, provides cost-shared funding to consortia of industry and university participants attempting to conduct precompetitive applied research. Funding for the program peaked at $341 million in 1995 and stood at $192.5 million in 1998. Funding history is available online at <http://www.atp.nist.gov/atp/budget.gif>.

16.   Two bills were introduced in the Senate in 1997 and 1998, calling for a doubling of the federal funding for basic scientific and precompetitive engineering research. In October 1997, Senators Gramm, Lieberman, and 18 other cosponsors introduced the National Research Investment Act of 1998. The plan called for the doubling of funds over a 10-year period. The bill was referred to the Senate Committee on Labor and Human Resources. In June 1998, Senator Frist submitted similar legislation entitled the Federal Research Investment Act along with 26 co-sponsors. In addition to doubling federal funding for research to 2.6 percent of the federal budget, the bill also called for new evaluation processes to provide better oversight of funding programs. The bill also called for the President to provide a strategic plan for proposed R&D funds as well as an analysis of current funds as part of the annual budget. The bill was referred to the Committee on Commerce. A companion bill in the House was introduced in August of 1998.

17.   Early in 1997, Vernon Ehlers, vice chairman of the House Science Committee, initiated the National Science Policy Study, which was intended to provide a new rationale for federal funding of science. The study examined issues in mathematical and scientific education, funding for R&D, cooperation among government, industry, and the international community. The chair of the Science Committee, James Sensenbrenner, hoped that the study would justify the proposed funding increases for research that were introduced in the Senate in 1997 and 1998. The final report was released on September 24, 1998 (Committee on Science, 1998).

18.   Each agency was required to submit by September 1997 strategic plans that outlined the agency's mission statement, goals and objectives, and strategies it would use to achieve them. The first annual performance plans were due when the President submitted the 1998 budget to Congress and were to include measures that the agency would use to gauge performance toward meeting those goals, and the resources to be used in doing so.

2

Economic Perspectives on
Public Support for Research

This chapter examines the economic logic of public subsidies for research and development (R&D) activities in general. The first section notes a number of serious theoretical objections that can be raised against public support of R&D, and it reviews empirical considerations that reaffirm the general presumption that, without government support, market failures will result in too few resources being allocated to expanding scientific and technological knowledge. The second section takes up the special considerations that bear on the economic case for public support of exploratory, open research—the sort that is usually designated as basic science, however unsatisfactory that label may be. That discussion emphasizes the complementarities and guidance that such research creates for private-sector, applications-oriented, proprietary R&D, rather than the possibilities of spin-off products that may compete with results targeted by industrial research organizations. It also highlights the contribution federal funding makes to the education of the scientific and engineering workforce.

THE ECONOMIC RATIONALE FOR PUBLIC SUPPORT
OF CIVILIAN R&D

During the past 30 years, economists have worked out cogent reasons why the price system and competitive markets should not be expected to do a good job in producing or distributing knowledge and information—certainly not by comparison with markets' performance in similarly allocating resources in more conventional, tangible commodities such as fish or chips (of both the computer and the potato varieties).[1] This conclusion rests on the fundamental insight that ideas—especially ideas tested and reduced to codified scientific and technological information through R&D activities—have some important attributes found in public goods, goods that are widely available to individuals whether or not they paid for them. Correspondingly, they may be better understood by studying other public goods, such as a smog-free environment or defense against nuclear missile attack.

Information and Knowledge as Commodities

An idea is a thing of remarkable expansiveness: it can spread rapidly from mind to mind without any reduction in its meaning and significance for those into whose possession it comes. Thomas Jefferson remarked upon this attribute, which permits the same knowledge to be used jointly by many individuals at once: "He who receives an idea from me, receives instruction himself without lessening mine; as he who lights his taper at mine receives light without darkening me. . . ." Economists have pointed out that the potential value of an idea to any individual buyer generally would not match its value to the social whole. The latter value, however, is not readily expressed in a willingness to pay on the part of all who would gain from the illuminating idea. Once a new bit of knowledge is revealed by its discoverer(s), some benefits will instantly spill over to others who are therefore able to share in its possession. Commodities that have the property of expansibility, permitting them to be used simultaneously for the benefit of a number of agents, are sometimes described as being nonrival in use: although the cost of the first instance of use of new knowledge may be large, in that it includes the cost of its generation, further instances of its use impose at most a negligible incremental cost.[2]

This formulation ignores the cost of training potential users to be able to use new information. Although it is correct that there can be fixed costs of access to the information, these costs do not invalidate the proposition that reuse of the information will neither deplete it nor impose further costs. It may be costly to teach someone how to read the table of the elements or use differential calculus, but any number of individuals thus instructed can go on using that knowledge without incurring further costs.

The second feature of ideas is that it is difficult, indeed costly, to retain exclusive possession of them while putting them to use. Another disadvantage of exclusivity is that results obtained by methods that are not or cannot be revealed often are felt to be less reliable. Of course, it is possible to keep a piece of information or a new idea secret. Producing results not achievable otherwise, however, indicates the existence of a method for doing so. Even a general explanation of the basis for achieving the observable result jeopardizes the exclusivity of its possession, for knowing that something can be done is an important step toward discovering how it may be done.

The dual properties of nonrival usage and costly exclusion of others from possession define what is meant by a pure public good. The term "public good" does not imply that such a commodity cannot be supplied privately, nor does it mean that government must produce it. But competitive market processes will not do an efficient job of allocating resources for producing and distributing pure public goods, because such markets work well when the incremental costs and benefits of using a commodity are assigned to the users.

Capturing the Benefits of Research Investments

One may see the problem posed by the public goods characteristics of knowledge by asking how ideas can be traded in competitive markets, except by having aspects of their nature and significance disclosed before the transactions are consummated. Rational buyers of ideas, no less than buyers of coal, and of fish and chips, first want to know something about what they will be getting for their money. Even if the exchange fell through, the potential purchaser would enjoy (without paying) some benefits from what economists refer to as transactional spillovers. These occur because there may be significant commercial advantages from acquiring even general information about the nature of a discovery, or an invention—especially one that a reputable seller has thought it worthwhile to bring to the attention of people engaged in a particular line of business.

This analysis leads to the conclusion that the findings of scientific research, being new knowledge, would be seriously undervalued were they sold directly through perfectly competitive markets. Some degree of exclusivity of possession of the economic benefits derived from ideas is necessary if the creators of new knowledge are to derive any profit from their activities under a capitalist market system. Firms can protect their knowledge either by seeking patent or copyright protection or by trying to keep it secret. Patents and copyrights provide legally enforceable means of protecting knowledge, but they require that inventors publicly disclose the workings of their inventions (e.g., through a patent application), enabling others to learn from their work and to find alternative means of achieving the same end (i.e., reverse engineering a particular device). Keeping a trade secret (if done effectively) avoids public disclosure, but offers little means for legal recourse if others learn the secret (unless they use unlawful means to do so). Industries vary in the degree to which firms prefer to seek intellectual property protection versus keeping trade secrets. Patents tend to be very important in pharmaceuticals, for example, but less so in computing. Regardless of the mechanism chosen for protection, imposing restrictions on how ideas may be used saddles society with the inefficiencies that arise when monopolies are tolerated, a point belabored by economists ever since Adam Smith.

Technical Standards as Public Goods

Technical standards also demonstrate characteristics of public goods in that competitive markets often fail to produce them without public assistance. Technical standards acquire economic value for their possessors only as a consequence of being publicly disclosed and jointly used, and they actually grow in utility for the individual user in proportion to the degree of universality in their adoption. Many technological and engineering reference standards, such as those for the thread sizes of nuts and bolts, or the diameter of optical fiber (to permit splicing without degrading the light signal that is propagated through the inner core), benefit buyers and vendors by reducing transactions costs and permitting economies of scale in production, especially when they are widely adopted.

It should be noted that many other reference standards have emerged from the work of scientific communities, such as the units in which electrical current, resistance, and power are measured. The ampere, ohm, and watt, like the joule, angstrom, and countless other precisely specified units, provide a standardized terminology that facilitates scientific communications. They thus enable individuals in a distributed research network to work together (i.e., become interoperable) in the way that compatibility standards enable interacting components of systems to achieve greater functionality. As is the case with other standards, market incentives are weak for producing and distributing scientific reference standards.

Firms that know of and wish to use technical standards would have every incentive to freely share that information, in order to encourage others to follow suit. Hence, an adequate supply of reference standards and related technologies may not be forthcoming through individual private enterprise, as it may not be worthwhile for any single firm to undertake the cost of designing a reference standard that would be useful for the industry as a whole and redistributed freely.

Governmental support for the collaborative development of reference standards, or direct funding of agencies such as national standards institutes that undertake such work, constitutes a mechanism for rectifying this market failure. The alternative of using intellectual property rights protection to grant monopoly privileges to private developers of such standards has a perverse effect. It tends to restrict the extent of the standards' use, and therefore deprives even those who do pay the monopolist's charges, imposed by licensing of patent-protected standards, from enjoying the added benefits that would accrue to all users from enlarging the user community. This is a generic problem with standards for systems, such as telephone and other communication systems, whose value to individual subscribers is enhanced by being able to connect with, and be contacted by, a larger number of network members.

Secrecy and Intellectual Property Rights

Some suggest that the problems of incomplete appropriability of benefits from research are overstated, or indeed nonexistent, because industrial secrecy is sufficient to protect against some firms free-riding on the R&D investments of others. But other factors must also be considered. First, one has to consider what costs a strategy of secrecy imposes upon private enterprise, and whether such practices can be totally effective in the face of the mobility of technical personnel and reverse engineering. Second, one must look at the matter from the societal viewpoint. On the supposition that extensive secrecy was a viable policy for firms engaged in research, what is the potential for wasting R&D resources by duplicating research, not to mention potential injury to consumers, were the developers of new products and processes actually able to maintain indefinite secrecy about their research results?

The economic logic of providing intellectual property rights in science and technology is that this is a better choice, from the societal standpoint, than secrecy. Modern economic analysis has come to view the granting of patent and copyright monopolies as a sacrifice of short-run consumer interests that may be justified by far greater long-run gains derived from giving creators of new, useful knowledge more secure pecuniary incentives to reveal it rapidly to the public. Still, in order to pursue research profitably, it is necessary for firms to be able to control the flow of information about work that is in progress, and to build an inventory of potential future projects that they can expect to exploit, rather than seeing these walk out the door with their research personnel.

Consequently, trade secrecy protections are in this respect complementary to intellectual property protection in the production process for new research findings whose benefits the firm expects to be able to appropriate. This reinforces the argument made for strengthening intellectual property rights in patents, and their enforcement, on the grounds that reliance upon secrecy is reduced thereby. Although the disclosure of codified information is augmented by patent systems, so is the inducement to curtail the transmission of tacit knowledge that might reduce the commercial value of the patents that are being sought.[3]

Common Pool Problems, Patent Races, and
Potential Overinvestment in R&D

Market failures do not necessarily result in underinvestment in R&D by profit-seeking firms. There also is a potential for excessive private investment when expected private marginal rates of return are not matched by the marginal social value expected to result from those expenditures. Economists have been aware for some time of three main situations in which that is likely to be the case, and, although these are thoroughly treated in the technical literature, they often go unmentioned in public testimony on the subject. These overinvestment pathologies of market competition through R&D go under the labels of business stealing, common pool problems, and racing behavior.

Business stealing refers to the situation that arises when research that is directed toward displacing a competitor from the market entails developing a new product or process that largely duplicates the functions of things that already exist, but adds some distinctive additional features. Achieving a marginal improvement in quality may be sufficient to capture a rival's share of the market, and so may justify the private investment in completely redesigning a product or system to accommodate the new feature, or to overcome the barriers that an incumbent has erected through secrecy or patent protection. But the social value of the added features for consumers may be much smaller than the private benefits of a successful attack on the incumbent's market position.

Common pool problems arise because individual competitors may vie for market position based upon R&D without taking into account the effect of their entry on the expected returns on the investments that others are making. Not every entrant will get a prize, but every entrant can believe in having just as good a chance, if not a better chance, for success than the others. The result can be duplicative investment in areas in which the anticipated prizes are large. The rivalries for certain prescription drug markets in the pharmaceutical industry often are cited as a classic manifestation of this problem: billions are spent to develop the next blockbuster therapy, whereas little investment may be devoted to products of lesser commercial value.

Racing behavior is another form of duplicative investment and is driven by the desire to beat one's rival to market. The value of being a week earlier at the patent office window, or 6 months in advance of competitors to launch a new software application, can be very large in comparison with the incremental social value of letting consumers use the innovation that much sooner. Firms then have an incentive to structure their R&D programs for speed, rather than cost minimization. They try to bluff the opposition into quitting by establishing a lead and displaying a commitment to maintain it, whatever the cost.

It is clear that such effects, like the appropriability problem, will lead to inefficiencies in the detailed allocation of private-sector research outlays: excess correlation of research strategies, excessively duplicative funding in some areas, and inattention to other areas in which the marginal social value of new technologies may be quite high. What is less clear is whether these tendencies to overinvestment are so powerful that they destroy the presumption that private markets will, on balance, fail to allocate enough to creating new scientific and engineering knowledge. Some recent analytical work suggests this is not the case—except in circumstances where the real interest rate is so high that the value of knowledge spillovers to future generations should, in fact, be heavily discounted by the present generation, and where the impact of additional R&D funding on the creation of knowledge is rather weak (Jones and Williams, 1996).

Thus, the accrued wisdom from the economics profession regarding the aggregate tendency to underinvestment, and the corresponding case for government support of research as a stimulus to economic growth, still stands. But these qualifications point to the need for greater attention to where the publicly funded research is to be directed.

THE BENEFITS OF PUBLIC SUPPORT OF RESEARCH

The development of scientific and technological knowledge is a cumulative process, one that depends on the prompt disclosure of new findings so that they can be tested and, if confirmed, integrated with other bodies of reliable knowledge. In this way open science promotes the rapid generation of further discoveries and inventions, as well as wider practical exploitation of additions to the stock of knowledge.

The economic case for public funding of what is commonly referred to as basic research rests mainly on that insight, and on the observation that business firms are bound to be considerably discouraged by the greater uncertainties surrounding investment in fundamental, exploratory inquiries (compared to commercially targeted R&D), as well as by the difficulties of forecasting when and how such outlays will generate a satisfactory rate of return.

The proposition at issue here is quantitative, not qualitative. One cannot adequately answer the question "Will there be enough?" merely by saying, "There will be some." Economists do not claim that without public patronage (or intellectual property protection), basic research will cease entirely. Rather, their analysis holds that there will not be enough basic research—not as much as would be carried out were individual businesses (like society as a whole) able to anticipate capturing all the benefits of this form of investment. Therefore, no conflict exists between this theoretical analysis and the observation that R&D-intensive companies do indeed fund some exploratory research into fundamental questions. Their motives for this range from developing a capability to monitor progress at the frontiers of science, to identifying ideas for potential lines of innovation that may be emerging from the research of others, to being better positioned to penetrate the secrets of their rivals' technological practices (Nelson, 1990).

Nevertheless, funding research is a long-term strategy, and therefore sensitive to commercial pressures to shift research resources toward advancing existing product development and improving existing processes, rather than searching for future technological options. Large organizations that are less asset constrained, and of course the public sector, are better able to take on the job of pushing the frontiers of science and technology. Considerations of these kinds are important in addressing the issue of how to find the optimal balance for the national research effort between secrecy and disclosure of scientific and engineering information, as well as in trying to adjust the mix of exploratory and applications-driven projects in the national research portfolio.

Direct Contributions to the Scientific Knowledge Base

When asked to demonstrate the usefulness of exploratory research that is undertaken to discover new phenomena, or explain fundamental properties of physical systems, scientists often point to discoveries and inventions generated by research projects that turned out to have immediate economic value. Many important advances in instrumentation, and generic techniques such as the polymerase chain reaction (PCR) and the use of restriction enzymes in gene-splicing, are such examples. These by-products of the open-ended search for basic scientific understanding also might be viewed as contributing to the knowledge infrastructure required for efficient R&D that might result in exploitable commercial innovations. Occasionally, such new additions to the stock of scientific knowledge are of immediate commercial value and yield major economic payoffs. Though few and far between, they can have far-reaching consequences.

There is no dearth of examples testifying to the practical value and commercial benefits that have followed serendipitously from exploratory, or curiosity-driven, scientific inquiries. The chance finding of bacteria surviving in and near the thermal vents in Yellowstone Park may be offered as a striking recent instance of a scientific discovery having an important and economically valuable field of application that hardly could be anticipated. The bacteria in question turned out to be crucial in the development of the PCR process for replication of specific pieces of DNA, a generic technique that is now the basis of many commercial biotech-nology applications, ranging from diagnostic kits to forensic medicine. What the developers of PCR required was an enzyme that would be stable at high temperatures, and the Yellowstone bacteria produced just what was needed.

The experience of the 20th century also testifies to the many contribu-tions of practical value that trace their origins to large, government-funded research projects that were focused upon developing new enabling tech-nologies for public-mission agencies (Rosenberg, 1987). Consider just a few recent examples from the enormous and diverse range that could be noted in this connection: airline reservation systems, packet switching and the Internet communication protocols, the Global Positioning Sys-tem, and computer simulation methods for visualization of molecular structures.

At issue is whether a more directed search for the solutions to these applied problems would have been less costly and more expedient than waiting for scientists with quite different purposes in mind to come up with these commercially useful findings. Indeed, the theme of such spin-off stories is their unpredictability. The argument that the new applica-tions are in some sense free requires that the research program to which they were incidental was worth undertaking for its own sake, so that whatever else might be yielded as by-products was a net addition to the benefits derived. Yet, the reason those examples are being cited is the skepticism as to whether the knowledge that was being sought by explor-atory science was worth the cost of the public support it required. Per-haps this is why the many examples of this kind that scientists have brought forward seem never enough to satisfy the questioners.

The discovery and invention of commercially valuable products and processes are seen from the viewpoint of the new economics of science[4] to be among the rarer of the predictably useful results that flow from the conduct of exploratory, open science. Without denying that research sometimes yields immediate applications around which profitable busi-nesses spring up, it can be argued that those direct fruits of knowledge are not where the quantitatively important economic payoffs from basic science are to be found. Much more critical over the long run than spin-offs from basic science programs are their cumulative *indirect* effects in raising the rate of return on proprietary R&D performed by business firms. Among those indirect consequences, attention should be directed not only to informational spillovers, but to a range of complementary "externalities" that are generated for the private sector by publicly funded activities in the sphere of open science, where research and training are tightly coupled.

Indirect Effects of Government-sponsored Research

Federally funded R&D provides a number of indirect benefits to private R&D beyond direct transfers of knowledge. These include intellectual assistance that can guide private R&D programs toward potentially more productive areas of inquiry and assistance in training researchers. Although resources are limited, and research conducted in one field and in one organizational mode is therefore performed at the expense of other kinds of R&D, exploratory science and academic engineering research activities support commercially oriented and mission-directed research that generates new production technologies and products. As such, public support of research in many ways complements, rather than competes with, private R&D efforts.

Intellectual Assistance

First among the sources of this complementary relationship is the intellectual assistance that fundamental scientific knowledge (even that deriving from contributions made long ago) provides to applied researchers—whether in the public or private sector. From the expanding knowledge base it is possible to derive time- and cost-saving guidance as to how best to proceed in searching for ways to achieve some prespecified technical objectives. Sometimes this takes the form of reasonably reliable guidance as to where to look first, and much of the time it takes the form of valuable instructions as to where it will be *useless* to look. One effect this has is to raise the expected rates of return and reduce the riskiness of investing in applied R&D. Gerald Holton, a physicist and historian of science at Harvard University, recently has remarked that if intellectual property laws required all photoelectric devices to display a label describing their origins, "it would list prominently: 'Einstein, Annalen der Physik 17 (1905), pp. 132-148.'" Such credits to Einstein also would have to be placed on many other practical devices, including all lasers.

The central point that must be emphasized here is that, over the long run, the fundamental knowledge and practical techniques developed in the pursuit of basic science serve to keep applied R&D as profitable an investment for the firms in many industries as it has proved to be, especially during the past half-century. In this role, modern science continues in the tradition of the precious, if sometimes imprecise, maps that guided parties of exploration in earlier eras of discovery, and in that of the geological surveys that are still of such value to prospectors searching for buried mineral wealth.

Research as Training

A second and no less important source of the complementary relationship between public and private research is the nexus between university research and training. The profitability of corporate R&D is closely tied to the quality of the young researchers who are available for employment. Seen from this angle, government funding of open exploratory science in the universities today is subsidizing the R&D performed by the private business sector. Properly equipped research universities have turned out to be the sites of choice for training the most creative and most competent young scientists and engineers, as many a corporate director of research well knows. This is why graduates and postdoctoral students in those fields are sent or find their own way to university laboratories in the United States. It explains why businesses participate in (and sponsor) industrial affiliates programs at research universities. It also is part of the reason for U.S. industrial research corporations' broadly protective stance in regard to the federal budget for scientific research. Acknowledgment of it has had a great deal to do with the recent announcement by the Japanese government of a dramatic reversal of its former policies and the initiation of a vast program of support for *university-based* research.

A key point deserving emphasis in this connection is that a great deal of the scientific expertise available to a society at any point in time remains *tacit,* rather than being fully available in codified form and accessible in archival publications. It is embodied in the knowledge of the researchers about such things as the procedures for culturing specific cell lines, or building a new kind of laser that has yet to become a standard part of laboratory repertoire. This is research knowledge, much of it very technological in nature—in that it pertains to how phenomena have been generated and observed in particular, localized, experimental contexts— that is embodied in people. Under sufficiently strong incentives it would be possible to express more of this knowledge in forms that would make it easier to transmit, and eventually that is likely to happen. But, being possessed by individuals who have an interest in capturing some of the value of the expertise they have acquired, this tacit knowledge is transmitted typically through personal consultations, demonstrations, and the movement of people among institutions.

The circulation of postdoctoral students among university research laboratories, between universities and specialized research institutes, and, no less important, the movement of newly trained researchers from the academy into industrial research organizations, are therefore important aspects of technology transfer—diffusing the latest techniques of science and engineering research. The incentive in this mode of transfer is a very powerful one for ensuring that the knowledge will be successfully translated into practice in the new location, for the individuals involved are unlikely to be rewarded if they are not able to enhance the research capabilities of the organization into which they move.

A similarly potent incentive may exist when a fundamental research project sends its personnel to work with an industrial supplier from which critical components for an experimental apparatus are being procured. Ensuring that the vendor acquires the technical competence to produce reliable equipment within the budget specifications is directly aligned with the interests of both the research project and the business enterprise. Quite obviously, the effectiveness of this particular form of user-supplier interaction is likely to vary directly with the commercial value of the procurement contracts and the expected duration and continuity of the research program.

For this reason, big science projects or long-running public research programs may offer particular advantages for the collaborative mode of technology transfers, just as major industrial producers—such as the large automotive companies in Japan—are seen to be able to set manufacturing standards and provide the necessary technical expertise to enable their suppliers to meet them. By contrast, the transfer of technology by licensing intellectual property is, in the case of process technologies, far more subject to tensions and deficiencies arising from the absence of complete alignment of the interests of the involved individuals and organizations. But, as has been seen, the latter is only one among the economic drawbacks of depending upon the use of intellectual property to transfer knowledge from nonprofit research organizations to firms in the private sector.

NOTES

1.   Economic theory describing the reasons industry will underinvest in research was first developed in the late 1950s and early 1960s. See Nelson (1959) and Arrow (1962).

2.   Economists refer to this characteristic as a form of nonconvexity or an extreme form of decreasing marginal costs as the scale of use is increased.

3.   For further discussion of the inefficiencies of using intellectual property protection to stimulate innovation (especially in regard to the adverse effects on the use of existing knowledge that is relevant to research), see David and Foray (1996).

4.   See, for example, Dasgupta and David (1987, 1994), David et al. (1992), and Grossman and Helpman (1991).

3

Federal Support for Research Infrastructure

Research infrastructure consists of many elements. Primary among them are research funding, human resources, and physical facilities for conducting research. Historically, the U.S. government has been a partner with industry and universities in creating the infrastructure for many critical new industries, ranging from agriculture to aircraft to biotechnology.[1] Computing is no exception. Government, industry, and universities have all contributed to the research infrastructure that underlies the innovative capacity of the nation's computing industry. Funding for the research infrastructure in computing comes largely from industry and government sources, with small contributions from universities and nonprofit organizations. Private industry invests in research, develops human resources, and builds physical infrastructure for research and development (R&D) primarily to serve commercial purposes. Public support for research infrastructure is, in contrast, intended to create a pool of resources that can be drawn upon by a variety of users in the private and public sectors. For example, substantial public investment is made in universities that train students, conduct research, and build research laboratories.

This chapter explores the federal government's contributions to the research infrastructure, examining the government's support for research, human resources, and research equipment. Although computing technology draws on research in a number of academic disciplines—from computer science, electrical engineering, mathematics, materials science and engineering, and cognitive science and psychology—this chapter examines federal contributions in the areas of computer science and electrical engineering, which are the most directly relevant. Computer science includes work on the theory of computing; design, development, and application of computer capabilities to data storage and manipulation; information science and systems; programming languages; and systems analysis. Research in electrical engineering includes work in communications, semiconductor technology, and electronic circuits, which is relevant to computing, as well as work in electric power, which is not.[2] Data on research funding is categorized according to the National Science Foundation's definitions of basic research, applied research, and development uses. Although the distinctions among these categories are increasingly difficult to make in the computing industry, they reflect the manner in which federal statistics are currently collected (see Chapter 1).[3]

FEDERAL RESEARCH FUNDING[4]

Levels of Federal Support

Since the end of World War II, the federal government has been a strong supporter of computing research. Between 1976 and 1995 (the earliest and latest years for which consistent data are available), federal funding for research in computer science increased by a factor of five, from $180 million to $960 million in constant 1995 dollars (Figure 3.1). Growth has occurred in both basic and applied research, with basic research jumping from $65 million to $265 million and applied research rising from $116 million to almost $700 million over the 19-year period. Roughly 35 to 45 percent of total federal research funding for computer science has gone to universities, with industry and government laboratories garnering the remaining 55 to 65 percent; about 70 percent of the basic research funding went to universities during this period.[5]

In contrast to computer science, federal funding for research in electrical engineering remained essentially flat between 1972 and 1995. From a peak of $1.1 billion (in constant 1995 dollars) in 1972, the real dollar level of federal funding for research in electrical engineering dropped below $800 million in 1976 and, after exceeding the $1 billion mark again in 1987 and 1989, dipped back below $800 million in 1995. Despite the overall decline, obligations for basic research in electrical engineering grew during this time frame, from about $130 million in the 1970s and early 1980s to about $200 million after 1985 (Figure 3.2). As a result, the share of total research funding in electrical engineering going to basic research increased from 12 to 25 percent, and the share of total research funding going to universities rose from 10 to 23 percent.

Federal expenditures on computing research represent just a portion of the federal budget for scientific and technological research. Combined federal obligations for computer science and electrical engineering research climbed from just under $1 billion to $1.7 billion between 1976 and 1995, growing from 5 percent to almost 7 percent of the federal research budget. Several other fields, such as biology and physics, have historically maintained higher levels of federal investment than computer science and electrical engineering, although growth in physics research funding slowed after the mid-1980s (Figure 3.3).

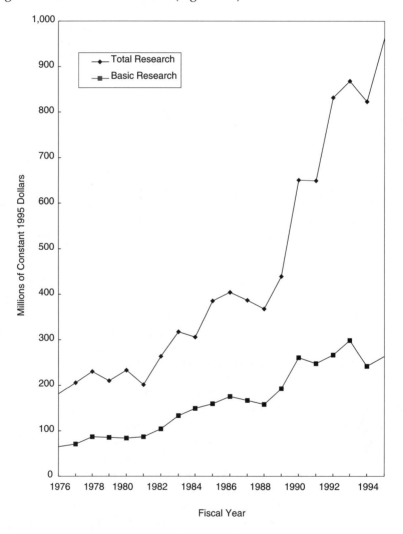

FIGURE 3.1 Federal funding for research in computer science, 1976-1995.
SOURCE: NSF (1998b), Tables 25 and 35.

Sources of Federal Support

Federal funding for research in computer science and electrical engineering has come through several federal agencies whose roles and levels of support have shifted over time. Because of the emphasis it placed on computing as a means of enhancing U.S. military capabilities during the Cold War, the U.S. Department of Defense (DOD) has long been the largest funder of computing and communications research. Early funding

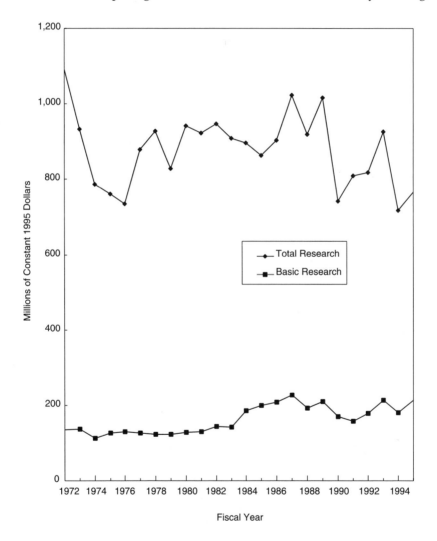

FIGURE 3.2 Federal funding for research in electrical engineering, 1971-1995.
SOURCE: NSF (1998b), Tables 25 and 35.

came from the Army and Office of Naval Research, but within 2 years of establishing its Information Processing Techniques Office in 1962, the Defense Advanced Research Projects Agency (DARPA) became the dominant source of funding, providing more support for computer science research than all other federal agencies combined. Between 1976 and 1995, DOD provided some 60 percent of total federal research funding in computer science and over 75 percent of total research funding in electrical engineering (Figures 3.4, 3.5).

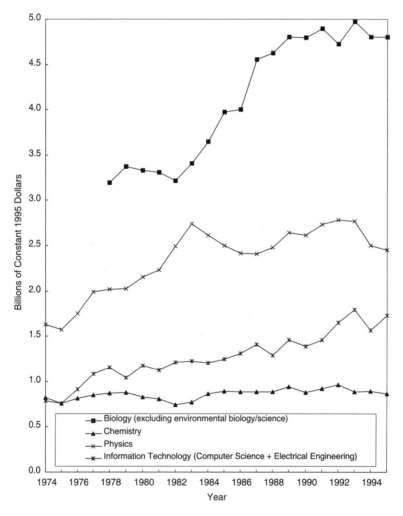

FIGURE 3.3 Federal funding for scientific research, 1974-1995.
SOURCE: NSF (1998b), Tables 25 and 35.

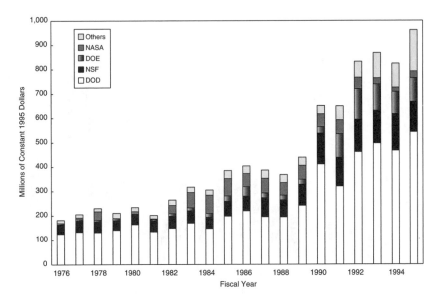

FIGURE 3.4 Federal funding for research in computer science by agency, 1976-1995.
SOURCE: NSF (1998c), Table 1.

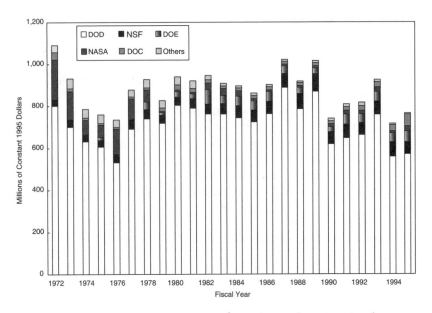

FIGURE 3.5 Federal funding for research in electrical engineering by agency, 1972-1995.
SOURCE: NSF (1998c), Table 1.

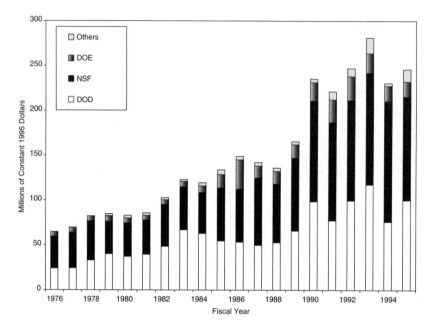

FIGURE 3.6 Federal funding for basic research in computer science by agency, 1976-1995.
SOURCE: NSF (1998c), Table 2.

By the 1970s, the National Science Foundation (NSF) emerged as the second largest supporter of research in computing and communications, providing 20 percent of all federal support for computer science research and 5 percent of federal support for electrical engineering research between 1976 and 1994. In contrast to DOD, NSF has concentrated its efforts on funding basic and university research in computer science, for which its research expenditures have generally equaled or exceeded those of DOD (Figure 3.6).[6] With the exception of a 4-year period between 1983 and 1987, NSF has provided between 40 and 45 percent of all basic research funding in computer science, and it has consistently provided about 40 percent of university research funding in computer science. In electrical engineering, NSF contributed just under 30 percent of the funding for basic research and 30 to 40 percent of the funding for university research, but it lagged behind DOD by a wide margin (Figure 3.7).

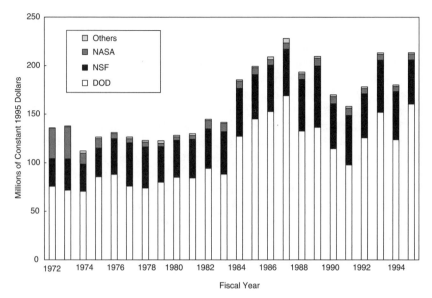

FIGURE 3.7 Federal funding for basic research in electrical engineering by agency, 1972-1995.
SOURCE: NSF (1998c), Table 2.

Comparisons to Industrial Research Funding

Federal funding has supported a substantial fraction of all research conducted in computing. In 1950, government funding for research and development dominated the computer world: it exceeded all industrial R&D spending on computing by a factor of three. As late as 1963, government still funded 35 percent of IBM's R&D in computing, 50 percent at Burroughs, and 40 percent at Control Data. But even by the 1960s the distribution was uneven, and several commercial suppliers, notably Honeywell and RCA, financed most of their R&D internally. Thus, the overall percentage of computer R&D supported by government declined dramatically from the late 1960s, both because of an absolute decline in government support and because of the rapid growth of the industry. In the mid-1970s, federal support represented only about 25 percent of computer R&D, and then shrank to a postwar low of 15 percent in 1979. With new programs and the Reagan administration's defense buildup, the level was restored to about 20 percent by 1983 (Flamm, 1987, p. 102).

These numbers alone, however, can be deceiving. Very little R&D performed in industry is research; most, in fact, counts as development. Even applied research accounts for only about 10 to 15 percent of industrial R&D in computing. Flamm estimates that the ratio of development to research in the computer industry was about seven to one in the early 1980s, and within the research category it was about seven to one of applied to basic (that is, basic research in industry is only about 2 percent of total R&D). Thus, when one excludes development from consideration, government support represented about 40 percent of all computer research, and half of that was basic research (Flamm, 1987, pp. 104-105).

Direct comparisons between federal and industrial research funding are hard to make because of differences in the way data are collected from federal and industry sources.[7] Nevertheless, a rough estimate of the federal share can be made by comparing federal funding for research in computer science to company funding for research in the office, computing, and accounting machinery industry.[8] This comparison shows that federal funding constituted roughly one-third of total computer-related research funding in the late 1970s (Figure 3.8). The federal share dipped

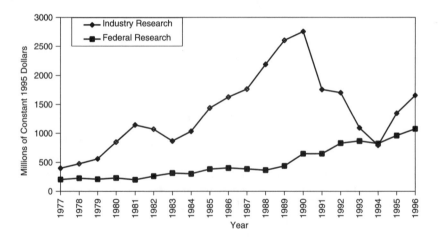

FIGURE 3.8 Federal and industrial funding for computing research, 1977-1996. Industry research, as shown, consists of company-funded research in computing and office equipment industry; it does not include company-funded research in other computing-related industries such as communications equipment, semiconductors, or computing and communications services. Government-funded research, as shown, consists of total federal funding for research in computer science. Industrial research data for 1978, 1980, 1982, 1985-1987, and 1989 were estimated from data on industry research and development expenditures and from the ratio of research to research and development in expenditures in years for which actual data were available.
SOURCE: Federal research funding from NSF (1998b), Table 25; industry research funding compiled from the 1979-1998 editions of the annual National Science Foundation report *Research and Development in Industry*.

to 15 percent in the early 1980s as industrial research funding expanded and federal funding stagnated, but by 1992 federal funding again constituted one-third of the total, owing to rapid growth in federal funding and restructuring and cutbacks in industry support.[9] Not included in this estimate are research expenditures financed by universities and nonprofit organizations, which tend to be much smaller than the amounts provided by federal agencies or industry.

Government also directed significant research funding to industry—even as the computer industry grew during the late 1970s. While the share of the computer industry's total R&D funds coming from government sources declined dramatically between 1975 and 1979, the share of the industry's *research* funding coming from the federal government remained high, declining only from 47 percent to 37 percent (Table 3.1). Flamm estimates that federal funding accounted for 40 percent of total computer industry research funding through the mid-1980s (Flamm, 1987, p. 104, Table 4-5). In the communications equipment industry, the federal role has been even larger and more pervasive.[10] In 1965, federal funds accounted for 66 percent of the industry's total R&D funding, a figure that declined to 40 percent by 1990. As a percentage of total industry *research*, federal funds declined steadily from 49 percent in 1965 to 19 percent in 1980, but then rebounded to account for half of all industry research funding in 1990 (Table 3.2). In contrast, federal funding has played a declining role in industrial R&D in the electronic components industry.[11] The percentage of industry R&D funding provided by government de-

TABLE 3.1 Funding for Industrial R&D and Research in Office and Computing Equipment, 1975-1979

	R&D		Research	
	Total Level (in millions of dollars)	Percent Federal	Total Level (in millions of dollars)	Percent Federal
1975	2,220	22	n.a.	n.a.
1976	2,402	21	269	47
1977	2,655	16	313	44
1978	2,883	11	n.a.	n.a.
1979	3,214	8	451	37

NOTE: Funding levels indicate total support for R&D and research conducted *by industry;* expenditures for research conducted by universities are excluded; n.a., data not available.
SOURCE: Data compiled from the National Science Foundation's biennial reports, *Research and Development in Industry,* issued between 1979 and 1992.

TABLE 3.2 Funding for Industrial R&D and Research in
Communications Equipment, 1965-1990

	R&D		Research	
	Funding (in millions of dollars)	Percent Federal	Funding (in millions of dollars)	Percent Federal
1965[a,b]	1,912	66	425	49
1970[a,b]	2,578	54	522	41
1975[b]	2,385	44	569	27
1979[c]	3,635	44	787	19
1985	9,397	45	1,674	30
1990	5,928	40	1,321	51

NOTE: Funding levels indicate total support for R&D and research conducted *by industry;* expenditures for research conducted by universities are excluded.

[a]Includes funding for electronic components, which had $330 million in R&D funding in 1972.

[b]Includes funding from the communications services industry.

[c]Data for 1979 are shown because complete data are not available for 1980.

SOURCE: Data compiled from the National Science Foundation's biennial reports, *Research and Development in Industry,* issued between 1979 and 1992.

clined from 38 percent in 1972 to 11 percent in 1990 as total R&D funding grew from $330 million to $4 billion.

These figures suggest that federal funding continued to play an important role in the expanding computing industry. It created economic opportunities for industry to exploit and, as such, expanded the private investments made to seize these opportunities. As new ideas emerged from federally funded research, companies capitalized on them. Indeed, firms in computing-related industries tend to spend a greater percentage of their sales revenues on R&D than do firms in most other industries (Figure 3.9). Roughly 10 to 20 percent of corporate R&D funds is spent on research as opposed to development.[12] Such expenditures tend to derive from, and result in, the fast pace of innovation characteristic of the field.

HUMAN RESOURCES

Human resources are essential to innovation, especially in knowledge-intensive fields like computing and communications. Attracting and educating students to new areas of research opportunity (especially, but by no means exclusively, at the graduate level) is a vital task—both in maintaining progress at the research frontier and in transferring new knowledge to industry by providing trained scientific and engineering

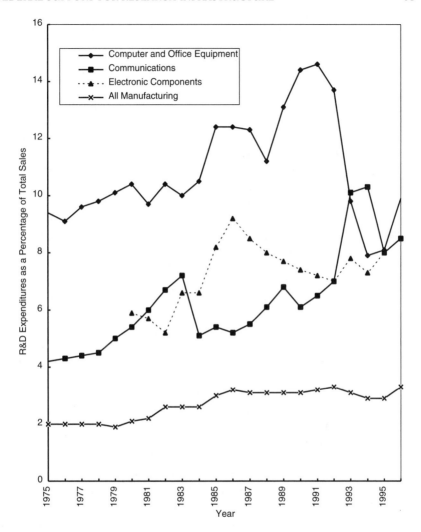

FIGURE 3.9 R&D intensity in computer-related industries, 1975-1996. Data for computing and office equipment between 1992 and 1996 reflect the reclassification of firms considered to be part of the industry.
SOURCE: NSF (1998a), Table A-18

personnel. In the United States, graduate education is tightly connected with university research, and university research budgets are an important driving force for graduate enrollment. The federal government has played an important role by supporting university research in computing and communications, which has directly and indirectly supported the education of graduate students and the creation of university departments in computer science.

Since 1965, the number of college and university departments in computer science and computer engineering has grown rapidly. The Taulbee surveys of U.S. and Canadian computer science and computer engineering departments show a steady growth in Ph.D.-granting departments, increasing linearly from 6 in 1965 to 56 in 1975 and to 148 in 1995 (Andrews, 1997).[13] Along with the expansion of academic computer science departments has been growth in enrollments at all levels, from undergraduate through doctorate. Between 1966 and 1986, the number of bachelor's degrees awarded in computer science skyrocketed from 89 to 42,000, surpassing the number of bachelor's degrees awarded in mathematics and electrical engineering (the largest engineering subdiscipline) in 1981 and in physics in 1982 (Figure 3.10). Electrical engineering also experienced significant growth, expanding at an average annual rate of 4 percent, from 11,000 to 27,000 during this period, while the total number of bachelor's degrees awarded in all academic fields rose at a 1 percent annual rate. Between 1987 and 1995, the number of bachelor's degrees awarded in both these fields declined precipitously, reflecting changing student preferences and shifts in the job market, as well as attempts by some universities to relieve the burden on electrical engineering and computer science departments by shifting students to other academic departments.[14] By 1995, the number of bachelor's degrees awarded in computer science and electrical engineering had declined to 25,000 and 18,000, respectively, although the decline showed evidence of leveling off.

Graduate student production also blossomed after 1965. In computer science, the number of master's degrees awarded climbed steadily at a rate of 14.5 percent a year between 1966 and 1995 (Figure 3.11). In electrical engineering, the number of master's degrees remained relatively constant at 4,000 per year from 1966 to 1980, and then began growing at a 6 percent annual rate. Such growth occurred despite the fact that the number of master's degrees awarded in all fields of science and engineering began to decline after 1977 and did not return to the 1977 level until 1990. At the Ph.D. level, the number of degrees awarded by U.S. universities in computer science grew from 19 in 1966 to over 900 in 1995, despite leveling off between 1976 and 1982 (Figure 3.12).[15] By comparison, the number of Ph.D.s awarded in electrical engineering and mathematics declined during the 1970s, although both fields began growing again in the 1980s and 1990s. Nevertheless, computer science has continued to lag behind both electrical engineering and mathematics in the total number of Ph.D.s awarded each year—despite leading in the number of bachelor and master degrees awarded. The percentage of Ph.D. recipients choosing a first job in industry (as opposed to academia) grew steadily between 1975 and

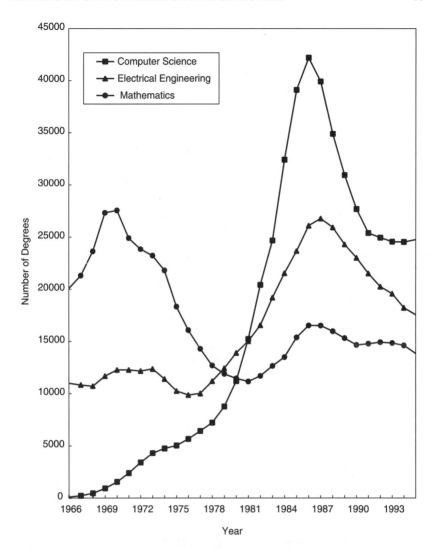

FIGURE 3.10 Bachelor's degrees awarded by field, 1966-1995.
SOURCE: NSF (1997b), Tables 30, 45, and 46.

1995, reflecting strong industrial demand for skilled computer scientists, and causing concern among universities about their ability to train the next generation of computer scientists (Table 3.3).

Foreign students have also played a large role in the growth of U.S. Ph.D. programs. The Taulbee surveys show that the percentage of Ph.D. recipients in computer science who are nonresident aliens increased from

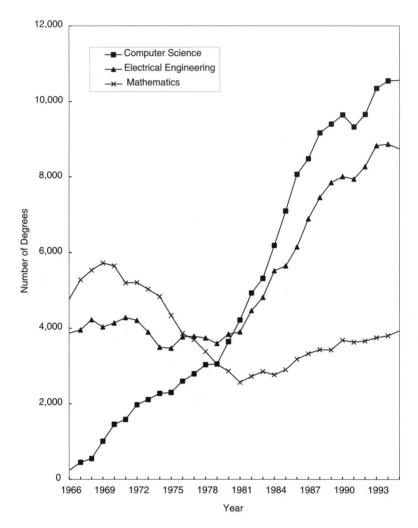

FIGURE 3.11 Master's degrees awarded by field, 1966-1995.
SOURCE: NSF (1997b), Tables 30, 45, and 46.

20 percent in the early 1970s to 40 percent in the 1980s and 1990s. In computer engineering the percentage reached as high as 64 percent. The United States has attracted a large number of foreign nationals, most of whom were first trained abroad before they entered graduate education in this country. These scientists and engineers have formed an important part of the nation's workforce in computing. It is reasonable to expect

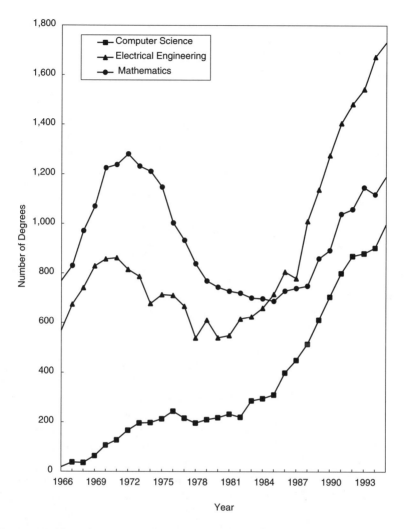

FIGURE 3.12 Doctoral degrees awarded by field, 1966-1995.
SOURCE: NSF (1997b), Tables 30, 45, and 46.

that fewer foreign students will decide to remain in the United States in
the future as opportunities for employment in their home countries increase. By 1997, U.S. industry was already seeing shortages of qualified
information technology personnel to fill job market vacancies, raising
questions about the need for policies to expand the proportion of the
labor force entrants who possess computing and related skills.[16]

TABLE 3.3 Employment, by Sector, for New Ph.D. Recipients in Computer Science and Engineering, 1970-1995

Sector	Number Employed (and percentage)				
	1970	1975	1985	1990	1995
Industry	37 (36)	69 (29)	145 (35)	355 (41)	375 (48)
Government	5 (5)	12 (5)	19 (5)	28 (3)	24 (3)
Academia	58 (56)	137 (57)	191 (46)	343 (40)	285 (37)
Other	3 (3)	24 (10)	38 (9)	131 (15)	92 (12)
TOTAL	103(100)	242(100)	412(100)	857(100)	776(100)

NOTE: Years refer to the start of the academic year for 1985, 1990, and 1995 and to the calendar year for 1970 and 1975. Totals do not include unknown employment, which totaled 9 in 1970, 12 in 1975, 15 in 1985, 217 in 1990, and 139 in 1995. Percentages may not add to 100 because of rounding.
SOURCE: Data compiled from annual Taulbee Surveys conducted between 1971 and 1996. See Note 12.

The federal government has directly and indirectly supported the creation of human resources in computing and communications. As early as the 1960s, federal agencies conducted or sponsored studies that identified human resource issues as matters of national concern.[17] Federal agencies have provided a number of fellowships for graduate students in computer science, and NSF has worked to develop curricula for university programs.[18] But the most important contribution has come indirectly through federal support of university research. Between 1976 and 1994, federal obligations for university research in computer science expanded from roughly $65 million to $360 million (Figure 3.13), and federal obligations for university research in electrical engineering more than doubled in real terms from $74 million to $161 million (Figure 3.14). Most of this funding has come from two sources, DARPA and NSF. Altogether, federal funding accounted for 70 percent of university research funding for computer science and between 65 and 75 percent of university research funding for electrical engineering from the mid 1970s through 1995 (Figure 3.15). The balance has come from a combination of industry, private foundations, state governments, and universities' own resources.

Federal funds play a significant role in supporting graduate students in electrical engineering and computer science. Data from the National Science Foundation indicate that between 1985 and 1996, the percentage

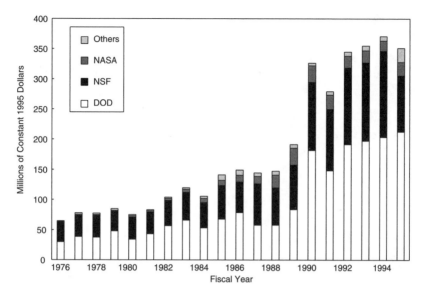

FIGURE 3.13 Federal funding for university research in computer science, 1976-1995.
SOURCE: NSF (1998d), Table 1.

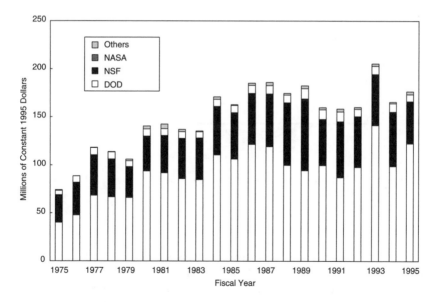

FIGURE 3.14 Federal funding for university research in electrical engineering, 1975-1995.
SOURCE: NSF (1998d), Table 1.

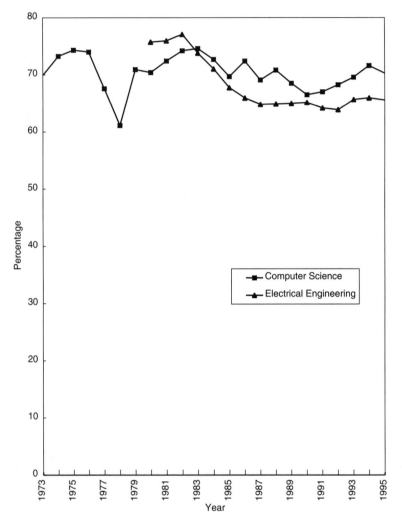

FIGURE 3.15 Portion of university research funding provided by the federal government, 1973-1995.
SOURCE: NSF (1998d), Table 2.

of graduate students in U.S. computer science and electrical engineering departments supported by federal funds (i.e., research assistantships, teaching assistantships, and fellowships) grew from 14 percent to 20 percent.[19] Over 75 percent of this support came in the form of research assistantships; over half of all research assistants in U.S. graduate programs between 1985 and 1996 received federal support.[20] In the nation's

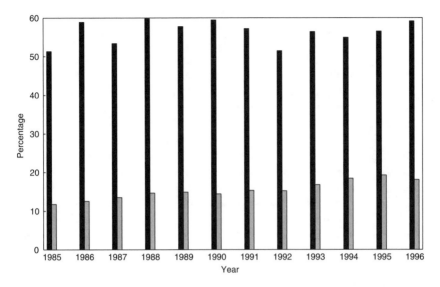

FIGURE 3.16   Computer science and electrical engineering graduate students supported by the federal government, 1985-1996.
SOURCE: Compiled from data in the National Science Foundation's online database of sources of support for science and engineering graduate students. The database is available via WebCASPAR at <http://caspar.qrc.com>.

top computer science departments, federal funding plays an even greater role (Figure 3.16). Between 1985 and 1995, approximately 56 percent of the graduate students in computer science and electrical engineering departments at the Massachusetts Institute of Technology (MIT), Carnegie Mellon University, and the University of California at Berkeley received federal funding, with research assistantships alone supporting 46 percent of them. At Stanford University, 27 percent of graduate students in electrical engineering and computer science received support from the federal government in 1997;[21] it is estimated that 50 to 60 percent of Stanford Ph.D. students in these departments receive federal funds.[22]

COMPUTER FACILITIES

Researchers need equipment and facilities with which to conduct their work. Acquiring and maintaining such equipment is especially challenging in computing and communications research because of the rapid growth of the field since the 1950s, the concomitant rise in the number of graduate students and faculty conducting research, and the rapid rate at which computing equipment becomes obsolete.[23]   In industry, support for research infrastructure is provided internally: corporate funds are used to build new facilities and to equip them with computers, networking equipment, and other research equipment, as needed. University infrastructure, on the other hand, relies on a mix of support from federal and state governments, university funds, and donations of equipment from industry. Since the 1960s, the federal government has been the dominant source of support for computing and communications research equipment.

Providing and supporting research infrastructure are expensive tasks. In 1988, for example, U.S. universities spent $187 million on equipment for academic computer centers and supercomputer centers, and an additional $334 million for maintenance, repair, and operations (Table 3.4). Computer science departments spent another $77 million on equipment purchases for research purposes and related maintenance, repair, and operational costs. Such expenditures are increasing faster than inflation as universities attempt to maintain state-of-the-art research centers and meet the demands of a growing pool of researchers. Between 1981 and 1995, expenditures for computer science research equipment alone (not including maintenance and operations) tripled in real terms from $25 million to $75 million. In electrical engineering, research equipment expenditures doubled during this same period to $68 million.

The federal government's support for financing the purchase of computing equipment by universities has taken a variety of forms, ranging from funding for general computing resources for universities, to financing of research-grant-related equipment in computer science departments, to establishing large supercomputer centers. While the first two of these missions required scientific or engineering computers of modest capabilities, the third required specialized computers to address large, complex

TABLE 3.4 University Expenditures for Computing Equipment, Maintenance, and Operations (in millions of dollars), 1988

Expenditure	Computer Science Departments	Computer Centers
Equipment	45	187
Maintenance and repair	17	84
Service contracts	12	58
Other (e.g., salaries, tools)	5	19
Operations	15	250
Technician salaries	12	156
Other (e.g., supplies)	3	94
TOTAL	77	521

SOURCE: NSF (1991), Tables 1 and 8.

problems of interest to DOD, other federal agencies (e.g., U.S. Meteorological Service), and academic research communities. All three required development of a networking infrastructure capable of linking researchers with resources that were geographically separated.

University Computing Centers

Among the first federal efforts to provide computing resources for universities was NSF's Institutional Computing Services program, established in 1956 to provide universities with computers for general educational use. Annual obligations expanded rapidly, and, between 1958 and 1970, NSF provided $66 million for such centers (Table 3.5). Other agencies also supported computing facilities on campuses during the 1960s. In fact, virtually all government-funded computer research included significant monies for equipment; one study estimated that in 1963 federal agencies were supplying about half the support for campus computing in the country. NSF support for computing facilities differed from that provided by other federal agencies because it was spread among a large number of universities and because it was not provided for use in any particular project sponsored by the government; rather, it supported general educational and scientific applications of computing. For example, NSF supported Philip Morse at MIT in his early work on time-sharing—a technology intended to improve the efficiency of facilities that NSF was already supporting at academic centers, by making them available to more users. DARPA support, in contrast, was aimed at a limited number

TABLE 3.5 National Science Foundation Obligations for Institutional Computing Services (in thousands of dollars)

Year	Funding
1958	200
1960	1,672
1962	2,975
1964	4,517
1966	8,899
1968	10,604
1970	6,563
TOTAL	65,913

SOURCE: Data for 1960-1967 compiled from the National Science Foundation's annual *Budget Request to Congress;* data for 1968-1970 compiled from the National Science Foundation's annual reports, *Grants and Awards.*

of select computer science departments (such as those at MIT, Carnegie Mellon University, and Stanford University) and was intended for use on DARPA projects, such as Project MAC and the ARPANET.

Departmental Computing

Other initiatives were targeted more specifically to computer science departments. Between 1981 and 1995, the federal government funded roughly 65 percent of the purchases of research equipment in computer science departments—providing 83 percent of such funding in 1985 (Figure 3.17). In electrical engineering, the share of equipment funds coming from the federal government declined from its 75 percent level in 1982, but remained at 60 percent in 1995 (Figure 3.18). Many government agencies provided funds for equipment in research contracts with universities, but NSF established two programs specifically designed to provide infrastructure for computer science departments: the Computer Research Equipment (CRE) program and the much larger Coordinated Experimental Research (CER) program.

The CRE program, initiated in the 1970s, provided basic computer support for computer science departments. Annual expenditures on the CRE between 1977 and 1985 grew to $1.4 million (Table 3.6). With the

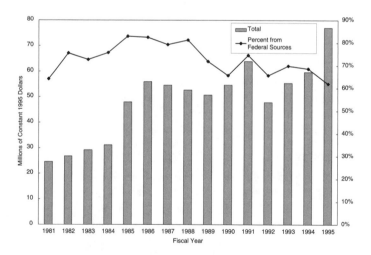

FIGURE 3.17 Expenditures for research equipment in computer science, 1981-1995. SOURCE: Compiled from data in the National Science Foundation's online database of current fund research equipment expenditures for computer science between fiscal years 1981 and 1995. The database is available via WebCASPAR at <http://caspar.qrc.com>.

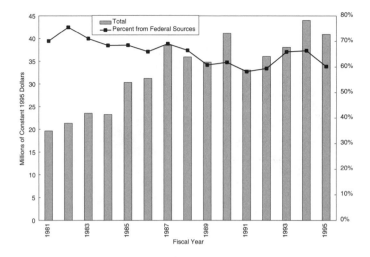

FIGURE 3.18 Expenditures for research equipment in electrical engineering, 1981-1995.
SOURCE: Compiled from data in the National Science Foundation's online database of current fund research equipment expenditures for electrical engineering between fiscal years 1981 and 1995. The database is available via WebCASPAR at <http://caspar.qrc.com>.

formation of the Computing and Information Science and Engineering (CISE) Directorate in 1986, CRE became the CISE Research Instrumentation Program. Program funding grew from $2 million to $3.8 million between 1987 and 1996.

The CER, started in 1981, was a response to growing concerns that computer science departments were not producing enough Ph.D.s in part because they lacked funds to pursue large-scale experimental computer research (NSF, 1981a). The majority of CER funds was allocated to the Experimental Computer Research Program, which provided "support of special purpose equipment needed by more than one computer research project and difficult to justify on a single project" (NSF, 1981b). This program also paid for recruitment and retention of quality faculty and technicians for the new computer science centers.[24] Another portion of the CER, the CSNET program (described in more detail below), although constituting less than 10 percent of the CER budget, made major strides in networking by linking computer science departments together to expedite research through a more open forum for ideas. The CER was renamed the CISE Institutional Infrastructure Program in 1986, and funding grew from $14 million to $23 million.

TABLE 3.6 National Science Foundation Expenditures on the
Coordinated Experimental Research and Computing Research
Equipment Programs (in millions of dollars), 1977-1985

Year	CRE	CER	Experimental Computer Research[a]	Total Budget of Computer Sciences Section (1977-1983) and Division of Computer Research (1984-1985)
1977	1.65			15.79
1978	1.55			16.63
1979	1.66			16.77
1980	1.97			18.17
1981	1.02	5.69	3.77	22.12
1982	1.21	8.55	7.10	25.59
1983	1.20	11.19	9.52	33.88
1984	1.39	13.50	12.74	33.79
1985	1.46	14.99	14.76	38.59
TOTAL	13.11	53.92	47.89	221.33

[a]Experimental Computer Research was the predominant source of infrastructure support
within the Coordinated Experimental Research Program. It does not include support for
faculty or CSNET.
SOURCE: Data for 1977-1993 compiled from the annual *Summary of Awards* for the National
Science Foundation's Mathematical Sciences Section. Data for 1984-1985 compiled from the
annual *Summary of Awards* of the National Science Foundation's Division of Computer
Sciences.

High-performance Computing

The government has been the largest supporter of access to high-
performance computers for researchers, especially those in universities.
Through the mid-1980s, government funding of the IBM 701, UNIVAC
LARC (Livermore Automatic Research Computer), Stretch, and later both
the CDC and the Cray series of computers created large systems that were
used for a variety of applications by researchers. In 1985, NSF launched a
program of supercomputer centers to provide access to high-performance
machines and to encourage development of useful technology and applications. Annual expenditures increased from $29 million to $71 million in
1996. This funding originally created five centers nationwide that provide researchers in many disciplines with access to supercomputer time.[25]
The centers were intended to allow for advanced computationally complex research that cannot be carried out on regular computers. Over time,
the centers became the early proving grounds of a long-developing new

architecture for high-performance computing—parallel computing. The centers also play an important educational role for some computer science departments teaching parallel computing (CSTB, 1992, p. 225), and they became the spur for additional supercomputer centers, paid for by state and private sources, to be established in other universities. Some computer scientists contend, however, that the supercomputers offered little value to researchers in computer science and that their primary use was by scientists in other disciplines. There has been a long-standing tension in the computer programs about support for computer research and provision of computer facilities to support research in other scientific and engineering disciplines.

Nevertheless, numerous innovations emanated from these centers. They catalyzed work leading to modeling and visualization tools, motivated development of the browser technology for the World Wide Web, and introduced industry to large-scale scientific and engineering calculation on an impressive scale. Both university and government laboratory computer centers were in the forefront of availing themselves of new communications technology to link users and providers and to make more efficient use of computer power on a national level. Many of the centers were used by researchers in the oil, automotive, and pharmaceutical industries whose companies had joined the centers as industrial partners so that they might explore the benefits of supercomputers in their research, development, and manufacturing efforts. As such, the supercomputer sites brought together academic and industry researchers to work on problems of mutual benefit and filled a much-needed gap for computing resources. In doing so, the centers generated scientific and technical benefits as well as economic ones.

Network Infrastructure

Federal agencies have long supported development and deployment of networking infrastructure to assist the research communities in computing and communications. As early as 1973, NSF initiated a program called Networking for Science, which provided between $600,000 and $750,000 per year to create computer networks for university researchers. More significant support for network infrastructure followed upon the development of packet-switched networking technologies by DARPA in the late 1960s and 1970s. This technology formed the basis of the ARPANET, which connected researchers at universities supported by DARPA research funding (see Chapter 7).

Use of the ARPANET expanded to the computer science research community and other scientific research communities starting in the 1970s. After management of the ARPANET was transferred to the Defense Communications Agency (now the Defense Information Systems Agency) in 1975, a number of federally supported, discipline-specific networks were established. These included (1) MFEnet, funded by the Department of Energy (DOE) to give academic physicists working on nuclear fusion access to supercomputers at Lawrence Livermore National Laboratory; (2) HEPnet, also funded by DOE to support research in high-energy physics; and (3) Space Physics Analysis Network, funded by the National Aeronautics and Space Administration (NASA). In the early 1980s, NSF established the CSNET to link computer science researchers at different universities who were not attached to the ARPANET. CSNET combined access to ARPANET, TELENET (a commercial packet-switched system run by a subsidiary of Bolt, Beranek, and Newman), and PhoneNet (an e-mail-only system for other academic departments). By 1985, CSNET had links to over 170 university, industrial, and government research organizations. In 1987, it merged with BITNET, another network serving users from academic institutions. CSNET operations were continued under the Corporation for Research and Education Networking until the fall of 1991 (CSTB, 1994, p. 238). The success of the CSNET convinced researchers of the value of a national computer network and therefore provided the impetus for NSF's more notable networking project, the NSFNET (Hafner and Lyon, 1996, pp. 241-245).

In 1986, NSF launched NSFNET, the backbone of a network that connected hundreds of colleges and universities in the United States with high-speed links and was used by departments of all varieties, including computer science and engineering. NSFNET linked NSF's five super-computing centers and, in coordination with the connections programs of the late 1980s, provided seed funding to allow regional networks (such as the New York State Education and Research Network, or NYSERNet) and universities to interconnect. The connections program provided 2 years of financial support, after which participants were expected to assume financial responsibility. Under the federal government's National Research and Education Network program, different federal agencies, including NSF, NASA, DOE, DARPA, and the National Library of Medicine, launched or expanded separate, interconnected networking efforts that served specific communities. NSF's funding for NSFNET grew from $6.5 million in 1987 to $25 million in 1992, during which time the capacity of the backbone was upgraded several times. With the commercialization of the Internet in 1993, NSF's responsibility for managing the network declined, but it continued to fund development and deployment of high-speed network infrastructure, including the very high speed backbone networking system and the Next-Generation Internet. Expenditures on such network infrastructure reached $42 million in 1996.

EFFECTS OF FEDERAL INVESTMENTS IN
RESEARCH INFRASTRUCTURE

The effects of federal investments in research infrastructure have been felt throughout the computing industry. Many concepts that were developed by industry and designed into products received their initial impetus from government-sponsored research and large-scale government development programs. Examples include core memories, computer time-sharing, the mouse, packet switching, computer graphics and virtual reality, speech recognition software, and relational databases. Chapter 4 and Chapters 6 through 10 of this report trace the influences of federal research funding upon the development of the particular technologies described above.

A more general sense of the broader linkages between federally funded research and innovation in computing can be derived from patent statistics. Although not an entirely satisfactory measure of innovation, patents can provide a rough measure of invention and, through the references cited within them, they can help in tracing the intellectual inputs to inventions.[26] Recent studies by CHI Research, Inc., suggest a significant—and growing—linkage between publicly funded research and patents (and by extension, innovation). Between 1985 and 1994, the number of scientific or technical papers cited in individual patents rose from 0.4 to 1.4 in the United States.[27] Of these papers, almost 75 percent were written by public-sector researchers in the United States or abroad (the public sector includes government laboratories, universities, and federally funded research and development centers). For the specific industries analyzed, reliance on public science was highest in drugs and medicines (79 percent of referenced papers) and lowest in electrical components (49 percent of referenced papers). Data for IBM indicate that only 21 percent of the papers referenced in its patents in 1993-1994 were written by IBM employees; 25 percent referenced papers by researchers at U.S. universities (Narin et al., 1997).

Similar figures hold for the computer industry. Between 1993 and 1994, 1,619 patents were issued in the United States containing references to papers published in computing-related journals, such as *IEEE Transactions on Computers*, the *IBM Journal of Research and Development*, *Communications of the ACM*, and *Computer*. Despite the fact that 75 percent of these patents were issued to U.S. companies, the majority of the papers cited by these patents were written by university or government researchers (Table 3.7). Moreover, of the papers for which funding information is available, 51 percent acknowledged funding from the federal government, whereas 37 percent acknowledged industry funding. NSF support was acknowledged in 22 percent of the papers, DARPA support in 6 percent.[28] These

TABLE 3.7 Authorship and Source of Financial Support for Computer-related Papers Cited in U.S. Patents Granted in 1993-1994

Sector of Author(s)	Number of Papers Cited	Number of Acknowledgments per Source of Funding								
		Industry	University	Government	Nonprofit	Foreign	Unknown	Total	NSF[a]	DARPA[a]
Industry	345	344	0	31	2	6	7	390	2	2
University	397	113	36	610	11	9	97	876	262	81
Industry and university	82	68	0	82	6	0	2	158	45	4
Government and university	7	4	0	9	0	0	4	17	2	1
TOTAL	831	529	36	732	19	15	110	1,441	311	88
Percent		37	3	51	1	1	8	100	22	6

[a]As a subset of the number acknowledging funding by the federal government.
SOURCE: Based on patent citation, authorship, and funding data provided by Francis Narin and Anthony Breitzman, CHI Research, Inc., Haddon Heights, N.J.

data are limited in that they reflect patenting behavior only during a recent 2-year period. Nevertheless, they suggest that federally sponsored research—especially that conducted at universities—continues to contribute to innovation in computing even as the computer industry has grown.

CONCLUSION

As this chapter demonstrates, the federal government has played an important role in helping to create the research infrastructure needed to support the nation's computing industry. The federal government became the primary source of funding for university research in computer science and electrical engineering and for research equipment in these disciplines. It also became the primary supporter of graduate students studying—and conducting research—in these fields. Such support complemented industry's efforts to build the much larger industrial infrastructure needed for successful innovation in computing and industry's contributions to public infrastructure (through equipment grants, tuition reimbursement, and sponsored research). Together, these investments created a publicly available pool of resources for others to draw upon. As subsequent chapters of this report describe in more detail, people with ideas and training made possible by public investments in research infrastructure helped staff the information revolution, disseminate its ideas, and chart its course. As part of the larger innovation process, they helped the nation to establish a dominant position in the international market for computing technology and to enjoy resulting social and economic benefits.

NOTES

1.   In aircraft, the government established the National Advisory Committee on Aeronautics in 1915 to address both instrumentation and generic design in the form of a wind tunnel and the design of an aerodynamic foil or wing. The National Aeronautics and Space Administration continues to play a role in aeronautics research. The former U.S. Bureau of Standards, now the National Institute of Standards and Technology, has undertaken much research in developing scientific and technical standards in the fields of metallurgy, optics, and electronics, as well as in computing hardware and software.

2.   The definitions of computer science and electrical engineering used in this report derive from those used by the National Science Foundation (NSF) in its surveys of federal research expenditures. See NSF (1997a).

3.   NSF defines basic research as research in which "the objective of the sponsoring agency is to gain more complete knowledge or understanding of the fundamental aspects of phenomena and of observable facts, without specific applications toward processes or products in mind." It defines applied research as work

in which "the objective of the sponsoring agency is to gain knowledge or under-standing necessary for determining the means by which a recognized need may be met." See NSF (1997a).

4.   Several shortcomings also exist in the data and statistics that follow. They are somewhat incomplete as data for the early years of computing are either poorly documented or intermixed with data from mathematics, electrical engineering, or other disciplines. Some data are not generally available. For example, data on the National Security Agency's expenditures on computer-related research, although early and extensive, are not publicly available.

5.   All data contained in this section derive from NSF (1997a) unless otherwise noted.

6.   It is notoriously difficult to distinguish among basic and applied research in DOD. While DOD divides its R&D expenditures into several categories, with 6.1 designating basic research, 6.2 designating applied research, and 6.3 designating advanced development, the classifications are often used in incompatible ways. Some of the work classified as 6.2 is often claimed to result in fundamental breakthroughs. Hence, comparisons among federal agencies are somewhat ambiguous.

7.   Statistics on federal and industry research spending are difficult to compare because they are compiled through different surveys (both administered by NSF), and because relevant spending is classified differently. Whereas federal research funding is classified by academic discipline (such as computer science or electrical engineering), industry research funding is classified by industry (computing and office equipment versus communications equipment). The comparison shown herein does not include industry-funded research for communications, electronic components, or related services, nor does it include the portion of federal funding of research in electrical engineering that might be relevant to those areas.

8.   Office, Computing, and Accounting Machinery is the industry defined in the standardized industrial classification (SIC) codes (used for classifying government statistics on industrial production, employment, trade, and so on) that is most closely aligned with computing. It includes electronic computers, computer storage devices, computer terminals, other computer peripheral equipment, calculating and accounting machines (except electronic computers), and other office machines. It does not include communications equipment, electronic components, or software, which are classified as part of other industries.

9.   The sharp decline in reported industry research expenditures in 1992-1994 resulted, in large part, from a reclassification of several companies into other industries (typically in the service sector). The reported rise in research spending between 1994 and 1996 reflects a combination of growing industry expenditures on research and the inclusion of several additional firms within the office and computing equipment industry category.

10.   The communications equipment industry, SIC code 366, includes manufacturers of telephone, networking, radio, and television broadcasting equipment. It does not include communications service providers, such as telephone companies, radio and television broadcasting stations, and cable television companies, which are separately classified under SIC code 48. Historical data on R&D ex-

penditures by communications service firms are not generally available, although they are included in the communications equipment totals prior to 1976.

11. The electronic components industry includes integrated circuits as well as discrete components, such as transistors, diodes, resistors, and capacitors. Statistics on federal and industrial support for research (as opposed to R&D) in this sector are not available.

12. This estimate is based on annual data compiled by the National Science Foundation and contained in its series of publications, *Research and Development in Industry,* between 1956 and 1998.

13. The Taulbee surveys of Ph.D.-granting departments were initiated and administered by Orin Taulbee at the University of Pittsburgh from 1970 through 1984. They were administered subsequently by David Gries and Dorothy Marsh at Cornell University through 1991 and are now administered by the Computing Research Association with assistance from David Gries. Results were originally presented in *Communications of the ACM* and now appear in *Computing Research News.*

14. For example, in the late 1980s, MIT established a program in mathematics with a focus on computer science and another program in physics with a concentration in semiconductor devices and electronics as a means of reducing enrollments in its departments of electrical engineering and computer science.

15. The leveling off of Ph.D. production around 1980 caused considerable concern in the computer science community.

16. See, for example, U.S. Department of Commerce (1997).

17. See, for example, NSF (1988).

18. Professional societies also played a role in developing curricula for computer science education. The Association for Computing Machinery (ACM), sponsored the first major work on curricula for computer science, Curriculum 68, which influenced the undergraduate curriculum in many departments formed in the 1970s. Later, the ACM and the Institute of Electrical and Electronics Engineers (IEEE) Computer Society worked together on curriculum efforts and jointly created the Computer Science Accreditation Board, which accredits undergraduate departments of computer science.

19. Data compiled from the National Science Foundation's database of sources of support for full-time science and engineering students, by academic discipline for fiscal years 1972-1996. The database is available online at <http://caspar.nsf.gov/cgi-bin/webic.exe?template=/nsf/srs/webcasp/start.wi>.

20. Between 20 and 23 percent of all graduate students in U.S. computer science and electrical engineering departments were supported by research assistantships during the time frame indicated.

21. Personal communication from Susan Clement, Stanford University, July 9, 1998. Statistics reported to NSF by Stanford University tend to underestimate the role of federal funding in supporting graduate students because they count only students supported by fellowships, not research assistantships. The Stanford figures cited in this chapter were provided directly by the university and count all forms of federal support.

22. Personal communication from John Hennessy, Dean of Engineering, Stanford University, June 22, 1998.

23. See Van Dam et al. (1991).

24. Personal communication with John R. Lehmann, Deputy Division Director for Computer-Communications Research, National Science Foundation, July 31, 1997.

25. In 1997, NSF restructured the Advanced Scientific Computing Centers program into the Partnership for Advanced Computation Infrastructure (PACI). Under the PACI program, each partnership operates a leading-edge site that maintains high-end hardware systems that are one or two orders of magnitude more capable than those typically available at a major research university. Non-leading-edge partners are expected to contribute to access, outreach, training, and software development. Two partnerships support two leading-edge centers and over 60 partners. These are the the the National Computational Science Alliance, which is anchored by the National Center for Supercomputing Applications in Urbana-Champaign, Illinois, and the National Partnership for Advanced Computational Infrastructure, anchored by the San Diego Supercomputing Center in California.

26. Invention refers to the creation of new products or processes that meet the test of novelty and utility and are not obvious to experts in the field. Innovation generally refers to the development and application of a new product, process, or service. As a result, patent statistics suffer from a number of shortcomings as a measure of innovation. Patents register new inventions, not innovation. Many inventions are never commercialized, and many innovations are never patented. For example, a firm may decide to keep its innovation a trade secret rather than filing a patent, which requires a disclosure of the operation of the new product, process, or service. Much technological progress emerges from incremental innovation, learning by doing, and adaptation of existing technologies. Patent statistics do not provide any indication of the economic value of the invention patented.

27. The vast majority of patents do not cite scientific or technical literature; they tend to cite previous patents, demonstrating the degree to which they represent incremental improvements to the state of the art.

28. The estimates of patents and cited papers contained in this paragraph derive from data provided by Francis Narin and Anthony Breitzman at CHI Research, Inc., in Haddon Heights, N.J.

4

The Organization of Federal Support: A Historical Review

Rather than a single, overarching framework of support, federal funding for research in computing has been managed by a set of agencies and offices that carry the legacies of the historical periods in which they were created. Crises such as World War II, Korea, Sputnik, Vietnam, the oil shocks, and concerns over national competitiveness have all instigated new modes of government support. Los Alamos National Laboratory, for example, a leader in supercomputing, was created by the Manhattan Project and became part of the Department of Energy. The Office of Naval Research and the National Science Foundation emerged in the wake of World War II to continue the successful contributions of wartime science. The Defense Advanced Research Projects Agency (DARPA) and the National Aeronautics and Space Administration (NASA) are products of the Cold War, created in response to the launch of Sputnik to regain the nation's technological leadership. The National Bureau of Standards, an older agency, was transformed into the National Institute of Standards and Technology in response to recent concerns about national competitiveness. Each organization's style, mission, and importance have changed over time; yet each organization profoundly reflects the process of its development, and the overall landscape is the result of numerous layers of history.

Understanding these layers is crucial for discussing the role of the federal government in computing research. This chapter briefly sets out a history of the federal government's programmatic involvement in computing research since 1945, distinguishing the various layers in the historical eras in which they were first formed. The objective is to identify the changing role the government has played in these different historical periods, discuss the changing political and technological environment in which federal organizations have acted, and draw attention to the multiplicity, diversity, and flexibility of public-sector programs that have stimulated and underwritten the continuing stream of U.S. research in computing and communications since World War II. In fulfilling this charge, the chapter reviews a number of prominent federal research programs that exerted profound influence on the evolving computing industry. These programs are illustrative of the effects of federal funding on the industry at different times. Other programs, too numerous to describe in this chapter, undoubtedly played key roles in the history of the computing industry but are not considered here.

1945-1960: ERA OF GOVERNMENT COMPUTERS

In late 1945, just a few weeks after atomic bombs ended World War II and thrust the world into the nuclear age, digital electronic computers began to whir. The ENIAC (Electronic Numerical Integrator and Computer), built at the University of Pennsylvania and funded by the Army Ballistic Research Laboratory, was America's first such machine. The following 15 years saw electronic computing grow from a laboratory technology into a routine, useful one. Computing hardware moved from the ungainly and delicate world of vacuum tubes and paper tape to the reliable and efficient world of transistors and magnetic storage. The 1950s saw the development of key technical underpinnings for widespread computing: cheap and reliable transistors available in large quantities, rotating magnetic drum and disk storage, magnetic core memory, and beginning work in semiconductor packaging and miniaturization, particularly for missiles. In telecommunications, American Telephone and Telegraph (AT&T) introduced nationwide dialing and the first electronic switching systems at the end of the decade. A fledgling commercial computer industry emerged, led by International Business Machines (IBM) (which built its electronic computer capability internally) and Remington Rand (later Sperry Rand), which purchased Eckert-Mauchly Computer Corporation in 1950 and Engineering Research Associates in 1952. Other important participants included Bendix, Burroughs, General Electric (GE), Honeywell, Philco, Raytheon, and Radio Communications Authority (RCA).

In computing, the technical cutting edge, however, was usually pushed forward in government facilities, at government-funded research centers, or at private contractors doing government work. Government funding accounted for roughly three-quarters of the total computer field.

A survey performed by the Army Ballistics Research Laboratory in 1957, 1959, and 1961 lists every electronic stored-program computer in use in the country (the very possibility of compiling such a list says a great deal about the community of computing at the time). The surveys reveal the large proportion of machines in use for government purposes, either by federal contractors or in government facilities (Weik, 1955, pp. 57-61; Flamm, 1988).

The Government's Early Role

Before 1960, government—as a funder and as a customer—dominated electronic computing. Federal support had no broad, coherent approach, however, arising somewhat ad hoc in individual federal agencies. The period was one of experimentation, both with the technology itself and with diverse mechanisms for federal support. From the panoply of solutions, distinct successes and failures can be discerned, from both scientific and economic points of view. After 1960, computing was more prominantly recognized as an issue for federal policy. The National Science Foundation and the National Academy of Sciences issued surveys and reports on the field.

If government was the main driver for computing research and development (R&D) during this period, the main driver for government was the defense needs of the Cold War. Events such as the explosion of a Soviet atomic bomb in 1949 and the Korean War in the 1950s heightened international tensions and called for critical defense applications, especially command-and-control and weapons design. It is worth noting, however, that such forces did not exert a strong influence on telecommunications, an area in which most R&D was performed within AT&T for civilian purposes. Long-distance transmission remained analog, although digital systems were in development at AT&T's Bell Laboratories. Still, the newly emergent field of semiconductors was largely supported by defense in its early years. During the 1950s, the Department of Defense (DOD) supported about 25 percent of transistor research at Bell Laboratories (Flamm, 1988, p. 16; Misa, 1985).

However much the Cold War generated computer funding, during the 1950s dollars and scale remained relatively small compared to other fields, such as aerospace applications, missile programs, and the Navy's Polaris program (although many of these programs had significant computing components, especially for operations research and advanced management techniques). By 1950, government investment in computing amounted to $15 million to $20 million per year.

All of the major computer companies during the 1950s had significant components of their R&D supported by government contracts of some type. At IBM, for example, federal contracts supported more than half of the R&D and about 35 percent of R&D as late as 1963 (only in the late 1960s did this proportion of support trail off significantly, although absolute amounts still increased). The federal government supported projects and ideas the private sector would not fund, either for national security, to build up human capital, or to explore the capabilities of a complex, expensive technology whose long-term impact and use was uncertain. Many federally supported projects put in place prototype hardware on which researchers could do exploratory work.

Establishment of Organizations

The successful development projects of World War II, particularly radar and the atomic bomb, left policymakers asking how to maintain the technological momentum in peacetime. Numerous new government organizations arose, attempting to sustain the creative atmosphere of the famous wartime research projects and to enhance national leadership in science and technology. Despite Vannevar Bush's efforts to establish a new national research foundation to support research in the nation's universities, political difficulties prevented the bill from passing until 1950, and the National Science Foundation (NSF) did not become a significant player in computing until later in that decade. During the 15 years immediately after World War II, research in computing and communications was supported by mission agencies of the federal government, such as DOD, the Department of Energy (DOE), and NASA. In retrospect, it seems that the nation was experimenting with different models for supporting this intriguing new technology that required a subtle mix of scientific and engineering skill.

Military Research Offices

Continuity in basic science was provided primarily by the Office of Naval Research (ONR), created in 1946 explicitly to perpetuate the contributions scientists made to military problems during World War II. In computing, the agency took a variety of approaches simultaneously. First, it supported basic intellectual and mathematical work, particularly in numerical analysis. These projects proved instrumental in establishing a sound mathematical basis for computer design and computer processing. Second, ONR supported intellectual infrastructure in the infant field of computing, sponsoring conferences and publications for information dissemination. Members of ONR participated in founding the Association for Computing Machinery in 1947.

ONR's third approach to computing was to sponsor machine design and construction. It ordered a computer for missile testing through the National Bureau of Standards from Raytheon, which became known as the Raydac machine, installed in 1952 (Rees, 1982). ONR supported Whirlwind, MIT's first digital computer and progenitor of real-time command-and-control systems (Redmond and Smith, 1980). John von Neumann built a machine with support from ONR and other agencies at Princeton's Institute for Advanced Study, known as the IAS computer (Goldstine, 1972; Rees, 1982). The project produced significant advances in computer architecture, and the design was widely copied by both government and industrial organizations.

Other military services created offices on a model similar to that of ONR. The Air Force Office of Scientific Research was established in 1950 to manage U.S. Air Force R&D activities. Similarly, the U.S. Army established the Army Research Office to manage and promote Army programs in science and technology.

National Bureau of Standards

Arising out of its role as arbiter of weights and measures, the National Bureau of Standards (NBS) had long had its own laboratories and technical expertise and had long served as a technical advisor to other government agencies. In the immediate postwar years, NBS sought to expand its advisory role and help U.S. industry develop wartime technology for commercial purposes. NBS, through its National Applied Mathematics Laboratory, acted as a kind of expert agent for other government agencies, selecting suppliers and overseeing construction and delivery of new computers. For example, NBS contracted for the three initial Univac machines—the first commercial, electronic, digital, stored-program computers—one for the Census Bureau and two for the Air Materiel Command.

NBS also got into the business of building machines. When the Univac order was plagued by technical delays, NBS built its own computer in-house. The Standards Eastern Automatic Computer (SEAC) was built for the Air Force and dedicated in 1950, the first operational, electronic, stored-program computer in this country. NBS built a similar machine, the Standards Western Automatic Computer (SWAC) for the Navy on the West Coast (Huskey, 1980). Numerous problems were run on SEAC, and the computer also served as a central facility for diffusing expertise in programming to other government agencies. Despite this significant hardware, however, NBS's bid to be a government center for computing expertise ended in the mid-1950s. Caught up in postwar debates over science policy and a controversy over battery additives, NBS research funding was radically reduced, and NBS lost its momentum in the field of computing (Akera, 1996).

Atomic Energy Commission

Nuclear weapons design and research have from the beginning provided impetus to advances in large-scale computation. The first atomic bombs were designed only with desktop calculators and punched-card equipment, but continued work on nuclear weapons provided some of the earliest applications for the new electronic machines as they evolved. The first computation job run on the ENIAC in 1945 was an early calculation for the hydrogen bomb project "Super." In the late 1940s, the Los Alamos National Laboratory built its own computer, MANIAC, based on von Neumann's design for the Institute for Advanced Study computer at Princeton, and the Atomic Energy Commission (AEC) funded similar machines at Argonne National Laboratory and Oak Ridge National Laboratory (Seidel, 1996; Goldstine, 1980).

In addition to building their own computers, the AEC laboratories were significant customers for supercomputers. The demand created by AEC laboratories for computing power provided companies with an incentive to design more powerful computers with new designs. In the early 1950s, IBM built its 701, the Defense Calculator, partly with the assurance that Los Alamos and Livermore would each buy at least one. In 1955, the AEC laboratory at Livermore, California, commissioned Remington Rand to design and build the Livermore Automatic Research Computer (LARC), the first supercomputer. The mere specification for LARC advanced the state of the art, as the bidding competition required the use of transistors instead of vacuum tubes (MacKenzie, 1991). IBM developed improved ferrite-core memories and supercomputer designs with funding from the National Security Agency, and designed and built the Stretch supercomputer for the Los Alamos Scientific Laboratory, beginning it in 1956 and installing it in 1961. Seven more Stretch supercomputers were built. Half of the Stretch supercomputers sold were used for nuclear weapon research and design (Pugh, 1995; pp. 222-223).

The AEC continued to specify and buy newer and faster supercomputers, including the Control Data 6600, the STAR 100, and the Cray 1 (although developed without AEC funds), practically ensuring a market for continued advancements (Pugh, 1995; p. 192). AEC and DOE laboratories also developed much of the software used in high-performance computing including operating systems, numerical analysis software, and matrix evaluation routines (Flamm, 1987, p. 82). In addition to stimulating R&D in industry, the AEC laboratories also developed a large talent pool on which the computer industry and academia could draw. In fact, the head of IBM's Applied Science Department, Cuthbert Hurd, came directly to IBM in 1949 from the AEC's Oak Ridge National Laboratory (Hurd, 1994). Physicists worked on national security problems with government support providing demand, specifications, and technical input, as well as dollars, for industry to make significant advances in computing technology.

Private Organizations

Not all the new organizations created by the government to support computing were public. A number of new private organizations also sprang up with innovative new charters and government encouragement that held prospects of initial funding support. In 1956, at the request of the Air Force, the Massachusetts Institute of Technology (MIT) created Project Lincoln, now known as the Lincoln Laboratory, with a broad charter to study problems in air defense to protect the nation from nuclear attack. The Lincoln Laboratory then oversaw the construction of the Semi-Automatic Ground Environment (SAGE) air-defense system (Box 4.1) (Bashe et al., 1986, p. 262). In 1946, the Air Force and Douglas Aircraft created a joint venture, Project RAND, to study intercontinental warfare. In the following year RAND separated from Douglas and became the independent, nonprofit RAND Corporation.

RAND worked only for the Air Force until 1956, when it began to diversify to other defense and defense-related contractors, such as the Advanced Research Projects Agency and the Atomic Energy Commission, and provided, for a time, what one researcher called "in some sense the world's largest installation for scientific computing [in 1950]."[1] RAND specialized in developing computer systems, such as the Johnniac, based on the IAS computer, which made RAND the logical source for the programming on SAGE. While working on SAGE, RAND trained hundreds of programmers, eventually leading to the spin-off of RAND's Systems Development Division and Systems Training Program into the Systems Development Corporation. Computers made a major impact on the systems analysis and game theoretic approaches that RAND and other similar think tanks used in attempts to model nuclear and conventional warfighting strategies.

Engineering Research Associates (ERA) represented yet another form of government support: the private contractor growing out of a single government agency. With ERA, the Navy effectively privatized its wartime cryptography organization and was able to maintain civilian expertise through the radical postwar demobilization. ERA was founded in St. Paul, Minnesota, in January 1946 by two engineers who had done cryptography for the Navy and their business partners (Cohen and Tomash,

BOX 4.1
Project Whirlwind and SAGE

Two closely connected computing projects, Whirlwind and SAGE, demonstrate the influence of federal research and development programs during the early days of computing. They not only generated technical knowledge and human resources, but they also forged a unique relationship among government, universities, and industry. The Whirlwind computer was originally intended to be part of a general-purpose flight simulator, but it evolved into the first real-time, general-purpose digital computer. SAGE, an air-defense system designed to protect against enemy bombers, made several important contributions to computing in areas as diverse as computer graphics, time-sharing, digital communications, and ferrite-core memories. Together, these two projects shared a symbiotic relationship that strengthened the early computer industry.

Whirlwind originated in 1944 as part of the Navy's Airplane Stability and Control Analyzer (ASCA) project. At that time, the Navy made extensive use of flight simulators to test new aircraft designs and train pilots; however, each new aircraft design required a separate computer specially created for its particular design. ASCA was intended to negate the need to build individual computers for the flight simulators by serving as a general-purpose simulator that could emulate any design programmed into it. Jay Forrester, the leader of the computer portion of the ASCA project, soon recognized that analog computers (which were typically used on aircraft simulators) would not be fast enough to operate the trainer in real time. Learning of work in electronic digital computing as part of ENIAC at the University of Pennsylvania, Forrester began investigating the potential for real-time digital computers for Whirlwind. By early 1946, Forrester decided to pursue the digital route, expanding the goal of the Whirlwind program from building a generalizable aircraft simulator to designing a real-time, general-purpose digital computer that could serve many functions other than flight simulation.

Pursuing a digital computer required dramatic increases in computing speeds and reliability, both of which hinged on development of improved computer memory—an innovation that was also needed to handle large amounts of data about incoming airplanes. Mercury delay-line memories, which used sonic pulses to record information and were being pursued by several other research centers, were too slow for the machine Forrester envisioned. He decided instead to use electrostatic storage tubes in which bits of information could be stored as an electrical charge and which claimed read-and-write times of a few milliseconds. Such tubes proved to be expensive, limited in storage capacity, and unreliable. Looking for a new memory alternative, Forrester came across a new magnetic ceramic called Deltamax and began working on the first magnetic core memory, a project to which he later assigned a graduate student, Bill Papian.

The expansion of Whirlwind's technical objectives resulted in expanding project budgets that eventually undermined support for the project. Forrester originally planned Whirlwind as a 2-year, $875,000 program, but he increased his cost estimate for the Whirlwind computer itself to $1.9 million in March 1946 and to almost $3 million by 1947 (Campbell-Kelly and Aspray, 1996, pp. 161-163). By 1949, Whirlwind made up nearly 65 percent of the Office of Naval Research (ONR) mathematics research budget and almost 10 percent of ONR's entire contract research budget (Edwards, 1996, p. 79). As a part of a general Department of Defense initiative to centralize computer research in 1951, ONR planned to reduce Whirlwind's annual budget from $1.15 million to $250 thousand in 1951, threatening the viability of the project (Edwards, 1996, p. 91). Support for the project was salvaged only after George Valley, Jr., a professor of physics at the Massachusetts Institute of Technology (MIT) and chairman of the Air Defense System Engineering Committee, realized that Whirlwind might play a critical role in a new air-defense program, SAGE, and convinced the Air Force to provide additional funding for the project, thereby adding to its credibility.

In 1949, Valley began lobbying the Air Force to improve U.S. air-defense capability in the face of the nation's growing vulnerability to Soviet bombers (Freeman, 1995, p. 2). Valley was put in charge of the Air Defense Systems Engineering Committee to investigate possible solutions. The resulting Project Charles Summer Study Group recommended that the Air Force ask MIT to build a laboratory to carry out the experimental and field research necessary to develop a system to safeguard the United States (Freeman, 1995, p. 6). In response, MIT created Project Lincoln, now known as Lincoln Laboratory, to create the Semi-Automatic Ground Environment, or SAGE, system.

Through SAGE, the Air Force became the major sponsor of Whirlwind, enabling the project to move toward completion. By late 1951, a prototype ferrite-core memory system was demonstrated, and by 1953, the Whirlwind's entire memory was replaced with core memory boasting a 9-microsecond access time, effectively ending the research phase of the program. The Air Force subsequently purchased production versions of the computer (designed in a cooperative effort between MIT and IBM) to equip each of its 23 Direction Centers. Each center had two IBM-manufactured versions of Whirlwind: one operating live and one operating in standby mode for additional reliability. The machines accepted input from over 100 different information sources (typically from ground, air, and seaborne radars) and displayed relevant information on cathode-ray-tube displays for operators to track and identify aircraft.

The first SAGE Direction Center was activated in 1958, and deployment continued until 1963, when final deployment of 23 centers was completed at an estimated cost of $8 billion to $12 billion. Although a technical success, SAGE was already outdated by the time of its completion. The launch of Sputnik shifted the most feared military threat to the United States from long-range bombers to intercontinental ballistic missiles. SAGE command centers continued to operate into the middle of the 1980s but with a reduced urgency.

All told, ONR spent roughly $3.6 million on Whirlwind, the Air Force, $13.8 million. In return, Whirlwind and SAGE generated a score of innovations. On the hardware side, Whirlwind and SAGE pioneered magnetic-core memory, digital phone-line transmission and modems, the light pen (one of the first graphical user interfaces), and duplexed computers. In software, they pioneered use of real-time software; concepts that later evolved into assemblers, compilers, and interpreters; software diagnosis programs; time-shared operating systems; structured program modules; table-driven software; and data description techniques. Five years after its introduction in Whirlwind, ferrite-core memory replaced every other type of com-

continued on next page

BOX 4.1 continued

puter memory, and remained the dominant form of computer memory until 1973. Royalties to MIT from nongovernment sales amounted to $25 million, as MIT licensed the technology broadly.[1]

In addition, SAGE accelerated the transfer of these technologies throughout the nascent computer industry. While Lincoln Laboratory was given primary responsibility for SAGE, the project also involved several private firms such as IBM, RAND, Systems Development Corporation (the spin-off from RAND), Burroughs, Western Electric, RCA, and AT&T.[2] Through this complex relationship between academia, industry, and the military, SAGE technologies worked their way into commercial products and helped establish the industry leaders. SAGE was a driving force behind the formation of the American computer and electronics industry (Freeman, 1995, p. 33). IBM built 56 computers for SAGE, earning over $500 million, which helped contribute to its becoming the world's largest computer manufacturer (Edwards, 1996, pp. 101-102; Freeman, 1995, p. 33). At its peak, between 7,000 and 8,000 IBM employees worked on the project. SAGE technology contributed substantially to the SABRE airline reservation system marketed by IBM in 1964, which later became the backbone of the airline industry (Edwards, 1996, p. 102). Kenneth Olsen, who worked on Whirlwind before founding Digital Equipment Corporation, called Whirlwind the first minicomputer and states that his company was based entirely on Whirlwind technology (Old Associates, 1981, p. 23).

SAGE also contributed to formalizing the programming profession. While developing software for the system, the RAND Corporation spun off the Systems Development Corporation (SDC) to handle the software for SAGE. SDC trained thousands of programmers who eventually moved into the workforce. Numerous computer engineers from both IBM and SDC started their own firms with the knowledge they acquired from SAGE.

SAGE also established an influential precedent for organizational management. Lincoln Laboratory was structured in the same style as MIT had run the Radiation Laboratory during World War II, in that it had much less management involvement than other equivalent organizations. As a result, researchers had a large amount of freedom to pursue their own solutions to problems at hand. Norman Taylor, one of the key individuals who designed SAGE at Lincoln Laboratory credited the management style for the projects' successes:

> I think Bob [Everett] put his finger on one important thing: the freedom to do something without approval from top management. Take the case of the 65,000 word memory. . . . We built that big memory, and we didn't go to the steering committee to get approval for it. We didn't go up there and say, "Now, here's what we ought to do, it's going to cost this many million dollars, it's going to take us this long, and you must give us approval for it." We just had a pocket of money that was for advanced research. We didn't tell anybody what it was for; we didn't have to. (Freeman, 1995, p. 20)

This management style contrasted with the more traditional bureaucratic style of most American corporations of the time. It was subsequently adopted by Digital Equipment Corporation (under Kenneth Olsen's leadership) and eventually imitated by many—if not most—of the information technology firms that dot the suburban Boston and Silicon Valley landscapes. Although not the first to pioneer this management style and the organizational ethos it engendered, Lincoln Laboratory had demonstrated its functionality in large computing systems development.

---

[1]MIT licensed the technology for core memories to several computer companies— IBM, Univac, RCA, General Electric, Burroughs, NCR, Lockheed, and Digital Equipment Corporation—and memory suppliers, including Ampex, Fabri-TEk, Electronic Memory & Magnetics, Data Products, General Ceramics, and Ferroxcube. See Old Associates (1981), Figure 2 and p. 3.

[2]Although AT&T is a private company, much of its research was supported through a tax on customers. Hence, its research is often considered quasi-public.

1979). The Navy moved its Naval Computing Machine Laboratory from Dayton to St. Paul, and ERA essentially became the laboratory (Tomash, 1973; Parker 1985, 1986). ERA did some research, but it primarily worked on task-oriented, cost-plus contracts. As one participant recalled, "It was not a university atmosphere. It was 'Build stuff. Make it work. How do you package it? How do you fix it? How do you document it?'"(Tomash, 1973). ERA built a community of engineering skill, which became the foundation of the Minnesota computer industry. In 1951, for example, the company hired Seymour Cray for his first job out of the University of Minnesota (ERA, 1950; Cohen, 1983; Tomash 1973).

As noted earlier, the RAND Corporation had contracted in 1955 to write much of the software for SAGE owing to its earlier experience in air defense and its large pool of programmers. By 1956, the Systems Training Program of the RAND Corporation, the division assigned to SAGE, was larger than the rest of the corporation combined, and it spun off into the nonprofit Systems Development Corporation (SDC). SDC played a significant role in computer training. As described by one of the participants, "Part of SDC's nonprofit role was to be a university for programmers. Hence our policy in those days was not to oppose the recruiting of our personnel and not to match higher salary offers with an SDC raise." By 1963, SDC had trained more than 10,000 employees in the field of computer systems. Of those, 6,000 had moved to other businesses across the country (Baum, 1981, pp. 47-51).

Observations

In retrospect, the 1950s appear to have been a period of institutional and technological experimentation. This diversity of approaches, while it brought the field and the industry from virtually nothing to a tentative stability, was open to criticisms of waste, duplication of effort, and ineffectiveness caused by rivalries among organizations and their funding sources. The field was also driven largely by the needs of government agencies, with relatively little input from computer-oriented scientists at the highest levels. Criticism remained muted during the decade when the military imperatives of the Cold War seemed to dominate all others, but one event late in the decade opened the entire system of federal research support to scrutiny: the launch of Sputnik in 1957. Attacks mounted that the system of R&D needed to be changed, and they came not only from the press and the politicians but also from scientists themselves.

1960-1970: SUPPORTING A CONTINUING REVOLUTION

Several significant events occurred to mark a transition from the infancy of information technology to a period of diffusion and growth. Most important of these was the launching of Sputnik in 1957, which sent convulsions through the U.S. science and engineering world and redoubled efforts to develop new technology. President Eisenhower elevated scientists and engineers to the highest levels of policy making. Thus was inaugurated what some have called the golden age of U.S. research policy. Government support for information technology took off in the 1960s and assumed its modern form. The Kennedy administration brought a spirit of technocratic reform to the Pentagon and the introduction of systems analysis and computer-based management to all aspects of running the military. Many of the visions that set the research agendas for the following 15 years (and whose influence remains today) were set in the early years of the decade.

Maturing of a Commercial Industry

Perhaps most important, the early 1960s can be defined as the time when the commercial computer industry became significant on its own, independent of government funding and procurement. Computerized reservation systems began to proliferate, particularly the IBM/American Airlines SABRE system, based in part on prior experience with military command-and-control systems (such as SAGE). The introduction of the IBM System/360 in 1964 solidified computer applications in business, and the industry itself, as significant components of the economy (Pugh, 1995).

This newly vital industry, dominated by "Snow White" (IBM) and the "Seven Dwarfs" (Burroughs, Control Data, GE, Honeywell, NCR, RCA, and Sperry Rand), came to have several effects on government-supported R&D. First, and most obvious, some companies (mostly IBM) became large enough to conduct their own in-house research. IBM's Thomas J. Watson Research Center was dedicated in 1961. Its director, Emanuel Piore, was recruited from ONR, and he emphasized basic research. Such laboratories not only expanded the pool of researchers in computing and communications but also supplied a source of applied research that allowed or, conversely, pushed federal support to focus increasingly on the longest-term, riskiest ideas and on problems unique to government. Second, the industry became a growing employer of computer professionals, providing impetus to educational programs at universities and making computer science and engineering increasingly attractive career paths to talented young people.

These years saw turning points in telecommunications as well. In 1962, AT&T launched the first active communications satellite, Telstar, which transmitted the first satellite-relay telephone call and the first live transatlantic television signal. That same year, a less-noticed but equally significant event occurred when AT&T installed the first commercial digital-transmission system. Twenty-four digital speech channels were time multiplexed onto a repeatered digital transmission line operating at 1.5 megabits per second. In 1963, the first Stored Program Control electronic switching system was placed into service, inaugurating the use of digital computer technology for mainstream switching.

The 1960s also saw the emergence of the field called computer science, and several important university departments were founded during the decade, at Stanford and Carnegie Mellon in 1965 and at MIT in 1968. Hardware platforms had stabilized enough to support a community of researchers who attacked a common set of problems. New languages proliferated, often initiated by government and buoyed by the needs of commercial industry. The Navy had sponsored Grace Hopper and others during the 1950s to develop automatic programming techniques that became the first compilers. John Backus and a group at IBM developed FORTRAN, which was distributed to IBM users in 1957. A team led by John McCarthy at MIT (with government support) began implementing LISP in 1958, and the language became widely used, particularly for artificial intelligence programming, in the early 1960s. In 1959, the Pentagon began convening a group of computer experts from government, academia, and industry to define common business languages for computers. The group published a specification in 1959, and by 1960 RCA and Remington Rand Univac had produced the first COBOL compilers (ACM Sigplan, 1978). By the beginning of the 1960s, a number of computer languages, standard across numerous hardware platforms, were beginning to define programming as a task, as a profession, and as a challenging and legitimate subject of intellectual inquiry.

The Changing Federal Role

The forces driving government support changed during the 1960s. The Cold War remained a paramount concern, but to it were added the difficult conflict in Vietnam, the Great Society programs, and the Apollo program, inaugurated by President Kennedy's 1961 challenge. New political goals, new technologies, and new missions provoked changes in the federal agency population. Among these, two agencies became particularly important in computing: the new Advanced Research Projects Agency and the National Science Foundation.

The Advanced Research Projects Agency

The founding of the Advanced Research Projects Agency (ARPA) in 1958, a direct outgrowth of the Sputnik scare, had immeasurable impact on computing and communications. ARPA, specifically charged with preventing technological surprises like Sputnik, began conducting long-range, high-risk research. It was originally conceived as the DOD's own space agency, reporting directly to the Secretary of Defense in order to avoid interservice rivalry. Space, like computing, did not seem to fit into the existing military service structure.[2] ARPA's independent status not only insulated it from established service interests but also tended to foster radical ideas and keep the agency tuned to basic research questions: when the agency-supported work became too much like systems development, it ran the risk of treading on the territory of a specific service.

ARPA's status as the DOD space agency did not last long. Soon after NASA's creation in 1958, ARPA retained essentially no role as a space agency. ARPA instead focused its energies on ballistic missile defense, nuclear test detection, propellants, and materials. It also established a critical organizational infrastructure and management style: a small, high-quality managerial staff, supported by scientists and engineers on rotation from industry and academia, successfully employing existing DOD laboratories and contracting procedures (rather than creating its own research facilities) to build solid programs in new, complex fields (Barber Associates, 1975). ARPA also emerged as an agency extremely sensitive to the personality and vision of its director.

ARPA's decline as a space agency raised questions about its role and character. A new director, Jack Ruina, answered the questions in no uncertain terms by cementing the agency's reputation as an elite, scientifically respected institution devoted to basic, long-term research projects. Ruina, ARPA's first scientist-director, took office at the same time as Kennedy and MacNamara in 1961, and brought a similar spirit to the agency. Ruina decentralized management at ARPA and began the tradition of relying heavily on independent office directors and program managers to run research programs. Ruina also valued scientific and technical merit above immediate relevance to the military. Ruina believed both of these characteristics—independence and intellectual quality—were critical to attracting the best people, both to ARPA as an organization and to ARPA-sponsored research (Barber Associates, 1975, Chapter V). Interestingly, ARPA's managerial success did not rely on innovative managerial techniques per se (such as the computerized project scheduling typical of the Navy's Polaris project) but rather on the creative use of existing mechanisms such as "no-year money," unsolicited proposals, sole-source procurement, and multiyear forward funding.

ARPA and Information Technology.   From the point of view of computing, the most important event at ARPA in the early 1960s, indeed in all of ARPA's history, was the establishment of the Information Processing Techniques Office, IPTO, in 1962. The impetus for this move came from several directions, including Kennedy's call a year earlier for improvements in command-and-control systems to make them "more flexible, more selective, more deliberate, better protected, and under ultimate civilian authority at all times" (Norberg and O'Neill, 1996, p. 10). Computing as applied to command and control was the ideal ARPA program—it had no clearly established service affinity; it was "a new area with relatively little established service interest and entailed far less constraint on ARPA's freedom of action," than more familiar technologies (Barber Associates, 1975, p. V-5). Ruina established IPTO to be devoted not to command and control but to the more fundamental problems in computing that would, eventually, contribute solutions.

Consistent with his philosophy of strong, independent, and scientific office managers, Ruina appointed J.C.R. Licklider to head IPTO. The Harvard-trained psychologist came to ARPA in October 1962, primarily to run its Command and Control Group. Licklider split that group into two discipline-oriented offices: Behavioral Sciences Office and IPTO. Licklider had had extensive exposure to the computer research of the time and had clearly defined his own vision of "man-computer symbiosis," which he had published in a landmark paper of 1960 by the same name. He saw human-computer interaction as the key, not only to command and control, but also to bringing together the then-disparate techniques of electronic computing to form a unified science of computers as tools for augmenting human thought and creativity (Licklider, 1988b, 1960). Licklider formed IPTO in this image, working largely independently of any direction from Ruina, who spent the majority of his time on higher-profile and higher-funded missile defense issues. Licklider's timing was opportune: the 1950s had produced a stable technology of digital computer hardware, and the big systems projects had shown that programming these machines was a difficult but interesting problem in its own right. Now the pertinent questions concerned how to use "this tremendous power. . . for other than purely numerical scientific calculations" (Barber Associates, 1975).[3] Licklider not only brought this vision to IPTO itself, but he also promoted it with missionary zeal to the research community at large. Licklider's and IPTO's success derived in large part from their skills at "selling the vision" in addition to "buying the research."

Another remarkable feature of IPTO, particularly during the 1960s, was its ability to maintain the coherent vision over a long period of time; the office director was able to handpick his successor. Licklider chose Ivan Sutherland, a dynamic young researcher he had encountered as a graduate student at MIT and the Lincoln Laboratory, to succeed him in 1964. Sutherland carried on Licklider's basic ideas and made his own impact by emphasizing computer graphics. Sutherland's own successor, Robert Taylor, came in 1966 from a job as a program officer at NASA and recalled, "I became heartily subscribed to the Licklider vision of interactive computing" (Taylor, 1989). While at IPTO, Taylor emphasized networking. The last IPTO director of the 1960s, Lawrence Roberts, came, like Sutherland, from MIT and Lincoln Laboratory, where he had worked on the early transistorized computers and had conducted ARPA research in both graphics and communications.

During the 1960s, ARPA and IPTO had more effect on the science and technology of computing than any other single government agency, sometimes raising concern that the research agenda for computing was being directed by military needs. IPTO's sheer size, $15 million in 1965, dwarfed other agencies such as ONR. Still, it is important to note, ONR and ARPA worked closely together; ONR would often let small contracts to researchers and serve as a talent agent for ARPA, which would then fund promising projects at larger scale. ARPA combined the best features of existing military research support with a new, lean administrative structure and innovative management style to fund high-risk projects consistently. The agency had the freedom to administer large block grants as well as multiple-year contracts, allowing it the luxury of a long-term vision to foster technologies, disciplines, and institutions. Further, the national defense motivation allowed IPTO to concentrate its resources on centers of scientific and engineering excellence (such as MIT, Carnegie Mellon University, and Stanford University) without regard for geographical distribution questions with which NSF had to be concerned. Such an approach helped to create university-based research groups with the critical mass and stability of funding needed to create significant advances in particular technical areas. But although it trained generations of young researchers in those areas, ARPA's funding style did little to help them pursue the same lines of work at other universities. As an indirect and possibly unintended consequence, the research approaches and tools and the generic technologies developed under ARPA's patronage were disseminated more rapidly and widely, and so came to be applied in new nonmilitary contexts by the young M.S. and Ph.D. graduates who had been trained in that environment but could not expect to make their research careers within it.

ARPA's Management Style. To evaluate research proposals, IPTO did not employ the peer-review process like NSF, but rather relied on internal reviews and the discretion of program managers as did ONR. These program managers, working under office managers such as Licklider, Sutherland, Taylor, and Roberts, came to have enormous influence over their areas of responsibility and became familiar with the entire field both personally and intellectually. They had the freedom and the resources to shape multiple R&D contracts into a larger vision and to stimulate new areas of inquiry. The education, recruiting, and responsibilities of these program managers thus became a critical parameter in the character and success of ARPA programs. ARPA frequently chose people who had training and research experience in the fields they would fund, and thus who had insight and opinions on where those fields should go.

To have such effects, the program managers were given enough funds to let a large enough number of contracts and to shape a coherent research program, with minimal responsibilities for managing staffs. Program budgets usually required only two levels of approval above the program manager: the director of IPTO and the director of ARPA. One IPTO member described what he called "the joy of ARPA . . . . You know, if a program manager has a good idea, he has got two people to convince that that is a good idea before the guy goes to work. He has got the director of his office and the director of ARPA, and that is it. It is such a short chain of command" (Taylor, 1989).

Part of ARPA's philosophy involved aiming at radical change rather than incremental improvement. As Robert Taylor put it, for example, incremental innovation would be taken care of by the services and their contractors, but, ARPA's aim was "an order of magnitude difference."[4] ARPA identified good ideas and magnified them. This strategy often necessitated funding large, group-oriented projects and institutions rather than individuals. Taylor recalled, "I don't remember a single case where we ever funded a single individual's work. . . . The individual researcher who is just looking for support for his own individual work could [potentially] find many homes to support that work. So we tended not to fund those, because we felt that they were already pretty well covered. Instead, we funded larger groups—teams." NSF's peer-review process worked well for individual projects, but was not likely to support large, team-oriented research projects. Nor did it, at this point in history, support entire institutions and research centers, like the Laboratory for Computer Science at MIT. IPTO's style meshed with its emphasis on human-machine interaction, which it saw as fundamentally a systems problem and hence fundamentally team oriented. In Taylor's view, the university reward structure was much more oriented toward individual projects, so "systems research is most difficult to fund and manage in a university" (Taylor, 1989). This philosophy was apparent in ARPA's support of Project MAC, an MIT-led effort on time-shared computing (Box 4.2).

ARPA, with its clearly defined mission to support DOD technology, could also afford to be elitist in a way that NSF, with a broader charter to support the country's scientific research could not. "ARPA had no commitment, for example, to take geography into consideration when it funded work"(Taylor, 1989). Another important feature of ARPA's multi-year contracts was their stability, which proved critical for graduate students who could rely on funding to get them through their Ph.D. program. ARPA also paid particular attention to building communities of researchers and disseminating the results of its research, even beyond traditional publications. IPTO would hold annual meetings for its contract researchers at which results would be presented and debated. These meetings proved effective not only at advancing the research itself but also at providing valuable feedback for the program managers and helping to forge relationships between researchers in related areas. Similar conferences were convened for graduate students only, thus building a longer-term community of researchers. ARPA also put significant effort into getting the results of its research programs commercialized so that DOD could benefit from the development and expansion of a commercial industry for information technology. ARPA sponsored conferences that brought together researchers and managers from academia and industry on topics such as time-sharing, for example.

Much has been made of ARPA's management style, but it would be a mistake to conclude that management per se provided the keys to the agency's successes in computing. The key point about the style, in fact, was its light touch. Red tape was kept to a minimum, and project proposals were turned around quickly, frequently into multiple-year contracts. Typical DOD research contracts involved close monitoring and careful adherence to requirements and specifications. ARPA avoided this approach by hiring technically educated program managers who had continuing research interests in the fields they were managing. This reality counters the myth that government bureaucrats heavy-handedly selected R&D problems and managed the grants and contracts. Especially during the 1960s and 1970s, program managers and office directors were not

BOX 4.2
Project MAC and Computer Time-sharing

The development of computer time-sharing and the advent of minicomputers set the technological stage for the 1970s. Time-sharing systems divide computation power cyclically between many users over a network. Properly designed time-sharing computers can switch among processes quickly enough so that users do not recognize any delay, making it appear as though each user has the computer's full attention. Such systems took advantage of design and manufacturing peculiarities of mainframes that resulted in the power of a mainframe computer varying as the square of cost of the computer.[1] Therefore, building one computer for twice the cost of a smaller machine created four times the power. Time-sharing systems took advantage of this phenomena by allowing several users to share a single larger computer instead of several smaller machines. Development of such systems emerged from the complementary efforts of industry, universities, and government. Key to these efforts were Project MAC and its predecessors, funded by the Advanced Research Projects Agency and the National Science Foundation (NSF). While Project MAC was not responsible for the first time-sharing system, it played a significant role in the technology's development.

Project MAC was started by IPTO in 1963, with funding going to the Massachusetts Institute of Technology (MIT). MAC stood for Man and Computer, Machine-Aided Cognition, and Multi-Access Computer. J.C.R. Licklider chose MIT as the site for Project MAC because of the large variety of computer disciplines being studied at MIT. Project MAC brought together, for example, Marvin Minsky's artificial intelligence work, Douglas Ross's computer-aided design systems, Herbert Teager's studies in languages and devices, and Martin Greenberger's work with human-machine systems. While the program was justified to the military as a command-and-control program, Licklider's goal was much broader. He sought "the possibility of a profound advance, which will be almost literally an advance in the way of thinking about computing." In an interview with the Charles Babbage Institute, Licklider said, "I wanted interactive computing, I wanted time-sharing. I wanted themes like: computers are as much for communication as they are for calculation" (Norberg and O'Neil, 1996, pp. 97-98). Project MAC would eventually receive $25 million in total from 1963 to 1970 (Reed et al., 1990, Chapter 19, p. 14).

The core of Project MAC involved the design of a time-sharing computer system. Project MAC was not the first time-sharing initiative, but it significantly pushed the state of the art. Time-sharing systems had previously been developed in the MIT Computation Center, at System Development Corporation, and at Bolt, Beranek and Newman. At first, Project MAC used the MIT Computation Center's Compatible Time-Sharing System (CTSS), which had been designed under a grant from NSF. The system was built on an IBM 7090/94 and became operational in 1961. This was the first system enabling users to write their own programs online (Reed et al., 1990, pp. 19-2 to 19-3). In 1964, CTSS was connected to 24 terminals across the MIT campus. Eventually, 160 terminals were in place and 30 could be in use at one time. However, the CTSS still could not provide as much power as researchers desired, and it lacked necessary data access security.

continued on next page

BOX 4.2 continued

Beginning in 1965, Project MAC began to create a second system with the help of General Electric and Bell Laboratories: MULTICS (Multiplexed Information and Computing Service), was completed in 1969 and would eventually support 1,000 terminals at MIT with 300 in use at any one time (Campbell-Kelly and Aspray, 1996, pp. 214-215). MULTICS also incorporated a multiuser file system and a complex virtual-memory system that allowed application programs to function as if available memory were much larger than the memory actually attached to the processor. It featured an automatically managed three-level memory system, controlled sharing and protection of data and programs accessed by multiple users, and the ability to reallocate its resources dyamically without interruption. MULTICS had a multiuser file system that allowed each user to work as if on an independent computer (Flamm, 1987, p. 58).

Project MAC led to many advances beyond time-sharing. MIT's Artificial Intelligence Laboratory received $1 million in funding through Project MAC for work to further the objectives of interactive computing (of which time-sharing was an integral part) and intelligent assistance (Norberg and O'Neill, 1996). Funds also went toward research in input/output devices. One of the earliest computer-aided design systems, KLUDGE, was developed through Project MAC. Project MAC's ability to compose and edit programs and documents online laid the groundwork for word processors and interactive programming. The idea for the spreadsheet, later popularized by Lotus 123 and subsequently Microsoft's Excel, also came from two students who worked on Project MAC. This idea spurred development of the first spreadsheet on the personal computer, VisiCalc, from Software Arts. The first real networking of the personal computer (the first version of Internet protocols for the PC) also came from MIT's Project MAC (renamed the Laboratory for Computer Science by then), which led to the company called FTP Software. FTP sold the first Internet protocol suite for DOS.

Another lasting spin-off from Project MAC was the popular operating system, Unix. The difficulty that Bell Laboratories had in developing the MULTICS operating system led to a new philosophy of software design stressing simplicity and elegance. In 1969, when Bell Laboratories realized that a commercial product was still many years away, it withdrew from Project MAC. Over the next 5 years, Bell researchers Kenneth Thompson and Dennis Ritchie, along with others who had been working with MAC and had become frustrated with MULTICS's complexity, developed Unix, which was based on MULTICS but was much simpler. It offered quick responses, had minimal system overhead, and ran on minicomputers instead of more expensive mainframes with special memory management systems.

Beyond the technical advances in time-sharing, Project MAC influenced an industrywide movement toward developing time-sharing computers. When searching for a contractor to supply the hardware for MULTICS, MIT turned down its traditional supplier, IBM, and hired General Electric (GE) because of IBM's unwillingness to modify their machines for the project. The early results of Project MAC, though, convinced IBM and other manufacturers that they would have to pursue time-sharing (Campbell-Kelly and Aspray, 1996, p. 215). By 1967, 20 firms were competing for a $20 million industry providing time-shared computer services to businesses across the nation including GE, Telcomp, Tymshare, Keydata, and University Computing

Company. By the mid-1970s, almost every mainframe computer sold incorporated time-sharing technology (Reed et al., 1990, pp. 9-14).

Project MAC was largely responsible for bringing the computer out of the laboratory and business and leading it to the home. Licklider's desire to create a "new way of thinking" about computers succeeded. Project MAC developed technology and ideas that allowed interactive computing to become a reality. . . ." As a result of Project MAC and other computer time-sharing research programs in the late 1960s, the concept of computer utilities became widely accepted in the computer and business world. In 1964, only one year after Project MAC began, Martin Greenberger wrote, "Barring unforeseen obstacles, an on-line interactive computer service, provided commercially by an information utility, may be as commonplace by 2000 A.D. as the telephone service is today" (Campbell-Kelly and Aspray, 1996, p. 217). The image Greenberger described is remarkably similar to the Internet. Before time-sharing became a reality, computing remained available only to large businesses, academic institutions, and the government. However, as more users could simultaneously use a single machine, the cost of computing dramatically decreased, and usage increased accordingly. Project MAC played a large role in the public's change of philosophy regarding the use of computers.

---

[1]This relationship between cost and the power of mainframes was often referred to as Grosch's law.

bureaucrats but were usually academics on a 2-year tour of duty. They saw ARPA as a pulpit from which to preach their visions, with money to help them realize those visions. The entire system displayed something of a self-organizing, self-managing nature. As Ivan Sutherland recalled, "Good research comes from the researchers themselves rather than from the outside."[5]

National Science Foundation

While ARPA was focusing on large projects and systems, the National Science Foundation played a large role in legitimizing basic computer science research as an academic discipline and in funding individual researchers at a wide range of institutions. Its programs in computing have evolved considerably since its founding in 1950, but have tended to balance support for research, education, and computing infrastructure. Although early programs tended to focus on the use of computing in other academic disciplines, NSF subsequently emerged as the leading federal funder of basic research in computer science.

NSF was formed before computing became a clearly defined research area, and it established divisions for chemistry, physics, and biology, but not computing. NSF did provide support for computing in its early years, but this support derived more from a desire to promote computer-related activities in other disciplines than to expand computer science as a discipline, and as such was weighted toward support for computing infrastructure (NSF, 1956, p. 57). For example, NSF poured millions of dollars into university computing centers so that researchers in other disciplines, such as physics and chemistry, could have access to computing power. NSF noted that little computing power was available to researchers at American universities who were not involved in defense-related research and that "many scientists feel strongly that further progress in their field will be seriously affected by lack of access to the techniques and facilities of electronic computation" (NSF, 1958, p. 103). As a result, NSF began supporting computing centers at universities in 1956 and, in 1959, allocated a budget specifically for computer equipment purchases. Recognizing that computing technology was expensive, became obsolete rapidly, and entailed significant costs for ongoing support, NSF decided that it would, in effect, pay for American campuses to enter the computer age. In 1962, it established its first office devoted to computing, the program for Computers and Computing Science within the Mathematical Sciences Division (Aspray and Williams, 1994). By 1970, the Institutional Computing Services (or Facilities) program had obligated $66 million to university computing centers across the country.[6] NSF intended that use of the new facilities would result in trained personnel to fulfill increasing needs for computer proficiency in industry, government, and academia.

NSF provided some funding for computer-related research in its early years. Originally, such funding came out of the mathematics division in the 1950s and grew out of an interest in numerical analysis. By 1955, NSF began to fund basic research in computer science theory with its first grants for the research of recursion theory and one grant to develop an analytical computer program under the Mathematical Sciences Program. Although these projects constituted less than 10 percent of the mathematics budget, they resulted in significant research.

In 1967, NSF united all the facets of its computing support into a single office, the Office of Computing Activities (OCA). The new office incorporated elements from the directorates of mathematics and engineering and from the Facilities program, unifying NSF's research and infrastructure efforts in computing. It also incorporated an educational element that was intended to help meet the radically increasing demand for instruction in computer science (Aspray and Williams, 1994). The OCA was headed by Milton Rose, the former head of the Mathematical Sciences Section, and reported directly to the director of NSF.

Originally, the OCA's main focus was improving university computing services. In 1967, $11.3 million of the office's $12.8 million total budget went toward institutional support (NSF, 1967, pp. 53-54). Because not all universities were large enough to support their own computing centers but would benefit from access to computing time at other universities, the OCA also began to support regional networks linking many universities together. In 1968, the OCA spent $5.3 million, or 18.6 percent of its budget, to provide links between computers in the same geographic region (NSF, 1968). In the 1970s, the computer center projects were canceled, however, in favor of shifting emphasis toward education and research.

Beginning in 1968, through the Education and Training program, the OCA began funding the inauguration of university-level computer science programs. NSF funded several conferences and studies to develop computer science curricula. The Education and Training program obligated $12.3 million between 1968 and 1970 for training, curricula development, and support of computer-assisted instruction.[7]

Although the majority of the OCA's funding was spent on infrastructure and education, the office also supported a broad range of basic computer science research programs. These included compiler and language development, theoretical computer science, computation theory, numerical analysis, and algorithms. The Computer Systems Design program concentrated on computer architecture and systems analysis. Other programs focused on topics in artificial intelligence, including pattern recognition and automatic theory proving.

1970-1990: RETRENCHING AND INTERNATIONAL COMPETITION

Despite previous successes, the 1970s opened with computing at a critical but fragile point. Although produced by a large and established industry, commercial computers remained the expensive, relatively esoteric tools of large corporations, research institutions, and government. Computing had not yet made its way to the common user, much less the man in the street. This movement would begin in the mid-1970s with the introduction of the microprocessor and then unfold in the 1980s with even greater drama and force. If the era before 1960 was one of experimentation and the 1960s one of consolidation and diffusion in computing, the two decades between 1970 and 1990 were characterized by explosive growth. Still, this course of events was far from clear in the early 1970s.

Computer Science, Computer Technology

By 1970, computer science was just emerging as a discipline. Many of the major computer science departments were established (at places like Stanford University, MIT, and Carnegie Mellon University), but computer science did not yet have the academic legitimacy of the older fields of physics, chemistry, and biology. Was computer science really a science? Although much theoretical work examined fundamental questions of computability that are independent of computing hardware, many problems for computing research stemmed from experience with the construction and use of actual computers (man-made instruments as opposed to naturally occurring phenomena).[8] During the 1970s, computer scientists would continue to answer these questions with a growing and mature body of theoretical work.

Technologically, the 1970s, like the 1950s, might be characterized as a decade of experiments. The Unix operating system grew to prominence during this decade, at first in research environments and then increasingly in industry. Although the minicomputer industry competed successfully with mainframes, it faced a threat of its own: Intel delivered the first microprocessor, the 4004, in 1971, soon followed by the 8-bit 8008, the basis of the first personal computers. Networking became an increasing focus of research and systems: the ARPANET, although formulated in the 1960s, became an operational system in the 1970s: it had 4 nodes in 1970, 23 in the next year, and was publicly demonstrated in Washington in 1972. In 1973, Xerox unveiled its Alto personal computer, a system of boxes, each of which was controlled with a graphical user interface and a mouse, with each box connected to others throughout the Palo Alto Research Center (PARC) through an Ethernet network. Still, it would take almost another 20 years before this visionary technology's prototype became the tangible reality of the world of business computing in the United States.

Also during the 1970s, a veritable computer culture emerged—hobbyists who touted computer liberation and experimentation with small microprocessor-based machines, often outside of institutional environments. It took Steve Jobs, Apple Computer, and the computerized spreadsheet, however, to turn the hobbyist personal computer into the ubiquitous piece of business equipment and consumer product it later became. Popular mythology celebrates the independent entrepreneurs who produced the personal computer (PC) revolution—Steve Jobs at Apple, Mitch Kapor at Lotus, and Bill Gates at Microsoft. These innovators built upon ideas developed previously, many of them with government funding (Box 4.3). IBM also played a critical role in making the new technology established and acceptable with its 1981 introduction of the IBM PC. Packaged with Lotus 123 and MS-DOS, the IBM PC gave the business marketplace what it wanted from a personal computer (Malone, 1995).

Until about 1980, truly capable computers remained large boxes. This began to change with the birth of the desktop workstation, based on the microprocessor. After Xerox built its Alto computers, it donated 10 machines to Stanford's Computer Science Department. They inspired Forest

BOX 4.3
Roots of the Personal Computer

The development of the personal computer (PC) is illustrative of the symbiosis between government and industry in the evolving computer industry. While the PC stands as a monument to industrial innovation and the foresight and tenacity of individual entrepreneurs, federally sponsored research also played a role. The Macintosh operating system and Microsoft Windows, which trace their lineage to the Alto computer developed by Xerox between 1973 and 1978, incorporate concepts first explored by researchers working with federal support.

In the 1960s, the Advanced Research Projects Agency (ARPA) and the National Aeronautics and Space Administration provided funding for Douglas Engelbart to create a new research program at the Stanford Research Institute to work on improving human-computer interactions. Engelbart's research concentrated on using computers to augment the abilities of an individual as opposed to automating those abilities. In 1968, at the Joint Computer Conference, Engelbart presented the NLS (On-Line System), a computerized office system that his group developed. The NLS was the first system to use a mouse and the first to use windows. The invention of the mouse and its use as part of a graphical user interface represented a dramatic change from the standard command-line operation of computers. Most mainframe and time-sharing systems at the time relied on typed commands that computer novices found cryptic and difficult to use. Text on the screen could often be edited only by referencing the line number as opposed to changing the text in place. The use of a mouse and graphical user interface began the trend to make computers usable by anyone.

Designers at the Xerox Palo Alto Research Center (PARC) later incorporated Engelbart's advances into a graphical user interface for Xerox's Alto computer. The Alto was designed for users including "children from age 5 or 6 and 'noncomputer adults' such as secretaries, librarians, architects, musicians, housewives, doctors and so on" (ACM, 1993, p. 29). The Alto also drew upon the ideas described in Alan Kay's doctoral thesis, work that was also supported by ARPA while Kay was at the University of Utah. Kay described a computer called FLEX that would act as "an interactive tool which can aid in the visualization and realization of provocative notions. It must be simple enough so that one does not have to become a systems programmer (one who understands the arcane rites) to use it. It must be cheap enough to be owned (like a grand piano). It must do more than just be able to realize computable functions; it has to be able to form the abstractions in which the user deals. FLEX is an idea debugger and as such, it is hoped that it is also an idea media."[1] Kay envisioned this computer of the future to be the size of a notebook, one that could handle all of an individual's personal information management and manipulation needs. Kay later called this computer the Dynabook. Kay was not able to build an operational Dynabook for his thesis, but the new computing context was influential. "Since at first people shared computers, the idea that everyone should have their own was a breakthrough" (ACM, 1993, p. 31).

Robert Taylor, the associate manager of the Computer Science Laboratory (CSL) at PARC recruited Alan Kay for the Xerox System Science Laboratory (SSL) in an attempt to integrate the SSL and CSL in working toward a shared goal. Taylor was a former director of ARPA's Information Processing Techniques Office and used his

continued on next page

BOX 4.3 continued

knowledge of the field and the key researchers in it to staff the laboratory and provide direction. He followed the same principles he used at ARPA: enlisting the most talented researchers and giving them the freedom to follow their own imagination.[2] Taylor planned for the CSL to create the hardware infrastructure for distributed personal computing and for SSL to design software and applications for it (Smith and Alexander, 1988, pp. 70-71). While working in the SSL, Kay developed the Small-Talk language on which most of Alto's software was developed. SmallTalk was the first object-oriented programming language.

Xerox was never able to market the Alto successfully, but its influence is noticeable in most business and home computers in use today. In 1979, Steve Jobs was invited to tour Xerox PARC. Jobs realized the potential for the Alto system. He told the demonstrator of the system, Larry Tesler, "Why isn't Xerox marketing this? . . . You could blow everything away" (Smith and Alexander, 1988, p. 241). Jobs then incorporated many aspects of the Alto into the Apple Lisa, first produced in 1983, and its successor, the MacIntosh. The popularity of graphical user interfaces grew rapidly. Eventually Microsoft introduced Windows, beginning the conversion of x86 PCs from the command-line operating system DOS to the operating systems prevalent today.

---

[1] Alan Kay as quoted in Smith and Alexander (1988).
[2] Taylor was not alone in his management style at IPTO. Other program managers and office managers at DARPA, including J.C.R. Licklider, used a similar style.

Baskett and student Andy Bechtolsheim to build a successor for engineering and scientific applications. The Stanford University Network (SUN) developed new desktop computers with Ethernet networking and high-resolution, high-speed graphics, tapping into DARPA's Very Large Scale Integrated Circuit (VLSI) program en route. In 1982, Bechtolsheim, Vinod Khosla, and Scott McNealy acquired venture capital to found Sun Microsystems, Inc.

By 1980, the sales of the computer equipment industry made up a significant share of the value of all domestically produced goods and services (GDP) (Table 4.1). The share of GDP contributed by the computing and office equipment industry continued to grow over the next decade, and investments in computing, communications, and office equipment began to absorb more than half of all gross fixed business investment in plant and equipment. The industry routinely built for commercial users complex systems combining computing and communications—technology once reserved for the military. Software became increasingly prominent, as a mass-market industry selling shrink-wrapped products, and as a subject of intellectual and managerial inquiry as the "software

TABLE 4.1 Computing and Related Equipment as a Share of the
National Economy

Year	Gross Domestic Product (GDP) (in billions of dollars)	Sales of Computing and Related Equipment (in billions of dollars)	Computer Equipment as a Percentage of GDP
1960	513	1.5	0.3
1970	1,010	10.5	1.0
1980	2,708	55.1	2.0
1990	5,546	154.8	2.8
1995	7,117	204.8	2.9

SOURCES: National Science Board (1996); ITI (1997).

crisis" increasingly demonstrated the difficulty of bringing in large programming projects on time and within budget. As the computer industry
exploded, traditional industrial research and development increased proportionally. But only the largest companies could afford broad-based
research efforts to rival those of universities and government laboratories.
In 1984, for example, IBM still conducted 50 percent of the R&D (by dollar
value) in the computer industry as a whole (Flamm, 1987).

The Changing Political Context

While the 1970s and 1980s saw explosions in the growth of technology,
they also witnessed a changing environment for government-supported
research. During the 1970s, the war in Vietnam became the driving force,
tending to redirect research toward military purposes and raising concerns about the effect of defense funding on university research. During
the 1980s, traditional defense concerns gave way to industrial competitiveness as the primary driver of research policy. Both these changes had
a significant effect on the nature, structure, and direction of federally
sponsored research in computing.

Science and Politics in the 1970s: A Changed Climate

Tension over the Vietnam War brought campus protests against the
war and against defense-related research on campus, forcing some universities to change their policies. As the costs of the war escalated, research budgets were increasingly squeezed within the Pentagon. In the
1970s, despite the fabulous success of the Apollo program in putting a
man on the moon in 1969, a general skepticism about the role of science in

society—and hence the role of scientific research—began to emerge. Divisions over Vietnam, heightened distrust of authority in the wake of Watergate, the oil crisis of 1973, and increased awareness of pollution and environmental damage all contributed to the changed role of science in the public sphere. DOD funding for mathematics and computer science reached a two-decade low in 1975. Government support for science and technology, although not necessarily in crisis, would never again enjoy the same prominence it had in the previous decade; the golden age of research support was over.

Politics intervened in other ways during this time, too. The Nixon administration, for example, did not think NSF should be in the business of developing computer networks, seeing such activities as the province of private business. As a result, NSF's activities were severely curtailed in this area. The Nixon administration also pushed for more directed research programs in computer science that addressed specific national problems, such as education and environment, rather than letting the research community have most of the role in defining research directions. These sentiments were matched by similarly motivated actions in Congress.

In 1969, Congress forbade military funding for any research that did not have a "direct or apparent relationship to a specific military function or operations." This legislation, enacted into law as the Mansfield Amendment (named after its sponsor) to the Defense Authorization Act of 1970 (Public Law 91-121), was short lived, but it sent a strong signal to the research community: it would have to demonstrate the military relevance of its work. Some program managers thought this would involve merely rewriting project descriptions with an emphasis on applications, and no doubt frequently they were correct. But the Mansfield Amendment, and the mood that gave rise to it, had the longer-term impact of shortening the time horizons for government research support in general and defense research in particular. Both ARPA and NSF materially felt the effects of this new climate in their computing programs.

Policy for the 1980s: Industrial Research and Competitiveness

In the 1980s, fears were raised that the microelectronics and computer industries seemed to be going the way of the auto industry—to Japan. Just as in the automobile industry, in which the Japanese had mastered manufacturing technology before turning their attention to design, the Japanese integrated- circuit companies first captured a dominant percentage of the dynamic random access memory (DRAM) industry. They began with the process-intensive memory chips and then turned their attention to more-design-intensive processors. As a result, many believed U.S.

industry to be in trouble in the early 1980s. Compounding the alarm was the declining market share of the semiconductor equipment industry, which makes the intricate manufacturing equipment for chips: its share of the world market fell from 75 percent to 40 percent during the 1980s (Alic et al., 1992). "Competitiveness" became the keyword for U.S. technology policy in the 1980s.

Much of the vast literature analyzing the competitiveness problem focused on the role of government and government-sponsored research. Japan's Ministry of Trade and International Development played a key role in bringing Japanese companies together to cooperate in targeting new markets and technologies. In the United States—amid calls for government action—joint ventures, cooperative agreements, university-industry collaborations, and industry consortia began to emerge to fight the Japanese threat. The National Cooperative Research Act of 1984 exempted research consortia from some antitrust laws and facilitated these mergers. The Microelectronics and Computer Technology Corporation, formed in January 1983, was entirely privately funded (at $60 million to $70 million in 1985) by its 12 member companies. Of these new initiatives, SEMATECH, the semiconductor manufacturing technology consortium, was most significant as a government-supported venture.

Changes in the Organization of Federal Research Support

Responses to the changing policy environment echoed throughout the federal research establishment. Significant changes in organization and management occurred at DARPA, NSF, and other federal agencies. New federal initiatives, such as SEMATECH and high-performance computing, began to dominate the research and policy agenda. These changes also reflected advances in computing technology and the evolution of the computing industry. New structures and missions allowed federal agencies to interact better with a growing industry that had an expanding range of capabilities and needs.

Changes at ARPA

ARPA's name was officially changed to DARPA (the Defense Advanced Research Projects Agency) in 1972, presaging changes in IPTO and its personnel as well. George Heilmeier, director of DARPA from 1975 to 1977, came, unlike his predecessors, from an industrial background. Heilmeier brought an emphasis on applications to DARPA and a more formalized management style to the agency. As one program manager recalled, "During the 1970s . . . there was tremendous pressure to produce stuff that looked like it had a short applications horizon."[9] The shortening time horizon had tangible effects, especially in IPTO. J.C.R. Licklider, who had started the office in the early 1960s, with a free hand and in his own image, returned for a stint as program director in 1974-1975 and found it a changed place (Norberg and O'Neill, 1996, pp. 37-38). After that, the agency had difficulty finding a successor to serve as director of IPTO.

These changes at DARPA, and in particular at IPTO, represented the natural evolution of an organization as it matures. IPTO's funding more than doubled from the $9 million of 1962 to $23 million in 1970, and it accounted for most of DOD's basic research and about half of the applied research in computing (Norberg and O'Neill, 1996, p. 55). In that sense Licklider and his cohort had been victims of their own success: IPTO leadership no longer had to evangelize and legitimate the field; they merely administered the research of an established area—an equally important, if perhaps less entrepreneurial, endeavor. Furthermore, Mansfield-era changes did bring some benefits. At first IPTO's computer research had all been classified as 6.1, DOD parlance for basic research. Now the emphasis shifted to 6.2, or "Exploratory Development," which expanded. Even in the early 1970s, 6.2 constituted more than half of the IPTO budget and after 1971 was responsible for most of its growth. As mentioned above, the shift also had the effect of transferring much of the basic research from DARPA to NSF.

Arguably, this change in the priority of applications and development, although potentially threatening to Licklider's original vision (and sometimes odious to academic investigators), built upon a decade of basic research. IPTO-sponsored research had created numerous new ideas that could now be tried on a large scale. Indeed, IPTO had several large, applications-oriented programs already under way in the early 1970s, including the ILLIAC IV and the ARPANET (see Chapter 7). The first was a modular parallel supercomputer being built at the University of Illinois. The second project, ARPANET, was built to demonstrate principles of computer networking that had been worked out in the previous decade. Both of these projects emphasized hardware, and both were built under large contracts let to industrial contractors (ILLIAC by Burroughs and ARPANET by Bolt, Beranek, and Newman). Together, ILLIAC IV and ARPANET consumed a significant portion of IPTO's budget in 1972. Nevertheless, the changes in DARPA's focus generated considerable controversy that continues to this day.

One man epitomized the new approach at DARPA. Robert Kahn joined the agency after a stint on the MIT faculty and at Bolt, Beranek, and Newman, where he worked on the construction of the original ARPANET. He joined DARPA as a program manager in 1972 and eventually took over as director of IPTO in 1979. Kahn embraced the new DARPA environment and turned it to IPTO's benefit. As a program manager and a technical leader, Kahn collaborated with contractors, defining systems for packet radio, networking, and eventually the internetworking protocols that became the Transmission Control Protocol/Internet Protocol (TCP/IP). On the latter effort, Kahn worked closely with Vinton Cerf, who was first at the University of California, Los Angeles, then at Stanford, and then assumed Kahn's networking responsibilities as a program manager at DARPA.

When Kahn became director at IPTO, his main direction from Heilmeier was to apply a "forcing function" to artificial intelligence (AI) "to produce something that would be useful" (Kahn, 1989). In addition to pushing AI, Kahn had two major goals of his own: (1) restoring, and then increasing, budgets for basic research (6.1), which had declined during the 1970s; and (2) increasing the involvement of industry in DARPA programs, creating overt links between universities and companies to transfer technology. "Transfer was all happening . . . by the invisible hand of the marketplace, or venture capital, or something. . . . But DARPA was not taking any role," Kahn recalled.

To accomplish his first goal, Kahn separated IPTO's applications programs from basic research so they could be managed in different styles. The Engineering Applications Office (EAO) split off for applications and "technology base" efforts. The move met with questionable success, and, when Saul Amarel succeeded Kahn as head of IPTO, he thought that EAO and IPTO were unnecessarily competing for resources. The two offices were recombined into the Information Systems Technology Office (ISTO). Kahn developed two major strategies to achieve his goals: the Very Large Scale Integrated Circuits program and the Strategic Computing Initiative.

Very Large Scale Integrated Circuits.[10] Efforts to develop very large scale integrated circuit (VLSI) technology demonstrate the role DARPA played in the growing computing industry by identifying technological developments of interest to DOD and the industry as a whole and helping them reach a state of greater maturity. Pioneering work in VLSI was conducted in the mid-1970s by Carver Mead, a professor at the California Institute of Technology (CalTech) with interests in semiconductor technology, and Lynn Conway, an expert in computer architecture at Xerox PARC. Encouraged by Bert Sutherland, Conway's laboratory manager at Xerox, and Bert's brother, Ivan Sutherland, chair of computer science at CalTech, Mead and Conway developed a simplified, standardized system design methodology and layout design rules for VLSI system and circuit design. Their design methods allowed integrated circuit (IC) designers to more quickly and easily design new ICs. Conway also innovated a new form of network-based, fast-turnaround VLSI prototyping service at PARC.

Called the MPC Implementation System, the service enabled chips designers at many locations around the country to submit design files over
the ARPANET for low-cost, rapid fabrication. The MPC system became
the basis of what was later called the Metal Oxide Silicon Implementation
Service, or MOSIS.

Mead and Conway propagated their new design methods and rules
through courses they taught during 1978 and 1979, first Conway's course
at MIT and then additional courses at other universities such as Stanford,
University of California at Berkeley (UC-Berkeley), and CalTech, exploiting prepublication versions of their new textbook about the methods. In
the fall of 1979, Conway and her group at Xerox PARC used the MPC
system to provide rapid chip prototyping for student design projects at
many universities. The success of the many MPC79 designs validated
their methods and quickly led to more widespread use of their design
methodology. Their book *Introduction to VLSI Systems* was published by
Addison-Wesley in 1980 (Mead and Conway, 1980).

The Mead-Conway approach also spurred development of a rich variety of computer designs as well as related supporting technologies for
checking and testing designs, for graphics editors, and for simulators.
The design methods and rules formed the basis of the specification language used in the MOSIS program and provided the essential ingredient
for developing computer-aided design tools for VLSI layouts. The first
such tool, ICARUS, resulted in 1976 from the work of Douglas Fairbairn
at Xerox PARC and James Rowson at CalTech. This tool was used in VLSI
design courses at Stanford and adopted by a number of researchers. James
Clark, then an associate professor at Stanford University, used VLSI tools
and techniques to develop a geometry engine for producing complex
computer graphic images. In 1982, Clark founded Silicon Graphics, Inc.,
which commercialized the technology and subsequently became a leader
in visual computing systems.[11]

DARPA's VLSI program built upon these early efforts. Formally initiated by Robert Kahn in 1978, the DARPA program grew out of a study it
commissioned at RAND Corporation in 1976 to evaluate the scope of
research DARPA might support in VLSI (Sutherland et al., 1976). The
final report, written by Ivan Sutherland, Carver Mead, and Thomas
Everhardt, concluded that continued attempts to increase computational
power by packing more devices onto a single integrated circuit—as industry was attempting—ignored the possibility of even greater gains
through wholly new computer architectures. As the report noted, the
advancement of VLSI technologies required new paradigms for integrated
circuit designs, because the circuit elements themselves would become
cheap, but the interconnections between them would become more expensive.[12] Sutherland and Mead published a derivative article in *Scien-*

tific American in September 1977 to gain an even broader audience for their ideas (Sutherland and Mead, 1977).

DARPA's plan for its VLSI program was to foster revolutionary advances by supporting university research and building bridges between research communities. To promote information sharing, DARPA maintained open, nonrestrictive policies on the publication of results, supported research with only indirect connections to military or defense applications, and refrained from classifying results.[13] These principles stood in direct contrast to DOD's other main semiconductor initiative of the time, the Very High Speed Integrated Circuit (VHSIC) program, which tried to advance industrial practices in a more incremental fashion, required direct defense relevance, and had a number of restrictions in place on publication of results.

DARPA played a strong role in identifying VLSI as an area for strategic direction but allowed much of the program content to emerge from the research community. Proposals were supported on the basis of their individual persuasiveness and the track record of the proposing institutions and principal investigators. Between 1978 and 1979, DARPA funded about a dozen programs in various aspects of VLSI technology at centers such as CalTech, Carnegie Mellon University, the Jet Propulsion Laboratory, MIT, Mississippi State University, University of North Carolina, Stanford University, UC-Berkeley, and the University of Utah. DARPA favored proposals drawn broadly to cover a range of related areas under the supervision of a single principal investigator. Many, if not most, of the participants were early adopters of the Mead-Conway design methods and thus had a common basis on which to build their research explorations.

Management of DARPA's VLSI program was turned over to Duane Adams in 1980 and to Paul Losleben in 1981 after Adams was promoted to deputy director of IPTO. Losleben came from the National Security Agency and brought expertise in semiconductor processing technology. Under their direction, the VLSI program evolved into four major lines of research: (1) computer architecture and system design; (2) microelectronic device fabrication process; (3) education and human resource development in microelectronics and computer science; and (4) fast-turnaround design fabrication, testing, and evaluation. The program made numerous contributions in each of these areas (Box 4.4 describes some prominent examples) and contributed to the commercialization of several VLSI-based technologies (Table 4.2). Part of this success resulted from the close ties between research and educational initiatives, with experimental classes leading to technologies such as reduced instruction set computing (RISC) processors, and research feeding back into the education and training of students.

TABLE 4.2 Representative VLSI Technologies and Resulting
Commercial Products

Technology	Investigator/Institution	Product/Company
RISC Architectures		
RISC I and RISC II	David Patterson, UC-Berkeley	SPARC, Sun Microsystems, Inc.
MIPS	John Hennessy, Stanford University	MIPS Computers, Inc. (now part of Silicon Graphics, Inc.)
Parallel Processors		
Connection Machine	Danny Hillis, MIT	Thinking Machines, Inc.
Cosmic Cube	Charles Seitz, CalTech	iPSC (Intel)
WARP	H.T. Kung, Carnegie Mellon University	iWARP (Intel)
Computer Systems		
Geometry Engine	Jim Clark, Stanford University	Silicon Graphics, Inc.
SUN (networked)	Forest Baskett, Stanford University	Sun Microsystems, Inc.
Design Tools		
Caesar	John Ousterhout, UC-Berkeley	Public domain
Magic	John Ousterhout, UC-Berkeley	Multiple[a]

[a]Valid Logic, Viewlogic, Mentor Graphics, Daisy, and Cadence all have products
essentially based on the Magic concept.
SOURCE: Van Atta et al. (1991a), Table 17-2, pp. 17-17 through 17-19.

On the technical side, the focus of the VLSI program expanded from
attempts to accelerate development of submicron semiconductor devices
to a broader set of improvements in computer capabilities based on submicron devices, with particular attention to computer design and architecture. DOD anticipated a range of uses for new-generation computers,
including signal processing and interpretation, aerodynamic simulation,
artificial intelligence, image and speech recognition, robotics, and high-
performance graphics (Van Atta et al., 1991a). Research it supported led
to a variety of new architectures that found acceptance both in DOD and
in the commercial marketplace (Box 4.4).

BOX 4.4
Accomplishments of DARPA's Very Large Scale
Integrated Circuit Program

DARPA's Very Large Scale Integrated Circuit (VLSI) program supported research on a number of innovations that revolutionized computing and computing research. Work on computer workstations, reduced instruction set computing, and semiconductor fabrication services for university researchers, in particular, benefited from DARPA support. In each of these areas, DARPA identified ongoing research of interest and provided the support necessary to bring the work to fruition.

Computer Workstations

Although industry efforts to develop computer workstations were under way at companies such as Apollo Computer, they received a significant boost from DARPA-sponsored research. DARPA supported the work of Forest Baskett, a specialist in computer architecture at Stanford University, who submitted a proposal to DARPA to create the Stanford University Network (SUN). As part of this effort, he planned to build a powerful single-user workstation, combining a 32-bit microprocessor (like Motorola's new 68000) and a wide-screen display. Baskett set Andreas Bechtolsheim to work on the hardware. He also interacted with James Clark, whose work on a high-speed graphics engine Baskett saw as critical to scientific and engineering applications of the system. The prototype SUN workstation was successfully demonstrated in 1981.

DARPA and Stanford University encouraged Bechtolsheim to commercialize the workstation, which he originally did through a company called VLSI Systems, which was to produce the workstation boards for other computer manufacturers. After reviewing proposals from potential computer manufacturers and seeing Apollo announce its own workstation, however, Bechtolsheim realized he would have to move quickly and design his own machines. Key to his plan was using Unix, recently expanded by Bill Joy at UC-Berkeley under another DARPA VLSI contract to enhance its multitasking, multiuser, and networking capabilities. With help from Vinod Khosla and Scott McNealy (both Stanford University MBAs), Bechtolsheim was able to solicit Joy's participation and attract needed venture capital. The team established Sun Microsystems, Inc., in February 1982, and its first product was launched in 1983.[1] DARPA extended funds to a number of academic institutions to allow them to purchase workstations for institutional users and networks. Such purchases accounted for 80 percent of Sun Microsystems' sales in its first year of business.[2] Since then, Sun has become a major force in the computing industry as both a manufacturer of computer workstations and the developer of the Java programming language.

RISC

Reduced instruction set computing (RISC) computers promised significant gains in performance by optimizing the flow of instructions through the processing unit.[3] Although pioneering work on RISC architectures was conducted by IBM as part of its 801 computer, IBM did not move quickly to commercialize the technology for fear that it would detract from burgeoning sales of its mainframe computers; nor was such

continued on next page

BOX 4.4 continued

work well publicized, although its existence became known in academic research circles (Hennessy and Patterson, 1990).[4] DARPA sponsored two university-based programs to develop RISC as a workable technology under VLSI: one, led by David Patterson at UC-Berkeley, developed the RISC I and RISC II architectures; the other, led by John Hennessy at Stanford University, resulted in the MIPS architecture. Both were general-purpose designs aimed at achieving more efficient interaction between computational, storage, and communications units within a device structure by employing pipelined architectures and processors closely linked with memory and communication circuits.

Both designs were adopted rapidly by industry. The newly formed Sun Microsystems, Inc., licensed the RISC II architecture from the University of California and hired Patterson as a consultant to help develop the scalable processor architecture, a RISC-based design that it subsequently incorporated into its workstations. This technology enabled Sun to fend off growing competition from companies such as Digital Equipment Corporation, Hewlett-Packard, and Steve Jobs' NeXT Corporation, which were planning their own entries into the workstation market. Hennessy and his colleagues at Stanford University founded MIPS Computer Systems to commercialize their RISC architecture. The company licensed five major chip producers to produce devices based on the technology and five other companies to use the MIPS architecture in their own computers. MIPS Computer Systems was subsequently purchased by Silicon Graphics, Inc. (SGI), although SGI is currently spinning off the company.

Other Architecture Projects

The VLSI program supported research on a number of innovative computer architectures other than RISC. Most of this work centered on designs for parallel computers. A range of projects supported a variety of configurations for linking microprocessors and memory, from the connection machine to the cube machines for general-purpose computing and the WARP architectures for special-purpose applications, such as signal processing. Several of these approaches were commercialized through start-up companies, such as Thinking Machines Corporation, or established firms, such as Intel Corporation. Although successful technologically, many of these designs failed to achieve commercial success.

MOSIS

DARPA also worked to establish ongoing technical and human infrastructure for VLSI. Of note was establishment of the Metal Oxide Silicon Implementation Service (MOSIS). Based on the innovative MultiProject Chip (MPC) service created by Lynn Conway at Xerox PARC (Conway, 1981), MOSIS provided university researchers with a means of quickly manufacturing limited numbers of custom or semicustom microelectronic devices at reasonable cost. New designs could be implemented in silicon within 4 to 10 weeks (less than the duration of an academic term). Prior to MOSIS (and the original MPC service), academic researchers had few economical ways of implementing and testing new semiconductor designs, few universities could afford their own fabrication lines, and the proliferation of different commercial systems of rules for specifying semiconductor circuit designs—most of which were kept proprietary—made collaboration between universities and industry difficult. With

MOSIS, researchers could submit designs for fabrication in a standardized format through the ARPANET or, subsequently, e-mail. Requests from different researchers were pooled into common lots and run through the fabrication process, after which completed chips were returned to the researchers. This system obviated the need for direct access to a fabrication line or for dealing with the complexity of arranging fabrication time at an industrial facility, by providing access to a qualified group of fabrication facilities through a single interface.

MOSIS was widely used by the academic research community and contributed to many novel systems. Access to MOSIS was originally limited to the VLSI research community and other Department of Defense contractors who linked to it through the ARPANET. After the National Science Foundation (NSF) assumed responsibility for administering MOSIS in 1982, access was expanded to include NSF-sponsored researchers and affiliated educational institutions. In 1984, access was expanded to other qualified users as well. Altogether, MOSIS was used by researchers at more than 360 institutions by 1989. The number of projects run through MOSIS increased from 258 in 1981 to 1,880 in 1989. RISC-based designs, such as RISC I, RISC II, and MIPS, and the geometry engine later commercialized by SGI were all run through MOSIS during their early design and testing phases. Prominent VLSI researcher Charles Seitz commented that MOSIS represented the first period since the pioneering work of Eckert and Mauchley on the ENIAC in the late 1940s that universities and small companies had access to state-of-the-art digital technology.[5]

Design Tools

DARPA also supported development of tools for designing VLSI devices. In 1978 and 1979, DARPA funded development of a program for step-level improvement in the layout of microelectronic devices. The result was Caesar, an interactive VLSI layout editor that was written in C, enabling it to run on VAX computers using the Berkeley version of Unix developed by Bill Joy. Caesar produced CalTech intermediate form files for use with the MOSIS system and was used to develop the RISC I, RISC II, and MIPS designs. Further modification made the tool suitable for more widespread use. A later, more advanced design technology created at UC-Berkeley, Magic, became even more widely used and formed the basis for several computer-assisted design systems, including those by VLSI Technology, Cadence, Valid Logic, Daisy, Mentor Graphics, and Viewlogic.

---

[1] S. Squires, chief scientist, DARPA, ISTO, October 19, 1990, as cited in Van Atta et al. (1991a).
[2] Vinod Khosla, as cited in Van Atta et al. (1991a).
[3] Ideally, all RISC processor instructions (for example, adding two registers) execute in one clock cycle. In actual practice, some instructions (such as multiplication and division) require additional clock cycles. Depending on the implementation, other instructions (such as shifts and register loads from memory) may require more than one clock cycle—this makes the distinction between RISC and complex instruction set computers (CISCs) somewhat gray. Mitchell Schnier, *Dictionary of PC Hardware*

continued on next page

DARPA was by far the largest federal supporter of VLSI research. Its
funding for the VLSI program grew from less than $15 million in 1979 to
over $93 million in 1982. But other organizations also played critical roles
in the success of the VLSI program. NSF assumed responsibility for
MOSIS. Its main objective was to pursue educational applications of
MOSIS, and it expanded the reach of the program to a wider set of academic institutions than DARPA had. ONR, too, funded several projects
in VLSI but with much smaller grants than DARPA. ONR funds were
often considered a "sandbox" for new ideas that, if successful, would
merit subsequent DARPA funding.[14] Similarly, industry contributed to
university research. The Stanford Center for Integrated Systems, for example, attracted funding in small amounts from 11 to 12 companies. This
money was generally used to support students and to fund faculty who
were starting new research areas and who lacked the long track record
needed to attract DARPA funding. Hence, while government research
funding dwarfed industry contributions, industry funding was key for
launching areas not mature enough to merit government support.[15]

Federal funding for VLSI began to decline in the mid-1980s. By 1983,
plans for DARPA's Strategic Computing Initiative evolved to the point
that the most promising ongoing architecture projects in the VLSI program (such as WARP, Butterfly, and Connection Machine) shifted to the
new program. The VLSI program became increasingly focused on semiconductor devices. Main elements of the program included computer-
aided design and manufacturing technology, test and evaluation tools,
and implementation and testing technologies, including ongoing support
for MOSIS.

Strategic Computing Initiative.   Kahn's second strategy was the Strategic Computing Initiative (SCI), which he formulated and proposed with

the support of Heilmeier's successor, DARPA director Robert Cooper. First presented to Congress in 1983, SCI aimed to spend $600 million by combining many of DARPA's computer research projects into an overall effort, with heavy emphasis on artificial intelligence. SCI responded to the growing unease about the apparent loss of U.S. leadership in the semiconductor and computer industries to Japan, following in the footsteps of the auto industry. Japan's "Fifth-Generation" computer program, run by the Ministry of International Trade and Industry, seemed a direct threat. Kahn and DARPA management argued that a strong, domestic electronics and computer industry was critical to national security. The argument succeeded: the project was budgeted originally at $145 million in 1986.

Kahn proposed four areas for SCI: microelectronics (based on the VLSI program), supercomputers, generic applications, and defense applications. The main goals were to create an industrial base for artificial intelligence, to implement multiprocessor technologies that could improve the speed of artificial intelligence programs by three orders of magnitude, and to develop advanced speech-understanding capabilities. Unlike the earlier, university-oriented IPTO, Kahn's vision incorporated industrial projects, with careful timelines and scheduled breakthroughs. In line with the shift to applications, industry would contribute to the production of three major "testbeds," or demonstration projects: the Autonomous Land Vehicle, to navigate hostile terrain based on visual sensors; the Pilot's Associate to respond to a fighter-pilot's verbal commands; and the Battle Management program, a series of expert systems to aid commanders in naval warfare. "The SCI proposed, for the first time, to place expert systems and other AI technology into central roles in military equipment and command" (Edwards, 1996, p. 295). Unlike the earlier university-based research programs, nearly half of SCI's funds went directly to industry, with corresponding emphasis on tangible results and applications. In the words of Kenneth Flamm, "economic and industrial spinoffs were a conscious objective of the program's planners"(Flamm, 1987, p. 75). In the words of Saul Amarel, who succeeded Kahn as IPTO program director, "the whole thing was motivated by developing an AI technology that would be richer, and more mature, building on what was done over the last twenty, twenty-five years, that would have an impact on applications, in particular, military applications . . . that would be used to help develop an industry of AI in the same way that an aeronautical industry was developed in this country" (Amarel, 1989).

The new approach at DARPA was a radical departure from the vision of its original founders, and it did not go without criticism. Some computer scientists were disturbed by what they saw as a shift away from intellectual research toward demonstrable results. Others were uncom-

fortable with the possibility that research products might actually some-
day pull the trigger in the envisioned autonomous robot weapons. Some
AI researchers saw expert systems as anathema to the fundamental goal
of building intelligent machines, and some went so far as to regard the
1980s as "years of distraction" because the emphasis on demonstrations
locked them into overly concrete promises for intelligent machines
(Norberg and O'Neill, 1996). Despite these concerns, the SCI coincided
with the early Reagan defense buildup and, hence, formed the center-
piece of DARPA computer research during that decade.

Making a Science, Funding a Science: The NSF in the 1970s and 1980s

The 1970s and 1980s saw a number of changes in NSF's support for
computing and communications, resulting in a vastly improved budget
for such activities. In 1970, the NSF's OCA lost its favored position below
the director and was placed under the Directorate for National and International Programs, marking the beginning of a decline for computing
within the NSF hierarchy. Soon, two other large changes to the OCA
followed as educational programs (approximately 40 percent of its budget) were spun off to another division. With the passage of the Mansfield
Amendment, OCA actually increased its basic research budget from $4.1
million in 1971 (23 percent of its budget) to $9 million dollars in 1973 (90
percent of its budget) (NSF, 1971, pp. 96-101; 1973, p. vii), but only as
incomplete compensation for cuts in basic research within DOD. This
increase in basic research support did not fully offset the loss of the educational programs, however, leaving the OCA with a budget of only $10
million in 1973, half the size of the 1972 figure. Computing funding did
not reach the $20 million mark again until 1981. This distillation of OCA's
objectives did, however, leave it as the only entity in the federal government whose primary function was to fund basic research in computer
science.

Subsequent changes recognized NSF's leading role in computer science, and, between 1973 and 1985, NSF's computing budgets qua-
drupled.[16] Changes included the creation of the Computer Sciences Section of the Division of Mathematical and Computer Sciences in 1975 and a
new Software Engineering Program created in 1977, which emphasized
symbolic manipulation, software tools, and programming environments.
Other divisions also conducted computer-related research (Box 4.5). By
1977, the Computer Sciences Section was the largest federal funder of
basic research in computer science. In its 1979 budget request to Congress, NSF stated that it "provides approximately 80 percent of the support [for theoretical computer science] except in numerical analysis . . . 50
percent of the federal support [for Software Systems Science] . . . almost

---

BOX 4.5
Computer Engineering at the National Science Foundation

Not all of the National Science Foundation's (NSF's) support for computing-related research came through the computer directorate. In 1973, the NSF created the Electrical Sciences and Analysis Section in its Engineering Division to fund electrical engineering research. Over the course of the next 10 years, the section's budget grew from $7.4 million dollars to $23.7 million in 1984 as NSF incorporated new programs. In 1979, the section was renamed the Division of Electrical, Computer, and Systems Engineering when it began to support computer engineering. The division supported research in very large scale integrated circuit technology, fiber-optic communications networks, and computer-aided drafting.

In 1986, many of the division's programs, including the Computer Engineering program, the Instrumentation, Sensing, and Measurement program, and the Automation, Instrumentation, and Sensing program, were shifted into the new microelectronics information processing system of the Computer and Information Sciences and Engineering Directorate. The communications programs were left behind, as most of their work focused on voice and video communication, rather than data networks.[1]

---

[1]Personal communication from Gordon Bell, former director of the Computer and Information Science and Engineering Directorate at the National Science Foundation, July 1998.

---

all of the support for basic research [in Software Engineering] . . . 60 percent of the support for basic research [in Computer Systems Design]" (NSF, 1979, p. B-II-3). NSF was also beginning to increase its support of intelligent systems as DARPA's support for basic AI declined.

Computer research support at NSF took on its current form in 1986. That year, NSF director Erich Bloch announced the creation of a new directorate entirely for computing, the Computer and Information Sciences and Engineering (CISE) Directorate (CSTB, 1992, p. 223). To lead the new directorate, Bloch recruited Gordon Bell, a pioneering system architect at Digital Equipment Corporation, who had been pushing NSF for several years to increase funding for computer science. Bell, like others in the computer industry, was still concerned that universities were not training enough Ph.D.s in computer science to continue advancing the field. He believed that the creation of CISE could help alleviate this problem.[17]

Unlike the more recent organizational changes in computing at NSF, CISE was more than a change of name and bureaucratic position. Much like the creation of OCA, CISE consolidated all the computer initiatives in NSF into one entity. The Division of Computer Research was combined with the computing portions of the Electrical, Computer, and Systems Engineering Division. CISE also absorbed the Office of Advanced Scientific Computing and the Division of Information Science and Technology. Monetary support for computing exploded immediately. CISE's 1986 budget was over $100 million, almost three times the Division of Computer Science's budget in 1984. CISE constituted 7 percent of the entire NSF budget as opposed to 3 percent in 1985.[18] In addition, attaining the level of NSF directorate symbolically marked the end of the uncertain position of computing within NSF. Computer science was formally on a par with the biological sciences, the physical sciences, and the other directorates of NSF.

Between 1987 and 1996, the CISE budget more than doubled from $117 million to $259 million, growing at about the same rate as NSF overall and remaining relatively constant at 7 to 8 percent of NSF's total budget. While all divisions within CISE grew during this period, the Division of Advanced Scientific Computing and the Division of Networking and Communications Research received the majority of the absolute dollar increases, reflecting the growing importance of NSF's infrastructure programs (Table 4.3). The Advanced Scientific Computing Division's budget increased from $42 million to $87 million between 1987 and 1996, making it by far the largest division within CISE, accounting for 35 percent of CISE's budget during that time. The Networking Division's budget increased from approximately 8 percent to almost 20 percent of the entire CISE budget, largely as a result of the NSFNET program and related networking infrastructure programs, which grew from $6.5 million in 1987 to $41.6 million in 1996 (NSFNET and the Advanced Scientific Computing program are discussed in Chapter 3). As a result, infrastructure programs grew from 42 percent to 50 percent of the CISE budget.[19]

Starting in 1989, CISE also began supporting a number of science and technology centers (STCs) whose goal was to promote collaborative, interdisciplinary research related to computer science. They include centers for computer graphics and scientific visualization, discrete mathematics and theoretical computer science, parallel computing, and research in cognitive science. These centers are supported not only by NSF but also by several other federal agencies, universities, and members of industry. Reviews of the STC program in 1995 and 1996 were highly supportive of the centers (National Academy of Public Administration, 1995; National Research Council, 1996).

Other Federal Agencies in the 1970s and 1980s

DARPA and NSF, of course, did not represent all federal funding of computer research during the 1970s and 1980s, though they clearly played

TABLE 4.3 Growth in the National Science Foundation's Computer and Information Sciences and Engineering Directorate Budget (millions of dollars), 1987–1996

	1987	1988	1989	1990	1991	1992	1993	1994	1995	1996
Computer and computation research	19	22	25	26	29	34	28	30	32	33
Cross-disciplinary activities	16	16	16	18	19	23	22	23	23	27
Advanced scientific computing	43	46	61	71	74	76	75	82	87	88
Information, robotics, and intelligent systems	17	17	18	19	22	25	26	29	30	31
Networking and communications research	10	11	16	20	29	34	39	50	56	54
Computer and information engineering	6	6	6	6	7	8	8	8	9	9
Microelectronics and information processing systems	6	7	8	10	11	13	13	15	16	17
TOTAL	117	124	152	169	190	210	212	236	254	259

NOTE: Totals may not add because of rounding.
SOURCE: Personal communication from Vernon Ross, NSF Office of Budget, Finance, and Award Management, July 1997.

a dominant role. Although SCI was formulated prior to and independent of the Strategic Defense Initiative (SDI), it could not but be partially absorbed (especially in the minds of the public) by the latter, despite the efforts of DARPA management to keep the programs distinct (Edwards, 1996, pp. 293-299). Reagan's $35 billion SDI program pumped tens of millions of dollars annually into computing.[20] SDI critically relied on command-and-control systems for its effectiveness, and doubts about software testing and reliability proved a major hurdle in implementation. SDI also supported work in parallel architectures, optical computing, and new semiconductor materials.

The VHSIC program, launched in 1980, focused on transferring technology from the commercial semiconductor industry into the largely separate military electronics industry. The long procurement cycle of military electronics meant that it was perpetually behind rapidly changing commercial technology. Under the VHSIC program, DOD, through the Office of the Secretary of Defense, spent more than $900 million over the course of the decade, but few new chips actually made their way into military systems. As one analyst wrote, "R&D could not solve a procurement problem" (Alic et al., 1992, p. 269). The Office of the Secretary of Defense (OSD) spent significant funds on the development of the Ada programming language, intended to be standard for all DOD computer applications. While Ada displaced a number of other programming languages in DOD applications, it did not achieve broad acceptance in the commercial marketplace as had been hoped.[21] OSD also made a significant investment in software production and maintenance techniques aimed at improving productivity and reliability ($60 million in 1984) (Flamm, 1987, p. 76).

NASA support for computing has varied considerably over the years. Overall, NASA has been more of a development than a research agency in computing: that is, it has focused on hardware and applications rather than basic research. In hardware, the agency built highly rugged and reliable machines to run its spacecraft but with conservative rather than cutting-edge technology. Although NASA tended to have little effect on computer architecture and design (although some significant impact in packaging), its software work in redundant and fault-tolerant computers, simulation, and program verifications made significant contributions to programming practice. The Saturn V computer pioneered triple redundancy and voter circuits (Tomayko, 1985, pp. 7-18). Some of this technology has been transferred to transaction processing in commercial units. Funding began to decline rapidly after the peak of the space program, in the late 1960s, and was virtually halted by 1972, at which point NASA's only computing program was the ILLIAC IV. It took off again in the early 1980s, focusing on image processing and supercomputers for modeling of aerostructures. The NASTRAN software package for finite element modeling of physical structures has become the most widely accepted such program in industry (Flamm, 1987, p. 85). Also during the 1980s, the National Institutes of Health (NIH) was a small but increasingly important player in developing computer applications for medicine and biology, particularly in innovative applications of expert systems (see Chapters 9 and 10 for a description of NIH's support for expert systems and virtual reality technology). The National Library of Medicine, along with DARPA and the National Institute of Standards and Technology (NIST), also supported work on information retrieval that has influenced the development of Internet search engines. Similarly, the Department of Energy invested in high-end and parallel machines, at about $7 million per year (Flamm, 1987, p. 93).

SEMATECH

In 1987, 14 U.S. semiconductor companies joined a not-for-profit venture, SEMATECH, to improve domestic semiconductor manufacturing. The joint nature of the effort, combined with member companies' willingness to put significant funds into SEMATECH and concerns over the nation's growing dependence on foreign suppliers for semiconductor devices, helped convince Congress to support the effort as well: in 1988, it appropriated $100 million annually for 5 years to match the industrial funding. The federal dollars for SEMATECH were funneled through DARPA because semiconductor manufacturing was seen as vital to the defense technology base. In the words of one analyst, "the half-billion-dollar federal commitment marks a major shift in U.S. technology policy: a turn toward explicit support for commercially oriented R&D carried out in the private sector" (Alic et al., 1992, p. 277).

SEMATECH originally planned to develop new production processes in-house for manufacturing next-generation semiconductor devices, but soon after decided to concentrate its efforts on strengthening the supplier base for the semiconductor industry. At the time, Japanese semiconductor manufacturing equipment suppliers were gaining market share at a rate of 3.1 percentage points a year, and U.S. semiconductor manufacturers planned to purchase the majority of their equipment from Japanese suppliers (SEMATECH, 1991).

Over the next several years, SEMATECH made several notable advances. It established partnerships with U.S. equipment suppliers to help them develop next-generation production tools, and it helped semiconductor manufacturers develop consensus regarding their future needs, especially those related to manufacturing equipment. These achievements allowed equipment manufacturers to meet one set of industry specifications rather than a variety of company specifications. SEMATECH also funded research and development efforts at supplier companies helping them improve their equipment and develop systems to make more advanced semiconductor devices. Perhaps most important, SEMATECH helped establish improved communication links between semiconductor manufacturers and their suppliers, allowing freer exchanges of information among users and suppliers of manufacturing equipment.

These efforts and others began to show benefits soon thereafter. Semiconductor equipment manufacturers regained market share against the Japanese, boasting 53 percent of the world market in 1992 versus 38 percent for Japanese suppliers (VLSI Research, 1992). Production yields for U.S. semiconductor manufacturers improved from 60 percent in 1987 to 84 percent in 1992, and U.S. market share in semiconductor devices also improved (GAO, 1992, p. 10). Clearly, other factors played a role, not the least of which was the relative rise of the market for microprocessors—in which U.S. firms developed a strong competitive advantage—versus memory chips. Nevertheless, SEMATECH has been cited as a factor in the resurgence of U.S. semiconductor equipment manufacturers. DARPA program managers also considered the effort successful, noting that many of DARPA's objectives were mentioned in SEMATECH's strategic plan, including efforts to rapidly convert manufacturing technology into practice and to develop technology for more flexible semiconductor production (OTA, 1993, p. 128).

DARPA continued its investment in SEMATECH beyond the original deadline, but, in 1995, SEMATECH announced that it would wean itself from public assistance. In doing so, it recognized that it had achieved most of its original objectives and believed it could remain self-sustaining with industry funds only. Doing so would also allow it greater freedom in establishing its research agenda, insulate it from continued uncertainty over federal funding, and reduce concerns about participating with foreign companies. In 1998, SEMATECH announced the establishment of SEMATECH International, a division of SEMATECH that would allow participation by foreign-owned companies.

High-performance Computing

The late 1980s saw a new theme emerge in government support of computing research: coordination among federal research agencies. The most visible example of this coordination, which also accounts for a significant percentage of today's federal support for computing R&D, is the High Performance Computing and Communications Initiative (HPCCI). Although this program focused on the highest-end computers and applications, it has much broader impact. The pace of microelectronics means that the evolution of a given capability (hardware and software) from supercomputer to desktop requires about a decade. Thus, today's high-performance applications are a glimpse into the future of computing.

In keeping with its traditional role of providing facilities for computer science in universities, in 1984 the NSF asked Congress to set up supercomputer centers so academic researchers could access state-of-the-art supercomputers. The result was the National Centers for Supercomputing Applications. NSF then established a high-speed network backbone to connect these centers, which itself became the seed of the high-speed Internet backbone. In 1988, the Office of Science and Technology Policy (OSTP) and the Federal Coordinating Council for Science, Engineering, and Technology (FCCSET) created the National Research and Education Network, a new system that built on earlier projects within NSF, DOE, NASA, and DOD that supported advanced scientific computing and human resource development for computer science. The result was the High Performance Computing Program, which also included an emphasis on communications.

In 1989, OSTP produced a formal program plan for high-performance computing. OSTP provided a vehicle for interagency coordination among the initial players, DOE, NASA, and NSF; the National Security Agency (NSA) has also been an influential player, although not a formal member. Thus, economies of scale and scope could be realized by avoiding duplication of effort across research agencies. Congress passed the High Performance Computing Act in 1991 as a 5-year program. This affirmed the interagency character of HPCCI, which by then had 10 federal agencies participating, including the Environmental Protection Agency, the National Library of Medicine (a branch of NIH), NIST, the National Oceanic and Atmospheric Administration, and later, the Department of Education, NSA, and the Veterans Administration.

Originally, HPCCI aimed at meeting several grand challenges, including scientific modeling, weather forecasting, aerospace vehicle design, and earth biosphere research. These goals have since been expanded to "National Challenges," which include digital libraries, electronic commerce, health care, and improvement of information infrastructure (CSTB, 1995a). Overall, the program achieved a number of notable results. The success of some applications and programming paradigms convinced people that parallel computing could be made to work. The program created and disseminated technologies to speed the pace of innovation, enhance national security, promote education, and better understand the global environment (see Chapter 3 for a discussion of some of the results of the high-performance computing effort).

1990 AND BEYOND

The 1990s have seen the continued evolution of computing and communications technology and a changing environment for federal support. The technological side has been characterized by an explosion in the use of computers and the Internet. Personal computers have continued to penetrate businesses and homes. By 1998, approximately 40 percent of U.S. households had at least one computer, and a growing number boasted a connection to the Internet. Building upon decades of federal research and development, the Internet itself emerged as a major force with the number of servers growing exponentially. With the emergence of the World Wide Web and browser technologies (also derivatives of federally sponsored research—see Chapter 7), the Internet has become a medium for disseminating information and conducting business. Companies such as Amazon.com formed solely as virtual entities, and many established firms created a presence on the Web to conduct business.

Development of networking technologies has also created new opportunities for new kinds of computing hardware and software. A number of companies developed and began offering network computers, machines designed specifically for use over the Internet and other corporate networks. Such machines rely on the network for much of their infrastructure, including application programs, rather than storing such files locally. Although it is not yet clear how well such computers will fare in the marketplace, especially as PC manufacturers expand their offerings of low-cost, scaled-down computers, network computers demonstrate the kinds of innovation that expansion of the Internet can motivate.

Component software also emerged as a new programming modality in the 1990s. Epitomized by the Java programming language, component software allows programs to be assembled from components that can run on a wide variety of computing platforms. Applications can be accessed, downloaded, and run over the network (e.g., the Internet) as needed for computations.

Along with these technological changes have come changes in the environment for federal research funding. With the fall of the Berlin Wall in 1989 and the subsequent demise of the Soviet Union, defense budgets began a slow, steady decline, placing additional pressure on defense research and development spending. At the same time, growing sentiment to reduce the federal deficit further squeezed federal budgets for science and technology generally in the first half of the decade. By 1997, the prospect of budget surpluses gave rise to the possibility of expanding budgets for science and technology spending and renewed attempts to develop a new framework for federal participation in the innovation process. Senator Phillip Gramm, along with Senators Joseph Lieberman,

Peter Domenici, and Jeffrey Bingaman, introduced a bipartisan bill in October 1997 to double federal spending for nondefense scientific, medical, and precompetitive engineering research over 10 years (the bill, S.1305, is called the National Research Investment Act of 1998). In early 1998, Congressman Vern Ehlers of the House Science Committee initiated a national science policy study to review the nation's science policy and develop a new, long-range science and technology policy that is "concise, comprehensive, and coherent" (Ehlers, 1998).

The structure of federal support for computing and communications also underwent modification in the 1990s. In place of the FCCSET committee, the Clinton administration established a National Science and Technology Council in 1993 to coordinate federal programs in science, technology, and space. Its Committee on Computing, Information, and Communications (CCIC), through the subcommittee on Computing, Information, and Communications R&D, coordinates computing- and communications-related R&D programs conducted by the 12 federal departments and agencies in cooperation with academia and industry. This group has restructured and expanded upon the HPCCI to organize programs in five areas: (1) high-end computing and computation; (2) large-scale networking; (3) high-confidence systems; (4) human-centered systems; and (5) education, training, and human resources. Further, in February 1997, President Clinton established an Advisory Committee on High Performance Computing and Communications, Information Technology, and the Next-Generation Internet. The committee's charge is to assist the administration in accelerating the development and adoption of information technology that is vital to the nation's future (NSTC, 1997).

Federal support for computing and communications infrastructure also changed in the 1990s. After opening the Internet to commercial use in 1992, NSF effectively privatized the network in 1995. Nevertheless, NSF and other federal agencies are pursuing development and deployment of the Next-Generation Internet (NGI), which will boast data rates 100 times those of the Internet. The NGI initiative will create an experimental, wide-area, scalable testbed for developing networking applications that are critical to national missions, such as defense and health care. Further, starting in December 1995, NSF began restructuring its support of national supercomputing centers, forming a new Partnerships for Advanced Computational Infrastructure program. The program will concentrate its resources on two groups of organizations, each with a leading-edge facility and several collaborators. One group, the National Partnership for Advanced Computational Infrastructure will have the San Diego Supercomputing Center in California as its leading-edge site. The other group, the National Computational Science Alliance, will have the National Center for Supercomputing Applications at Urbana-Champaign,

Illinois, as its leading-edge site. The objective is to equip these sites with high-end computing systems one to two orders of magnitude more capable than those typically available at major research universities. They will work in partnership with other organizations that are expected to contribute to access, to education, outreach, and training, and to software development that will facilitate and enhance both the overall infrastructure and access to that infrastructure (Cutter, 1997).

Funding for research in computer science weathered these changes reasonably well with basic and applied research posting real gains between 1989 and 1995 (see Chapter 3). Nevertheless, the research community expressed concerns that such funding may not be adequate to support the continuing growth of the field (and the rising number of researchers in academia and industry) and that the nature of such research is changing. Many researchers claim that federal funding is increasingly focused on near-term objectives and less radical innovation. Calls for greater accountability in the research enterprise, they claim, have led agencies to favor work that is less risky and that exploits existing knowledge, despite its potentially lesser payback. The implications of such changes are not yet clear, but they will become evident over the next several years and beyond.[22]

NOTES

1. Quoted in Edwards (1996), p. 122.

2. As President Eisenhower declared in the 1958 State of the Union message, "Some of the important new weapons which technology has produced do not fit into any existing service pattern. They cut across all services, involve all services, and transcend all services, at every stage from development to operation. In some instances they defy classification according to branch of service."

3. Quoted in Barber Associates (1975), pp. V-51 to V-52.

4. Quoted in Norberg (1996), pp. 40-53.

5. Quoted in Norberg and O'Neill (1996), p. 31.

6. Figure based on data for 1960-1968 in the National Science Foundation's annual *Budget Request to Congress* (1960-1969) and for 1968-1970 in its annual publication *Grants and Awards* (1968-1970). Both are available from the National Science Foundation.

7. Figure based on data from the 1968, 1969, and 1970 editions of the National Science Foundation's *Grants and Awards for the Fiscal Year Ended June 30*.

8. The fundamental discoveries of computability and complexity theory show precisely that the details of the computing machine do not matter in analyzing the most important properties of the function to be computed. The science of computing is the study of the consequences of certain basic assumptions about the nature of computation (spelled out most clearly in Turing's famous 1936 paper), not the study of particular artifacts. Of course, problems arising from the construction and use of actual computers are a main source of questions for the

science of computing, in the same way as problems in the physical sciences and engineering have been a main source of ideas and questions in mathematics.

9. Blue, quoted in Norberg and O'Neill (1996), p. 37.

10. Many of the details contained in this section derive from case studies of the VLSI program and MOSIS contained in Van Atta et al. (1991a), although the interpretation here differs in some respects.

11. Silicon Graphics, Inc. had sales of $3.1 billion and employed over 9,800 workers in 1998.

12. Charles Seitz in a presentation to the study committee, February 28, 1997, Stanford, Calif.

13. In order for the program to benefit U.S. industry more than its foreign competitors, there was a general understanding that investigators would delay open publication of results for roughly 1 year, during which time results would be circulated quickly within the community of DARPA-sponsored VLSI researchers (Van Atta et al., 1991a, pp. 17-10 and 17-13, based largely on comments by Robert Kahn on August 7, 1990).

14. Charles Seitz in a presentation to the study committee, February 28, 1997, Stanford, Calif.

15. John L. Hennessy in a briefing to the study committee, February 28, 1997, Stanford, Calif.

16. Data from "Compilation of Data" from the National Science Foundation's annual *Summary of Awards* between 1973 and 1985.

17. Personal communication from Gordon Bell, July 1998.

18. Personal communication from Vernon Ross, NSF Office of Budget, Finance, and Award Management, July 1997.

19. Personal communication from Vernon Ross, NSF Office of Budget, Finance, and Award Management, July 1997.

20. SDI budgets for computing are difficult to discern with accuracy, as they were buried within other types of contracts. One estimate is between $50 million and $225 million annually from 1985 to 1994 (Paul Edwards, 1996, p. 292).

21. For a discussion of Ada and its use in military and civilian applications, see CSTB (1997a).

22. The Computer Science and Telecommunications Board of the National Research Council has a project under way to document changes in support for information technology research in industry and government and evaluate their implications. For more information on this project, "Information Technology Research in a Competitive World," see <http://www4.nas.edu/cp.nsf >.

5

Lessons from History

The federal government has made significant contributions to the research base for computing technology. As detailed in Chapter 3, federal support has accounted for a substantial fraction of the total funding for computing research in the United States and the vast majority of all university research funds in the field. Such funding has supported both the development of new technologies and the training of students. The federal government has also paid for public research infrastructure, providing most of the funds for research equipment in university departments of computer science and electrical engineering, and has sponsored programs to provide access to and infrastructure for high-performance computing and networking. Such contributions did not single-handedly drive subsequent development of the nation's computing industry; rather, they formed part of the larger innovation system that combined the efforts of government, universities, and industry. They nevertheless played an important role in the industry's development.

What have been the results of federal investments? How can future federal programs be designed to enhance their effectiveness? The history described in this report can aid in answering these questions. History demonstrates by select examples the kinds of effects federal research funding has had on the innovation process in computing, and it illustrates some of the principles of sound project management. This chapter synthesizes the major lessons of this report. It attempts to characterize the effects of federal investments in computing research and to discuss the programmatic considerations that appear to have contributed to the success of the field. In doing so, the chapter draws on case studies from other sections of the report as needed for examples. Readers are referred to Chapters 6 through 10 and Chapter 4 for a more complete elaboration of the case studies.

THE BENEFITS OF FEDERAL RESEARCH INVESTMENTS

Government research funding has had a profound influence on the development of the computing industry in the United States. Federal research support has provided a proving ground for testing new concepts, designs, and architectures in computing, and it has helped hasten the commercialization of technology developed in industry laboratories. This influence has manifested itself in a variety of ways: (1) in the creation of new products, services, companies, and billion-dollar industries that are based on federally funded research; (2) in the expansion of university research capabilities in computer science and electrical engineering; (3) in the formation of human resources that have driven the computing revolution; and (4) in the ability of federal agencies to better accomplish their public missions.

Quantifying the benefits of federal research support is a difficult, if not impossible, task for several reasons. First, the output of research is often intangible. Most of the benefit takes the form of new knowledge that subsequently may be instantiated in new hardware, software, or systems, but is itself difficult to measure. At other times, the benefits take the form of educated people who bring new ideas or a fresh perspective to an organization. Second, the delays between the time a research program is conducted and the time the products incorporating the research results are sold make measurement even more difficult. Often, the delays run into decades, making it difficult to tell midcourse how effective a particular program has been. Third, the benefits of a particular research program may not become visible until other technological advances are made. For example, advances in computer graphics did not have widespread effect until suitable hardware was more broadly available for producing three-dimensional graphical images. Finally, projects that are perceived as failures often provide valuable lessons that can guide or improve future research. Even if they fail to reach their original objectives, research projects can make lasting contributions to the knowledge base.

Despite these difficulties, several observations can be made that provide a qualified understanding of the influence of federal research programs on industry, government, and universities. They demonstrate the effect federal funding has had on computing and, by extension, on society.

Providing the Technology Base for Growing Industries

Federal research funding has helped build the technology base on which the computing industry has grown. A number of important computer-related products trace their technological roots to federally sponsored research programs. Early mainframe computers were given a significant boost from federally funded computing systems of the 1950s, such as the U.S. Air Force's Semi-Automatic Ground Environment (SAGE) project. Although a command-and-control system designed to warn of attacks by Soviet bombers, SAGE pioneered developments in real-time digital computing and core memory (among other advances) that rapidly spread throughout the fledgling computer industry. Time-shared minicomputers, which dominated the market in the 1970s and early 1980s, exploited time-sharing research conducted in the 1960s under the Defense Advanced Research Projects Agency's (DARPA's)[1] Project MAC and earlier work sponsored by the National Science Foundation (NSF) on the Compatible Time-Sharing System at the Massachusetts Institute of Technology (MIT) (see Chapter 4). The Internet, which came of age in the early 1990s, was derived from DARPA's ARPANET program of the early 1970s, which created a packet-switching system to link research centers across the country, as well as from subsequent programs managed by NSF to expand and improve its NSFNET (see Chapter 7). Federal funding for relational databases helped move that technology out of corporate laboratories to become the basis of a multibillion-dollar U.S. database industry. The graphical user interface, which became commonplace on personal computers in the 1990s, incorporates research conducted at SRI International under a DARPA contract some 30 years earlier (Chapter 4).

The economic impact of federally funded research in computing is evident in the many companies that have successfully commercialized technologies developed under federal contracts. Examples include Sun Microsystems, Inc., Silicon Graphics, Inc., Informix Corporation, Digital Equipment Corporation, and Netscape Communications Corporation. Established companies, such as International Business Machines Corporation (IBM) and American Telephone and Telegraph Corporation (AT&T), also commercialized technologies developed with federal sponsorship, such as core memories and time-sharing operating systems. Clearly, federally sponsored research was only one element in the success of these companies. Private firms had to dedicate tremendous resources to bring these technologies successfully to market, investing in their research and development, establishing manufacturing capacity, and setting up marketing and distribution channels. But new technology created the seed for continued innovation.

Maintaining University Research Capabilities

Federal funding has also maintained university research capabilities in computing. Universities depend largely on federal support for research programs in computer science and electrical engineering, the two academic disciplines most closely aligned with computing and communications. Since 1973, federal agencies have provided roughly 70 percent of all funding for university research in computer science. In electrical engineering, federal funding has declined from its peak of 75 percent of total university research support in the early 1970s, but still represented 65 percent of such funding in 1995.[2] Additional support has come in the form of research equipment. Universities need access to state-of-the-art equipment in order to conduct research and train students. Although industry contributes some equipment, funding for university research equipment has come largely from federal sources since the 1960s. Between 1981 and 1995, the federal government provided between 59 and 76 percent of annual research equipment expenditures in computer science and between 64 and 83 percent of annual research equipment expenditures in electrical engineering.[3] Such investments have helped ensure that researchers have access to modern computing facilities and have enabled them to further expand the capabilities of computing and communications systems.

Universities play an important role in the innovation process. They tend to concentrate on research with broad applicability across companies and product lines and to share new knowledge openly.[4] Because they are not usually subject to commercial pressures, university researchers often have greater ability than their industrial counterparts to explore ideas with uncertain long-term payoffs. Although it would be difficult to determine how much university research contributes directly to industrial innovation, it is telling that each of the case studies and other major examples examined in this report—relational databases, the Internet, theoretical computer science, artificial intelligence, virtual reality, SAGE, computer time-sharing, very large scale integrated circuits, and the personal computer—involved the participation of university researchers. Universities play an especially effective role in disseminating new knowledge by promoting open publication of research results. They have also served as a training ground for students who have taken new ideas with them to existing companies or started their own companies. Diffusion of knowledge about relational databases, for instance, was accelerated by researchers at the University of California at Berkeley who published the source code for their Ingres system and made it available free of charge. Several of the lead researchers in this project established companies to commercialize the technology or brought it back to existing firms where they championed its use (see Chapter 6).

Creating Human Resources

In addition to supporting the creation of new technology, federal funding for research has also helped create the human resources that have driven the computer revolution. Many industry researchers and research managers claim that the most valuable result of university research programs is educated students—by and large, an outcome enabled by federal support of university research. Federal support for university research in computer science grew from $65 million to $350 million between 1976 and 1995, while federal support for university research in electrical engineering grew from $74 million to $177 million (in constant 1995 dollars).[5] Much of this funding was used to support graduate students. Especially at the nation's top research universities, the studies of a large percentage of graduate students have been supported by federal research contracts. Graduates of these programs, and faculty researchers who received federal funding, have gone on to form a number of companies, including Sun Microsystems, Inc. (which grew out of research conducted by Forest Baskett and Andy Bechtolsheim with sponsorship from DARPA) and Digital Equipment Corporation (founded by Ken Olsen, who participated in the SAGE project). Graduates also staff academic faculties that continue to conduct research and educate future generations of researchers.

Furthermore, the availability of federal research funding has enabled the growth and expansion of computer science and computer engineering departments at U.S. universities, which increased in number from 6 in 1965 to 56 in 1975 and to 148 in 1995 (Andrews, 1997, p. 5). The number of graduate students in computer science also grew dramatically, expanding more than 40-fold from 257 in 1966 to 11,500 in 1995, with the number of Ph.D. degrees awarded in computer science increasing from 19 in 1966 to over 900 in 1995 (NSF, 1997b, Table 46). Even with this growth in Ph.D. production, demand for computing researchers still outstrips the supply in both industry and academia (U.S. Department of Commerce, 1997).

Beyond supporting student education and training, federal funding has also been important in creating networks of researchers in particular fields—developing communities of researchers who could share ideas and build on each other's strengths. Despite its defense orientation, DARPA historically encouraged open dissemination of the results of sponsored research, as did other federal agencies. In addition, DARPA and other federal agencies funded large projects with multiple participants from different organizations. These projects helped create entire communities of researchers who continued to refine, adopt, and diffuse new technology throughout the broader computing research community. Development of the Internet demonstrates the benefits of this approach: by funding groups of researchers in an open environment, DARPA created an entire community of users who had a common understanding of the technology, adopted a common set of standards, and encouraged their use broadly. Early users of the ARPANET created a critical mass of people who helped to disseminate the technology, giving the Internet Protocol an important early lead over competing approaches to packet switching (see Chapter 7).

Scientific societies have also played a significant role in this respect. Groups such as the Association for Computing Machinery (ACM) and the Institute of Electrical and Electronics Engineers (IEEE) and their subgroups have helped create communities of researchers and facilitated communication among them. The development of virtual reality, for example, benefited enormously from the creation of SIGGRAPH, the ACM's special interest group for computer graphics. This organization brought together university and industry researchers, as well as users of computer graphics, from a variety of fields (e.g., arts, entertainment, medicine, and manufacturing). Its annual conferences have become a showcase of new technology and a primary forum for exchanging new ideas.

Accomplishing Federal Missions

In addition to supporting industrial innovation and the economic benefits that it brings, federal support for computing research has enabled government agencies to accomplish their missions. Investments in computing research by the Department of Energy (DOE), the National Aeronautics and Space Administration (NASA), and the National Institutes of Health (NIH), as well as the Department of Defense (DOD), are ultimately based on agency needs. Many of the missions these agencies must fulfill depend on computing technologies. DOD, for example, has maintained a policy of achieving military superiority over potential adversaries not through numerical superiority (i.e., having more soldiers) but through better technology. Computing has become a central part of information gathering, management, and analysis for commanders and soldiers alike (High Performance Computing Modernization Office, 1995).

Similarly, DOE and its predecessors would have been unable to support their mission of designing nuclear weapons without the simulation capabilities of large supercomputers. Such computers have retained their value to DOE as its mission has shifted toward stewardship of the nuclear stockpile in an era of restricted nuclear testing. Its Accelerated Strategic Computing Initiative builds on DOE's earlier success by attempting to support development of simulation technologies needed to assess nuclear weapons, analyze their performance, predict their safety and reliability, and certify their functionality without testing them.[6] In addition, NASA could not have accomplished its space exploration or its Earth observation and monitoring missions without reliable computers for controlling spacecraft and managing data. New computing capabilities, including the World Wide Web, have enabled the National Library of Medicine to expand access to medical information and have provided tools for researchers who are sequencing the human genome.

CHARACTERISTICS OF EFFECTIVE FEDERAL SUPPORT

The success of federal funding in computing research derives both from the kind of programs and projects it has supported and the ways it has structured those programs. By funding a mix of fundamental research and system development activities, for example, government was able to promote the long-term health of the field and to demonstrate new technologies. By funding a mix of work in universities and industry, it was able to marry long-term objectives to real-world problems. And, by channeling its funding through a variety of federal agencies, it was able to ensure broad-based coverage of many technological approaches and to address a range of technical problems. This section examines some of the key factors that have led to the success of federal research investments in the past and attempts to provide guidance for structuring future research programs.

Support for Long-range, Fundamental Research

A strength of federal research funding is that it complements, rather than competes with, private research investments. Successful government research programs have supported research that private industry has had little incentive or ability to support because the commercial applications of the research were too distant and too uncertain, or because the research itself was so fundamental that individual firms could not expect to capture the benefits themselves while preventing others from doing so (see Chapter 2). Private industry is generally not able to assume the risks inherent in such projects, nor does it continue funding research in a particular field over extended periods if the payback is unclear. In many such instances, federally sponsored research has laid the groundwork for new technologies that ultimately created not only new products, processes, and services, but also entire industries. Such investments were typically made years—if not decades—before practical applications became feasible; they helped advance knowledge of the field sufficiently so that firms could begin to make appropriate investments. This pattern has been repeated in numerous cases:

1. In artificial intelligence (AI), early funding came mostly from federal sources, primarily DARPA. Although large computing and communications companies, such as IBM and AT&T, established small programs for artificial intelligence research in the 1950s, these efforts were scaled back and redirected toward more practical topics (such as speech recognition) when it became evident that more fundamental research might not produce marketable results for more than a decade. The federal government, too, cut back on some programs that failed to show initial progress (such as machine translation and, for a time, speech recognition), but it continued to make strong investments in AI research to explore both fundamental research questions and applications of AI technology. These investments, combined with industry efforts, enabled sufficient progress for a number of AI-based products to begin entering the market place. Based on pioneering efforts such as DENDRAL, an expert (or rule-based reasoning) system for deducing the likely molecular structure of organic compounds, a number of firms began creating rule-based reasoning systems for engineering and medical applications in the mid-1970s and the 1980s. Building on work conducted with industry and federal funding, several companies, including IBM, Dragon Systems, and Lucent Technologies, introduced in the 1990s robust, continuous speech-recognition packages for use with personal computers. A range of other AI technologies began to appear as integral parts of other systems, such as grammar checkers in word processors, decision aids for troubleshooting software, and software agents for finding information on the World Wide Web (see Chapter 9).

2. Pioneering work in virtual reality was conducted by Ivan Sutherland, then at Harvard University, with support from several defense agencies. A handful of private firms, such as General Electric, established research programs to build on this work but soon realized that products incorporating such technology lay many years in the future. Subsequent research—funded by agencies such as DARPA and NSF and conducted at universities such as the University of Utah, California Institute of Technology, and the University of North Carolina at Chapel Hill—created a number of advances in hardware and software for rendering two- and three-dimensional computer graphics that have since been used widely in medicine, entertainment, and engineering applications. Federally funded research in these areas succeeded in developing the technology to the point that private companies could both develop products and invest in productive research. In virtual reality, for example, the entertainment industry has built on early university research to create systems for pro-

ducing computer-animated films. More recently, Microsoft established a large research group in computer graphics to help improve graphics for desktop computers. Its interest is now driven largely by the video game industry and the search for improved user interfaces (see Chapter 10 for a case study of the federal role in virtual reality research).

In both of these cases, industry had limited incentives to invest in research. The time needed for such programs to yield tangible results was often measured in decades, far beyond the planning horizons of many companies. Furthermore, early progress in these fields required fundamental advances that were applicable to a range of potential applications and were difficult for any single company fully to appropriate (or control). Because few mechanisms exist for companies to collectively fund fundamental research of mutual interest,[7] federal funding has often been the most appropriate mechanism for supporting research, especially if the research is applicable to government missions.

This is not to say that industry will not support long-term research. Many larger companies conduct fundamental research with broad applicability. IBM and AT&T are the most prominent examples. The ability of such companies to support fundamental research is closely linked to their ability to recoup their investments in these areas (see Chapter 2) and, hence, to their overall profitability and dominance in the marketplace. AT&T, for example, conducted long-term research at Bell Laboratories and for many years had a government-granted monopoly on the telephone industry. Its research expenditures were in effect a tax on consumers because they were paid for by AT&T's regulated rates for telephone service. Since divestiture, Bell Laboratories (now part of Lucent Technologies) has continued to fund long-term research, but a more conscious effort has been made to link that research to corporate needs and to capture the benefits of the research investment (Buderi, 1998). IBM maintained long-term research at its T.J. Watson Research Center and its other laboratories, and, given its market dominance, was able to appropriate many of the results of that research. However, as the computer industry has become more competitive and IBM's market dominance has declined, IBM's research has been reined in somewhat and redirected to specific strategic areas (Markov, 1996). Long-term fundamental research is still conducted, but it has greater relevance to IBM's interests. In contrast, as Microsoft has grown and its dominance has increased in the software industry, it has begun to fund more long-term research. Although Microsoft researchers have considerable flexibility in choosing research topics, they must demonstrate the relevance of the research to Microsoft's interests (Ziegler, 1997).

Support for Efforts to Build Large Systems

Although support for fundamental research is an important part of the government's research portfolio, many advances in computing have stemmed from projects aimed at building operational systems. Systems developed to meet the government's needs often resulted in pioneering advances that were subsequently incorporated into a range of commercial applications. Such system-building programs not only created new technology and know-how but also established networks of people that helped to rapidly disseminate knowledge broadly throughout the technical community. For example:

1. The development of SAGE stemmed from the needs of DOD for improved early warning capabilities against Soviet bomber attacks. It built on Project Whirlwind, an effort funded by the Office of Naval Research (ONR) to develop a general-purpose aircraft simulator and that pioneered real-time digital computing. Despite the fact that SAGE was almost obsolete when it was finished, it provided invaluable learning experiences for the engineers and scientists designing and developing the communications and computing technology. Countless graduate students and postdoctoral engineers and scientists, for instance, had their first hands-on experiences with computers while working on these projects (see Chapter 4).

2. The development of packet-switched networks and internetworking (the interconnection of multiple networks) can be traced to federal funding from DARPA and NSF. Packet switching was conceptualized by Paul Baran (then at RAND Corporation) in 1961 and independently by Donald Davies at the National Physical Laboratory in England in 1965. DARPA saw the technology as a means of allowing more efficient use of geographically separated computing resources and funded development of the first packet-switched network. Large telecommunications companies, such as AT&T, did not participate in DARPA's subsequent program to build a packet-switched network, the ARPANET, although they did conduct in-house research on packet-switched networks (AT&T's work on asynchronous transfer mode—or ATM switching—is an example). Instead, DARPA contracted with Bolt, Beranek, and Newman, which had been started by three MIT professors in 1948 and performed much of the work on the ARPANET in association with a handful of universities and private companies.[8] The ARPANET demonstrated the capabilities of packet switching and became a source for innovations such as e-mail. The protocols that allowed the flows of information packets through interconnected networks (internets) were developed jointly by Vinton Cerf, then at DARPA, and Robert Kahn (see Chapter 7). Continued efforts,

sponsored by NSF, to develop CSNET, and later NSFNET, demonstrated the value of internetworked communication systems and led to the eventual commercialization of the Internet.

The value of system-building efforts derives from the close linkages between research in computer engineering (as opposed to computer science) and the development of specific artifacts. Theory and practice are closely linked, and innovation tends to proceed in a highly nonlinear fashion, with attempts to build operational systems stimulating identification of new problems for further research. Development of new products or services can *precede* the development of the underlying science, pointing out potentially fruitful avenues of inquiry. For example, development of magnetic core memory for computers did not flow directly from advances in materials research (although it certainly drew upon such research), but from the need to develop a memory system with short enough access times and high enough reliability to support the real-time digital computing demanded by Project Whirlwind (see Chapter 4). Similarly, attempts to develop techniques for virtual surgery (see Chapter 10) motivated and accelerated research in areas such as high-resolution graphics, haptic interfaces, force-feedback systems, robotics, and control techniques.

Building on Industrial Research

Even in areas in which industry has a well-defined interest, government-sponsored research has been able to hasten the commercialization of new technology developed in industry laboratories. Some technologies, such as relational databases and reduced instruction set computing (RISC) computers, were invented by industry researchers but were not commercialized immediately because they either competed with existing product lines or were considered too risky for further development. In these cases, government funding has supported an independent community of technical experts who validated these technologies and provided a pool of talent that helped exploit the idea both in the corporation of origin and in competing corporations.

Early work on relational databases, for example, was conducted by Ted Codd at IBM, but IBM saw the technology as a threat to its established line of database products. Codd publicized the results of his work, seeding efforts in relational databases by several university researchers, including Michael Stonebraker and Eugene Wong at the University of California at Berkeley (UC-Berkeley). With subsequent funding from NSF, Stonebraker and Wong were able to develop a relational database system called Ingres (interaction graphics and retrieval system). To commercialize the technology, Stonebraker started Ingres Corporation, which demonstrated the viability of the relational approach and helped disseminate knowledge about it, building a community of researchers who further developed the relational database technology. This work, and efforts by other large database vendors, helped stimulate continued development of IBM's System R, which created the dominant query language for relational databases.

The development of RISC processing followed a similar history. John Cocke at IBM invented a RISC processor for IBM's Stretch computer, but IBM did not use the technology more widely because it might detract from sales of existing products. DARPA funding enabled university researchers to continue working on RISC. David Patterson at UC-Berkeley and John Hennessy at Stanford University developed RISC processor designs that were commercialized by Sun Microsystems, Inc., and MIPS Computer Systems, respectively. Other designs were offered by competing firms, such as Hewlett-Packard Company and IBM (see Chapter 4).

To some extent, this phenomenon is not unexpected. Large industry research groups produce more ideas than they can possibly exploit given time and financial constraints. These ideas sometimes find their way directly into the marketplace through start-up companies; at other times, however, the amount of research needed to demonstrate the feasibility and benefits of a technology is beyond the capabilities of start-up companies and direct commercialization is unlikely. In these cases, federal funding of university research can be an effective mechanism for helping bring new technology to the marketplace.

Not all pathbreaking research requires government assistance. For example, the development of the personal computer—which represented a significant departure from dominant modes of computing at the time— took place mostly in industry, with the Xerox Palo Alto Research Center and Apple Computer playing prominent roles (see Chapter 4). This work demonstrated the viability of personal computers, especially in the business marketplace, and IBM subsequently developed its own personal computer. Nevertheless, federal funding was important in supporting some of the early ideas on human-computer interaction (such as the computer mouse) that contributed to developing the personal computer.

Diverse Sources of Government Support

Between 1945 and 1995, federal support for computing was provided by a range of organizations, including DARPA, NSF, DOE, NASA, and NIH. This diversity of funding sources has had a salutary effect on computing research. Federal funding agencies differ widely in their cultures, goals, resources, and perspectives, and thus in the kinds of research projects they support. The result has been a federal research establishment that has nurtured diverse approaches to research. DARPA, for example, has tended to award contracts for large programs involving multiple researchers and research organizations. It has concentrated its funding for computer research on a limited number of centers of excellence, such as MIT, Stanford University, Carnegie Mellon University, and UC-Berkeley. Program managers have generally been given significant discretion in selecting and shaping new research initiatives. NSF, in contrast, has primarily supported individual investigators, with considerably smaller awards. Its funding has been purposely spread among researchers at a wide range of institutions, generally universities, and project selection has been based largely on peer review. NSF has also funded projects intended to support the broad educational and research missions of universities. Other agencies, such as NASA, DOE, and NIH, mostly concentrate their resources on research more directly applicable to their missions: space, energy, and health, respectively. As a result, federal funding agencies complement one another rather than compete in funding research, with each supporting work best suited to its particular needs. In the end, no single approach can support a vibrant research base; all are needed to play different roles.

The most obvious benefit of diverse sources of funding is the opportunity for researchers to seek support from multiple potential sponsors of their work. If a particular agency cannot support a worthy research project for any of several reasons—limited resources, poor match with agency objectives, or the judgments of individual program managers—another agency may continue to sponsor potentially fruitful lines of inquiry. For example, DARPA and ONR declined to fund Michael Stonebraker's work on relational databases because DOD was already supporting other database research (see Chapter 6). NSF, the Air Force Office of Scientific Research, and the Navy Electronic Systems Command, however, viewed the program as fitting well into their research portfolios and subsequently funded Stonebraker's Ingres project. With this funding, Stonebraker was able to demonstrate the merits of the relational approach, which later garnered much industry support and became a dominant way to design databases. The process of revising and resubmitting proposals for consideration by multiple sponsors also provides an opportunity for more fully exploring the applications of a technology and the different approaches that can be pursued. It is unlikely that any single agency has the expertise required to understand the varied needs and interests of potential users of new computing and communications technology in government and in industry.

Diverse modes of support for research (i.e., research funding vs. procurement contracts) have also been valuable in ensuring a balance between open-ended research and research directed toward specific sponsors' needs. In the late 1940s, the Office of Naval Research began to doubt the relevance of the Whirlwind computer to its mission of supporting computing for scientists and mathematicians. As the project evolved from a programmable flight simulator to a real-time digital computer, ONR was not convinced it could continue to support the work. At about the same time, the Air Force decided that Whirlwind was appropriate for its SAGE command-and-control project and maintained support for it. Subsequently, the SAGE project pioneered many advances in computing, from real-time computing to core memories to computer graphics. In the end, it also trained a generation of hardware and software engineers (Redmond and Smith, 1980).

Diversity in funding for research also widens the range of applications for new technology and the technological approaches taken. As Chapter 9 demonstrates, the majority of federal support for artificial intelligence research, for example, came from DARPA, but other agencies such as NSF, NASA, and ONR funded projects to pursue particular applications of interest to them. NASA supported development of the pioneering expert system DENDRAL, to deduce the likely structure of organic compounds from known chemical analyses and spectrometry data. The same is true in virtual reality research (see Chapter 10). DARPA, NSF, and NIH have all sponsored relevant research, but each with specific mission interests to motivate their investments: DARPA in helmet-mounted displays and applications for training and simulation, NSF in scientific visualization, and NIH in molecular design and manipulation of biomedical images. Such diversity of funding is important in the early stages of technological development when the uncertainty associated with any particular approach is high. Furthermore, some technologies become reliable or viable only if used in multiple applications, and funding agencies with different needs can help foster the pursuit of diverse, complementary approaches to a problem.

In addition, support from different agencies can be effective at different points in the innovation process. For example, work pioneered by one agency can lead to follow-up work supported by other agencies that allows the technology to mature. In some cases, small-scale efforts funded by NSF, ONR, or other agencies planted the seeds of larger DARPA-sponsored programs, as occurred in the development of computer time-sharing. NSF funded early work at MIT on its first time-sharing system, CTSS (Compatible Time-Sharing System), which by 1964 had connected 24 terminals across the MIT campus. The success of CTSS demonstrated the viability of time-sharing and created a nexus of researchers with expertise in developing and using time-shared systems. It also raised additional questions about the ability to scale up such systems to support a larger number of terminals and to provide adequate security to prevent users from corrupting each other's programs or data. DARPA built on the CTSS effort with Project MAC, a much larger program that received $25 million between 1963 and 1970. Project MAC had ambitious goals for exploring interactive computing, including time-sharing. By its end, the project not only had produced the MULTICS system, which eventually supported 1,000 users, but also had given impetus to the fledgling time-shared computer industry and helped bring computers out of the laboratory. A program of this scope was beyond the capabilities of NSF at the time, yet NSF played an important role in demonstrating, on a smaller scale, the viability of time-sharing.

At other times, DARPA has transferred programs to other agencies once they reached a certain level of maturity. In the case of the Internet, for example, DARPA supported development of hardware and software (e.g., network routers and transmission protocols) for the ARPANET. By 1975—7 years after DARPA awarded the first contract for work on the system—the project had reached a sufficient level of maturity for DARPA to transfer management of the network to the Defense Communication Agency. By the early 1980s, NSF was developing packet-switched networks to link university researchers, first through the CSNET (for computer science researchers) and later through the NSFNET. These networks were seen as a means of supporting the research community by providing a shared medium for exchanging information. In 1989, the ARPANET was absorbed by the NSFNET. Other discipline-specific networks that had been constructed by NASA, DOE, and other agencies were also linked to the NSFNET, and NSF became the government's primary supporter of networking infrastructure. It assumed responsibility for upgrading and expanding the network, which eventually became the backbone of the Internet.

Strong Program Managers and Flexible Management Structures

Scientific and technological research explores the unknown; hence, its outcomes cannot be predicted at the start—even if a clear, practical goal motivates the work. In fact, the outcomes anticipated at the start of a research project can differ from those eventually achieved or that prove to be most important. The Internet is a case in point. DARPA's early interest in packet-switched networks (such as the ARPANET) grew from a desire to use more efficiently the computing capabilities that were distributed among its many contractor sites. By allowing remote access to these disparate computers in a seamless fashion, DARPA program managers hoped to expand the number of researchers who could use them and increase their utilization rates. These results were achieved in the end, but, as the ARPANET was subsumed into the NSFNET, which later evolved into the Internet, the range of applications for packet-switched networks expanded in a number of unanticipated directions. Few could have predicted the popularity of electronic mail as a means of communicating among computer users; still fewer could have anticipated the emergence of the World Wide Web as a means for sharing information and conducting business. Although visions of expansive computer networks for public and private use existed, they were not part of DARPA's original plan, nor did they receive much attention then within the research community.

Moreover, even research projects that do not achieve their original objectives can produce meaningful results or generate valuable knowledge for guiding future research efforts. By some measures, Project Whirlwind and SAGE were failures (see Chapter 4). Planned as a computer-driven aircraft simulator, Whirlwind cost far more than expected and did not produce a simulator; rather, the attempt to develop the simulator resulted in the development of a real-time digital computer eventually used as part of the Air Force's SAGE command-and-control system. By the time it was deployed in the late 1950s and into the 1960s, SAGE's mission was largely obsolete, as intercontinental ballistic missiles were seen as a greater threat than Soviet bombers. Yet both these projects made tremendous contributions to computing that have paid back handsome dividends over time, far beyond the costs of research and development.

Other projects show meaningful returns only after a long time because their applications are not immediately recognized or other technological advances are needed to make their usefulness evident. Work on the mathematics of one-way functions, for example, was not appreciated fully until it was realized that it provided a basis for public-key cryptography (see Chapter 8). Twenty years passed before the benefits of work on the mathematics of hidden Markov models were incorporated into general-purpose speech-recognition systems for PCs. Only after continued increases in processing power and memory capacity did hidden Markov models become feasible for use in recognizing continuous speech on PCs.

Such difficulties frustrate attempts to meaningfully measure the performance of research and also highlight the need for ensuring flexibility in the management and oversight of federally funded research programs. Researchers need sufficient intellectual freedom to follow their intuition and to modify research plans based on preliminary results. Constraining research too narrowly can limit their ability and willingness to take risks in choosing new research directions. Building such flexibility into federal structures for managing research requires both skilled program managers—who understand, articulate, and promote the visions of researchers—and an organizational culture that accepts and promotes exploratory efforts.

These two elements complement one another: organizations that promote exploration and allow program managers to exercise their own discretion in selecting new directions for research tend to attract individuals who are effective program managers and who earn the respect of the research community.

DARPA and NSF both have incorporated these principles into their institutional structures. Especially in the 1960s and 1970s, DARPA gave program managers sufficient funds to shape coherent research programs, and program budgets required only two levels of approval: one by the office director and one by the DARPA director. The organization as a whole aimed to generate order-of-magnitude improvements in computing technology by funding a combination of fundamental research and large system-building efforts. It was able to attract visionary leaders, such as J.C.R. Licklider, Ivan Sutherland, Robert Taylor, Lawrence Roberts, Vinton Cerf, and Robert Kahn. Many of these leaders were drawn from the research community for short tours of duty. They brought to DARPA an understanding of current research challenges and a vision of the future. They were attracted to DARPA by the promise of being able to help implement a vision and lead the field. They maintained an interactive relationship with the research community, taking ideas from researchers and turning them into strategic directions, rather than trying to force their own agendas. They managed with a light touch, giving researchers room to pursue open-ended projects.

Clearly, there are limits to the flexibility that researchers and program managers can be allowed. In development-oriented programs, for example, program managers must ensure that specific objectives are met. In exploratory research, program managers must ensure that research funds are used prudently. But such accountability must be balanced against the unpredictability of research. Structures for managing and overseeing federally funded research need to allow program managers to alter programs midcourse in response to preliminary results and need to recognize that research projects can produce valuable results even if they do not achieve their original objectives. Failing to do so risks stifling creativity and innovation. The history of computing demonstrates the benefits of a flexible approach. By giving program managers greater discretion, federal agencies such as DARPA and NSF were able to support the development of the numerous innovations identified in this report.

Industry-University Collaboration

Collaboration among researchers from academia and industry often has been a successful way of linking practical goals with technical capabilities. Although tensions can exist relative to the differing time horizons between academic research and industry development cycles, collaboration between researchers and product developers has had salutary effects on computing research, helping to ensure the relevance of academic research and helping industry to take advantage of new academic research. Such collaboration allows government program managers to better leverage their resources by attracting industry contributions. Similarly, government funding can act as a "seal of approval" that encourages greater private investment. In this way, government funding, on average, spurs—rather than displaces—private research investments.

Collaboration between industry and universities builds communities of researchers who pursue a particular field and share a common vocabulary. Rapid advances in computing technology have resulted from the pace at which information has been exchanged between researchers and disseminated throughout the research and product development communities. IBM's ability to commercialize core memories rapidly, for example, was related to its participation in the SAGE project, which pioneered the innovation. Overall, the computing community has an impressive track record of transferring technology and knowledge successfully between the academic and industrial communities. As a number of researchers note, however, fruitful collaborations tend to evolve from research projects as the necessary skills to conduct a research or development program are assembled and as information about a research topic spreads throughout the research community. Researchers themselves often serve as the best means of technology transfer, taking knowledge with them as they move among posts in government, industry, and universities or as they start new companies to commercialize research results. Attempts to deliberately bring together university and industry researchers in collaborative projects can also be successful, but considerable flexibility must be allowed in specifying the nature of the collaboration.

Organizational Innovation and Adaptation

The history of computing is characterized by frequent modification of the structures for federal research support. As discussed in Chapter 4, new organizations have been created, and existing ones have been modified to better adapt to changing technology, political influences, and, most important, changing national needs.

Early work in computing, for example, was driven largely by defense interests. The ENIAC, the nation's first digital electronic computer, was developed with funding from the Army Ballistic Research Laboratory and produced its first operational calculations as part of the effort to develop the hydrogen bomb. Subsequently, DOD became the largest federal supporter of research in computer science and electrical engineering. In order to manage defense-related investments in computing, new organizations were needed. Immediately after World War II, the individual services established research offices (the Army Research Office, Office of Naval Research, and Air Force Office of Scientific Research) to manage their research portfolios. But the desire to prevent another technological surprise like Sputnik and to separate defense research from interservice rivalry and near-term operational considerations demanded the establishment of a separate agency, DARPA. As the importance of computing became increasingly apparent for defense applications, DARPA established the Information Processing Techniques Office to manage computing research. This office has changed names and structure over the past 30 years, to better reflect changes in the technology, and has continued to invest in an ever-changing array of computer-related technologies.

The founding of NSF in 1950 also followed from national imperatives, as policymakers and researchers alike tried to institutionalize and build on the many successes the nation had in mobilizing the research community during World War II (marked by the rapid development and introduction of innovations like the atomic bomb and radar). NSF established an Office of Computing Activities in 1967 to support research, education, and computing facilities. The components of this office were later dispersed among other NSF directorates. Recognizing the emergence of computing as an independent discipline with its own research needs, NSF established the Computer and Information Sciences and Engineering (CISE) Directorate in 1986. CISE, and its predecessors, carried out multiple missions: funding computing research, supporting educational initiatives, and maintaining computing and communications infrastructure for the research community.

Growing concerns over the competitiveness of U.S. industry in the 1980s and early 1990s produced a shift in federal policy for computing and a resultant shift in the organization of federal support for computing research. Greater emphasis was placed on partnerships among government, universities, and industry to facilitate more rapid transfer of technology into the marketplace and to tie research more closely to industrial needs. As a result, NSF established a number of Engineering Research Centers (ERCs) to better link academic research to industrial needs, and the National Institute of Standards and Technology began its Advanced Technology Program, which funded consortia working on precompetitive research projects of mutual interest. Loss of market share in memory chips and semiconductor manufacturing equipment prompted the government to invest $100 million annually for 7 years in SEMATECH, the semiconductor manufacturing technology consortium, which brought together 12 of the nation's largest semiconductor manufacturers to conduct precompetitive research that would strengthen the U.S. semiconductor industry.

The end of the Cold War and the dominance of U.S. firms in the global market for computing in the 1990s significantly altered the political environment for research funding after 1990. It is likely that computing research will be redirected to new missions, whether improving health, providing government benefits (social security, food stamps, and so forth), or supporting economic growth. DOD and other federal agencies will continue to demand advances in information technology to support their missions, but new organizational structures may also be needed to ensure that the research enterprise is well matched to research needs.

CONCLUDING REMARKS

Given the importance of computing to the nation's economy, security, and health, it is important to ensure that the United States maintains its leadership in the field. Doing so will require the concerted efforts of industry, universities, and government. As the lessons above suggest, each sector has an important role to play in the overall innovation process. While the information technology industry as a whole has evolved considerably over the past 50 years, opportunities for significant innovation continue to exist. Expanding and exploiting information infrastructure for a range of social, business, and personal needs will require continued research and development to make computing and communications systems more capable, more useful, and more reliable. The success of such efforts will depend in large part on resolving ongoing debates about the scope and direction of federal support for science and technology.

NOTES

1.   DARPA was named the Advanced Research Projects Agency, or ARPA, from the time of its establishment in 1958 until the word "Defense" was added in 1972. It became ARPA again between 1993 and 1995. For consistency, this chapter refers to the agency as DARPA, its name in 1998, regardless of the time period described.

2.   Estimates based on data extracted from the National Science Foundation's database on R&D Expenditures, total and federally financed, in electrical engineering and computer science between fiscal years 1972 and 1996. Online access to the database is available via WebCASPAR at <http://caspar.qrc.com>.

3.   Estimates based on data extracted from the National Science Foundation's database on Current Fund Research Equipment Expenditures in electrical engineering and computer science between fiscal years 1981 and 1995. Online access to the database is available via WebCASPAR at <http://caspar.qrc.com>.

4.   In recent years, a number of concerns have been raised about a reduction

in the openness of university research, owing to increased links to industry-funded research of a proprietary nature.

5.   Estimates based on data extracted from the National Science Foundation's database on Federal Research Obligations to Universities and Colleges for basic and applied research in electrical engineering and computer science between fiscal years 1981 and 1995.   Online access to the database is available via WebCASPAR at <http://caspar.qrc.com>.

6.   Additional information on DOE's Accelerated Strategic Computing Initiative is available online at <http://www.llnl.gov/asci/>.

7.   One notable exception is the Semiconductor Research Corporation, which funds university research of interest to its member companies—most of the large semiconductor companies.

8.   Researchers at Bolt, Beranek, and Newman modified Honeywell computers for use as switching devices, or routers, on the ARPANET.

Part II

Case Studies in Computing Research

Part II, Chapters 6 through 10, presents five case studies in computing research. These case studies are not meant to be definitive histories of the fields they address; rather, they are intended to illustrate the role the federal government has played in the innovation process by investing in computing research. They contain historical material that is important not only in indicating the government's role per se, but also in characterizing the larger innovation process, including the movement of researchers between universities and industry, the transfer of research results into practice, and the interrelationships among people and research in government, universities, and industry.

Taken together, the cases cover a range of technologies, time periods, and federal investments; individually, they differ considerably in their scope and emphasis. The case studies of relational databases and the Internet, for example, are relatively narrow in the sense that they trace the development of a particular technology or system. The innovations described have a fairly well defined beginning and end, although clearly the systems described in each will continue to evolve over time. The case study of theoretical computer science highlights the development of theory as well as its relationships to computer engineering and the construction of computer systems. It traces the refinement and dissemination of ideas throughout the research community and into educational curricula. The final two case studies, artificial intelligence (AI) and virtual reality (VR), address relatively broad areas of research that are motivated by a long-term vision: development of systems that display intelligent behavior in the AI case, and development of systems that generate synthetic environments meant to resemble the real world in the VR case. Progress in both these fields is marked by a series of research breakthroughs or technological advances that move ever closer to these objectives.

Each case study concludes with a summary of themes or lessons regarding the innovation process and the government's essential role within it. Because they derive from the individual case studies, these lessons reflect the particular conditions that prevailed at the time described, such as the nascent state of the computing field and dominant styles of federal research management in past decades. The case studies themselves do not attempt to discuss the relevance of these lessons to the current policy environment or to provide guidance regarding future federal support for research in computing. That task is taken up instead in Chapter 5 of this report, which synthesizes the lessons from all the case studies and attempts to consider their more general applicability.

6

The Rise of Relational Databases

Large-scale computer applications require rapid access to large amounts of data. A computerized checkout system in a supermarket must track the entire product line of the market. Airline reservation systems are used at many locations simultaneously to place passengers on numerous flights on different dates. Library computers store millions of entries and access citations from hundreds of publications. Transaction processing systems in banks and brokerage houses keep the accounts that generate international flows of capital. World Wide Web search engines scan thousands of Web pages to produce quantitative responses to queries almost instantly. Thousands of small businesses and organizations use databases to track everything from inventory and personnel to DNA sequences and pottery shards from archaeological digs.

Thus, databases not only represent significant infrastructure for computer applications, but they also process the transactions and exchanges that drive the U.S. economy. A significant and growing segment of the software industry, known as the database industry, generates about $8 billion in annual revenue. U.S. companies—including IBM Corporation, Oracle Corporation, Informix Corporation, Sybase Incorporated, Teradata Corporation (now owned by NCR Corporation), and Microsoft Corporation—dominate the world market. This dominance stems from a serendipitous combination of industrial research, government-funded academic work, and commercial competition.

Much of today's market consists of relational databases based on the model proposed in the late 1960s and early 1970s. This chapter provides background on early data management systems and then examines the emergence of the relational model and its rise to dominance in the database field, and the translation of this model into successful commercial products. The final section summarizes the lessons to be learned from history. It highlights the critical role of the government in advancing this technology. For instance, although the relational model was originally proposed and developed at IBM, it was a government-funded effort at the University of California at Berkeley (UC-Berkeley) that disseminated the idea widely and gave it the intellectual legitimacy required for broad acceptance and commercialization.

This case study does not address the entire database field (it omits topics such as transaction processing, distributed databases, and multimedia), but rather focuses on events that illustrate the ways in which synergistic interactions of government, universities, and industry built U.S. leadership in a particular subfield, largely through the work of individuals who developed and then transferred technology between firms and laboratories. As James Gray, a senior database researcher, has observed: "A very modest federal research investment, complemented by an also-modest industrial research investment, led directly to U.S. dominance of this market" (CSTB, 1995a).

BACKGROUND

Emergence of Computerized Databases

The U.S. government has always had significant requirements for the collection, sorting, and reporting of large volumes of data. In 1890, the Bureau of the Census encouraged a former employee, Herman Hollerith, to develop the world's first automated information processing equipment. The resulting punched-card machines processed the censuses of 1890 and of 1900. In 1911, Hollerith's company merged with another, also founded with Census support; the resulting company soon became known as International Business Machines (Anderson, 1988), now IBM.

During World War I, the government used new punched-card technology to process the various data sets required to control industrial production, collect the new income tax, and classify draftees. The Social Security Act of 1935 made it necessary to keep continuous records on the employment of 26 million individuals. For this, "the world's biggest bookkeeping job," IBM developed special collating equipment. The Census Bureau purchased the first model of the first digital computer on the commercial market, the UNIVAC I (itself based on the government-funded Electronic Discrete Variable Automatic Computer (EDVAC) project at the University of Pennsylvania). In 1959, the Pentagon alone had more than 200 computers just for its business needs (e.g., tracking expenses, personnel, spare parts), with annual costs exceeding $70 million. U.S. dominance of the punched-card data processing industry, initially established with government support, was a major factor in U.S. companies' later dominance in electronic computing.

By the early 1960s, substantial progress had been made in removing hardware-specific constraints from the tasks of programmers. The term "database" emerged to capture the sense that the information stored within a computer could be conceptualized, structured, and manipulated independently of the specific machine on which it resided. Most of the earliest database applications were developed in military command and intelligence environments, but the concept was quickly adopted by commercial users (System Development Corporation, 1964; Fry and Sibley, 1974).

Early Efforts at Standardization

As computing entered the mainstream commercial market, a number of techniques emerged to facilitate data access, ensure quality, maintain privacy, and allow for managerial control of data. In 1960, the Conference on Data Systems Languages (Codasyl), set up by the U.S. Department of Defense (DOD) to standardize software applications, established the common business-oriented language (COBOL) for programming (ACM Sigplan, 1978), incorporating a number of prior data-definition languages (Fry and Sibley, 1974). Magnetic disk drives, which could access data at random, began to replace magnetic tape drives, which required serial data access, for online storage. In 1961, Charles Bachman at General Electric Company introduced the integrated data store (IDS) system, a pioneering database management system that took advantage of the new storage technology and included novel schemas and logging, among other features.

During these early years, innovations in the practice-oriented field tended to be made by user groups and industrial researchers, with little academic involvement (CSTB, 1982; Wiederhold, 1984). In the mid-1960s, Bachman and others, largely from industry and manufacturing, set up the Database Task Group (DBTG) under Codasyl to bring some unity to the varied field (Olle, 1978). The group published a set of specifications for how computer languages, COBOL in particular, might navigate databases. In 1971, it published a formal standard, known colloquially in the industry as the Codasyl approach to database management. A number of Codasyl-based products were introduced for mainframe computers by Eckert-Mauchly Computer Corporation (the maker of Univac), Honeywell Incorporated, and Siemens AG, and, for minicomputers, by Digital Equipment Corporation (DEC) and Prime Computer Corporation.[1]

Notably missing from the list of vendors that supported Codasyl products was IBM, which had earlier (in 1968) introduced its own product, IMS, derived in part from a National Aeronautics and Space Administration (NASA) Apollo project. It ran on System/360 equipment. Whereas Codasyl was based on a network model of data, IBM's database used a hierarchical structure. (Cullinet Corporation provided a Codasyl-compatible database for IBM users.) Both the IBM and the Codasyl products were sometimes called navigational databases because they required the user to program or navigate around a data set. Bachman's Turing Award lecture in 1973, in fact, was entitled "The Programmer as Navigator" (Bachman, 1973; Cardenas, 1979).

EMERGENCE OF THE RELATIONAL MODEL

Codd's Vision

At least one researcher at IBM was dissatisfied with both the Codasyl products and IBM's database package. Edgar F. (Ted) Codd, an Oxford-trained mathematician, joined IBM in 1949 and later moved to IBM San Jose. Codd found existing and new database technologies "taking the old-line view that the burden of finding information should be placed on users. . . . [In this view, the database management system] should only recognize simple commands and it would be up to the users to put together appropriate commands for finding what was needed" (Codd, 1982).[2]

In a series of IBM technical reports and then a landmark paper, "A Relational Model of Data for Large Shared Data Banks," Codd laid out a new way to organize and access data. What Codd called the "relational model" rested on two key points:

It provides a means of describing data with its natural structure only—that is, without superimposing any additional structure for machine representation purposes. Accordingly, it provides a basis for a high level data language which will yield maximal independence between programs on the one hand and machine representation on the other. (Codd, 1970)

In other words, the relational model consisted of (1) data independence from hardware and storage implementation and (2) automatic navigation, or a high-level, nonprocedural language for accessing data. Instead of processing one record at a time, a programmer could use the language to specify single operations that would be performed across the entire data set. Codd's model had an immediate impact on research and, as described below, spawned a number of significant prototyping projects.

Given its eventual commercial success, the relational model might seem bound to emerge and even dominate the field without any government involvement in research. It was formulated, after all, entirely within the walls of an industrial laboratory. But Codd's model was long seen as something of an intellectual curiosity. To gain legitimacy within the field, it had to survive at least two battles—one in the technical community at large, and one within IBM. The relational model might not have survived either battle without government intervention, which, in this case, involved funding of a competing project at another institution.

Within IBM, the trouble was the existing database product, IMS. The company had already invested, both financially and organizationally, in the infrastructure and expertise required to sell and support it. A radical new technology had a great deal to prove before it could displace a successful, reliable, revenue-generating product such as IMS. Initially, the threat was minimal; Codd published his original paper in the open literature because no one at IBM (himself included) recognized its eventual impact. The response to this publication from the outside technical community, however, soon showed the company that the idea had great commercial potential. To head off this eventuality, IBM quickly declared IMS its sole *strategic* product, thus setting up Codd and his work to be criticized as counter to company goals. Internal politics further compounded the situation, as IBM was not accustomed to major software innovations coming from IBM San Jose, which until then had worked primarily on disk storage.

In spite of IBM's reaction, Codd spoke out zealously and promoted the virtues of the relational model to computer scientists. He arranged a public debate between himself and Charles Bachman, at that time the key proponent of the Codasyl-sponsored standard. The debate exposed Codd to criticism from within IBM that he was undermining the company's existing products, but it also achieved his intended effect on the technical community. In the early 1970s, two projects emerged to develop relational technology and prove its utility in practical applications. One, System R, began within IBM, and the other, Ingres, began at UC-Berkeley with military and National Science Foundation (NSF) funding. The synergy between the two projects, which were at once mutually reinforcing and competing, demonstrates the subtle but significant effects that government-supported research can have on computer technology.

System R

In the early 1970s, a group of IBM programmers moved from Yorktown to San Jose.[3] The group designed and built a prototype system to demonstrate relational ideas. Dubbed System R, this prototype was intended to provide a high-level, nonnavigational, data-independent interface to many users simultaneously, with high integrity and robustness (Astrahan et al., 1976). The first phase of the project, in 1974-1975, produced a quick prototype to demonstrate feasibility, but its code was eventually abandoned. The next phase produced a full-function, multiuser version, which was evaluated in subsequent trials in 1978-1979. Perhaps the most lasting development to come out of the project was the Structured Query Language (SQL), now a U.S. and international standard for database access (Chamberlin et al., 1981; McJones, 1995).[4]

On its own, System R did not convince IBM management to abandon its existing product and replace it with relational databases. IBM and its customers still had strong vested interests in the established IMS technology. It took outside efforts, funded by the government, to prove that relational databases could become viable commercial products.

Ingres

In 1973, about when System R was getting started at IBM, two scientists at UC-Berkeley, Michael Stonebraker and Eugene Wong, became interested in relational databases. Initially, they raised money to design a geographic data system for Berkeley's economics group (the name Ingres, which stood for interactive graphics and retrieval system, reflects this legacy). In search of further support, Stonebraker approached the Defense Advanced Research Projects Agency (DARPA), the obvious funding source for computing research and development. Both DARPA and the Office of Naval Research (ONR) turned Ingres down, however; they were already supporting database research elsewhere.

Stonebraker then introduced his idea to other agencies, and, with help from Wong and Berkeley colleague Lotfi Zadeh, he eventually obtained modest support from the NSF and three military agencies: the Air Force Office of Scientific Research, the Army Research Office, and the Navy Electronic Systems Command. The experience of acquiring support for Ingres illustrates the importance of maintaining diverse funding sources within the government. When a researcher can propose a new idea to several potential supporters, it not only increases the chances of funding a good idea but also provides a crucial learning process as proposals are rewritten and resubmitted.

Thus funded, Ingres was developed, during the mid-1970s, into a prototype relational database system that was similar to IBM's System R but based on different hardware and a different operating system. Ingres went through an evolution similar to that of System R, with an early phase demonstrating an initial solution in 1974 followed by significant revisions to make the code maintainable. Ingres was then disseminated to a small user community, both inside and outside academia, which provided feedback to the development group. The dissemination process was advanced by the proliferation of inexpensive DEC machines in universities. Members of the project team rewrote the Ingres prototype repeatedly during these years to incorporate accumulated experience, feedback from users, and new ideas. Ingres also included its own query language, QUEL, which was similar to, but still distinct from, IBM's SQL (Stonebraker, 1976, 1980).[5]

DIFFUSION AND COMMERCIALIZATION OF RELATIONAL DATABASES

Ingres technology diffused into the commercial sector through three major channels: code, people, and publications. Unlike the technical details of the IBM project, Ingres source code was publicly available, and about 1,000 copies were distributed around the world so that computer scientists and programmers could experiment with the system and adjust it to their own needs. Michael Stonebraker founded Ingres Corporation (purchased by Computer Associates in 1994) to commercialize the Berkeley code directly. Robert Epstein, the chief programmer at Ingres in the 1970s, went on to co-found Britton-Lee Incorporated and then Sybase. Both Britton-Lee and Sybase used ideas and experience from the original Ingres, and government agencies were early customers of both companies. Computer Associates released a commercial version of the Ingres code in the 1980s.

Continued movement of Ingres researchers throughout the database community spread the technology even farther. Jerry Held and Carol Youseffi moved from UC-Berkeley to Tandem Computers Incorporated, where they built a relational system, the predecessor to NonStop SQL. Until joining Kleiner, Perkins, Caufield & Byers in 1998, Held was senior vice-president of engineering at Oracle, where he headed that company's database efforts. Paula Hawthorn moved from Ingres to Britton-Lee (as did Michael Ubell) and eventually became a co-founder of Illustra Information Technologies Incorporated, now part of Informix. Stonebraker himself worked with Ingres Corporation, Illustra, and Informix. Other Ingres alumni went to AT&T, Hewlett-Packard Company (HP), IBM, and Oracle, bringing with them the lessons learned from Ingres. As Robert Epstein observed, "What came from Ingres was the experience of having built a prototype . . . to say what parts need to be done differently."[6]

The Ingres and System R development groups had a complex relationship that fostered a spirit of competition, as both groups worked on similar new technology. Both groups were relatively small and close-knit. Between 1973 and 1979, approximately 30 individuals cycled through the Ingres group, which never contained more than five or six programmers. The System R group included roughly 15 persons who wrote code and papers on System R and later worked with IBM's product development groups to commercialize the technology. Several members of the IBM group had Berkeley connections, and UC-Berkeley sent summer students to IBM. Timely publication and proper allocation of credit for new ideas became paramount concerns (McJones, 1995). Ingres's QUEL was in competition with IBM's SQL as a query language; the latter eventually won out and became the industry standard.

The success of SQL transpired almost in spite of IBM, which could have taken advantage of its query language several years sooner than it did. Oracle, founded by Larry Ellison, developed and began selling an SQL-compatible product even before IBM had an SQL product in the market. Ellison had learned of SQL through publications by the System R project team. IBM was compelled to develop its SQL/DS system by the threat of competing products from other established database companies, such as Software AG, a German company. Other fledgling companies, such as Informix and Ingres, also introduced relational systems, with Informix embracing the SQL model. System R programmers influenced the industry personally as well as by their writing.[7]

System R and Ingres were not the only relational database efforts to spring from Codd's work. Other research at the University of Toronto, IBM in the United Kingdom, the University of Utah, and the University of Wisconsin made contributions as well. It also became clear that the relational model has limitations, particularly in handling complex data. In 1982, the Ingres project ended, and in 1985 it was transformed into Postgres at UC-Berkeley, which sought to extend the relational model to objects. This change coincided with DARPA hiring its first program manager for databases, who funded Postgres. This project became a component of the digital library and scientific database efforts within the University of California system.

A landmark year for the relational model was 1980, when IBM's SQL/DS product hit the market for mainframes, smaller vendors began selling second-generation relational systems with great commercial success, and Codd was awarded the Association for Computing Machinery's (ACM) Turing Award. The relational model had come of age.

Today, relational databases are but one way of accessing the multiple types of information computers can handle. Related research in information retrieval, multimedia, scientific databases, and digital libraries is under way, supported by DARPA, NSF, and the National Library of Medicine, among others. Still, the history of the emergence of relational database technologies, products, and companies reveals a good deal about innovation in computing and communications.

LESSONS FROM HISTORY

The federal government had important effects on the development of relational databases. The earliest days of this subfield suggest that government missions can create new markets for technology, providing incentives for innovation. The Census Bureau's need to conduct a decadal census supported the information processing industry before computers were created to automate it.

Later on, government funding hastened commercialization. An example is the case of System R and Ingres. The critical issue is not which one was more successful or influential in the long run, but rather, to paraphrase a System R team member, whether either project would have succeeded in the absence of the other. The academic interest legitimized System R within IBM, and Ingres was bootstrapped off IBM's commercial influence.[8] Competitive pressure, combined with the legitimacy bestowed on the relational model by government funding and academic interest, finally convinced IBM to sell relational database products. Were it not for the government-funded effort at UC-Berkeley, such databases probably would have been commercialized anyway, but later—and time-to-market is, of course, a critical factor with new technology.

That same example shows that the commercial interests of firms such as IBM can impede the continued development and commercialization of technologies that compete with existing product lines. IBM and its customers had vested interests in the established IMS technology and resisted change until external events proved that relational databases could become viable commercial products.

This case history also suggests that the large numbers of researchers passing through university laboratories, their willingness to share data and code, and their publication imperatives make university researchers ideal sources of technology transfer to the broader technical community. Industrial laboratories, by comparison, rarely place significant technologies directly into the public domain and have lower rates of personnel turnover, although they often benefit from greater and more stable supplies of resources. Especially in the computing industry, employees may take ideas into the marketplace on their own, but industrial laboratories are likely to publish only information that concerns completed projects or is not deemed critical to the company's vital interests.

Academic research is important for other reasons as well. Because it can push the cutting edge of technology and produce results that may evolve into commercially viable products, existing commercial suppliers never have a lock on advanced technology and are forced to respond to the marketplace of ideas.

Finally, in pursuing new ideas and new areas of technology, academic research projects can benefit from access to multiple funding sources within the government, as any individual sponsor may assess the value of a new idea from a limited perspective. Although DARPA and ONR declined to support Ingres, for example, the NSF and three other military agencies agreed to do so.

NOTES

1.   For his work with IDS and the Codasyl group, Bachman was awarded the Association for Computing Machinery's A.M. Turing Award in 1973 (Bachman, 1973; King, 1983).

2.   Edgar F. Codd, in an interview with a representative of the Committee on Innovation in Computing and Communications, February 7, 1997.

3.   The group included Mike Blasgen, Ray Boyce, Donald Chamberlain, James Gray, Frank King, Leonard Liu, Raymond Lorie, and Franco Putzolu.

4.   Donald Chamberlin, in an interview with a representative of the Committee on Innovation in Computing and Communications, February 4, 1997.

5.   M. Stonebraker, in interviews with a representative of the Committee on Innovation in Computing and Communications, December 27, 1996, and February 26, 1997.

6.   Robert Epstein, in an interview with a representative of the Committee on Innovation in Computing and Communications, March 19, 1997.

7.   Kapali Eswaran left IBM in the late 1970s to form his own company, and its code eventually became part of HP and Cullinet products. Jim Gray moved from IBM to Tandem, where he worked on NonStop SQL, and he is now the senior database researcher at Microsoft. Franco Putzolu also went from IBM to Tandem, where he was a principal designer of NonStop SQL, and later went to Oracle as a senior database architect.

8.   Donald Chamberlin, in an interview with a representative of the Committee on Innovation in Computing and Communications, February 4, 1997.

7

Development of the Internet and the World Wide Web

The recent growth of the Internet and the World Wide Web makes it appear that the world is witnessing the arrival of a completely new technology. In fact, the Web—now considered to be a major driver of the way society accesses and views information—is the result of numerous projects in computer networking, mostly funded by the federal government, carried out over the last 40 years. The projects produced communications protocols that define the format of network messages, prototype networks, and application programs such as browsers. This research capitalized on the ubiquity of the nation's telephone network, which provided the underlying physical infrastructure upon which the Internet was built.

This chapter traces the development of the Internet,[1] one aspect of the broader field of data networking. The chapter is not intended to be comprehensive; rather, it focuses on the federal role in both funding research and supporting the deployment of networking infrastructure. This history is divided into four distinct periods. Before 1970, individual researchers developed the underlying technologies, including queuing theory, packet switching, and routing. During the 1970s, experimental networks, notably the ARPANET, were constructed. These networks were primarily research tools, not service providers. Most were federally funded, because, with a few exceptions, industry had not yet realized the potential of the technology. During the 1980s, networks were widely deployed, initially to support scientific research. As their potential to improve personal communications and collaboration became apparent, additional academic disciplines and industry began to use the technology. In this era, the National Science Foundation (NSF) was the major supporter of networking, primarily through the NSFNET, which evolved into the Internet. Most recently, in the early 1990s, the invention of the Web made it much easier for users to publish and access information, thereby setting off the rapid growth of the Internet. The final section of the chapter summarizes the lessons to be learned from history.

By focusing on the Internet, this chapter does not address the full scope of computer networking activities that were under way between 1960 and 1995. It specifically ignores other networking activities of a more proprietary nature. In the mid-1980s, for example, hundreds of thousands of workers at IBM were using electronic networks (such as the VNET) for worldwide e-mail and file transfers; banks were performing electronic funds transfer; Compuserve had a worldwide network; Digital Equipment Corporation (DEC) had value-added networking services; and a VNET-based academic network known as BITNET had been established. These were proprietary systems that, for the most part, owed little to academic research, and indeed were to a large extent invisible to the academic computer networking community. By the late 1980s, IBM's proprietary SNA data networking business unit already had several billions of dollars of annual revenue for networking hardware, software, and services. The success of such networks in many ways limited the interest of companies like IBM and Compuserve in the Internet. The success of the Internet can therefore, in many ways, be seen as the success of an open system and open architecture in the face of proprietary competition.

EARLY STEPS: 1960-1970

Approximately 15 years after the first computers became operational, researchers began to realize that an interconnected network of computers could provide services that transcended the capabilities of a single system. At this time, computers were becoming increasingly powerful, and a number of scientists were beginning to consider applications that went far beyond simple numerical calculation. Perhaps the most compelling early description of these opportunities was presented by J.C.R. Licklider (1960), who argued that, within a few years, computers would become sufficiently powerful to cooperate with humans in solving scientific and technical problems. Licklider, a psychologist at the Massachusetts Institute of Technology (MIT), would begin realizing his vision when he became director of the Information Processing Techniques Office (IPTO) at the Advanced Research Projects Agency (ARPA) in 1962. Licklider remained at ARPA until 1964 (and returned for a second tour in 1974-1975), and he convinced his successors, Ivan Sutherland and Robert Taylor, of the importance of attacking difficult, long-term problems.

Taylor, who became IPTO director in 1966, worried about the duplication of expensive computing resources at the various sites with ARPA contracts. He proposed a networking experiment in which users at one site accessed computers at another site, and he co-authored, with Licklider, a paper describing both how this might be done and some of the potential consequences (Licklider and Taylor, 1968). Taylor was a psychologist, not a computer scientist, and so he recruited Larry Roberts of MIT's Lincoln Laboratory to move to ARPA and oversee the development of the new network. As a result of these efforts, ARPA became the primary supporter of projects in networking during this period.

In contrast to the NSF, which awarded grants to individual researchers, ARPA issued research contracts. The IPTO program managers, typically recruited from academia for 2-year tours, had considerable latitude in defining projects and identifying academic and industrial groups to carry them out. In many cases, they worked closely with the researchers they sponsored, providing intellectual leadership as well as financial support. A strength of the ARPA style was that it not only produced artifacts that furthered its missions but also built and trained a community of researchers. In addition to holding regular meetings of principal investigators, Taylor started the "ARPA games," meetings that brought together the graduate students involved in programs. This innovation helped build the community that would lead the expansion of the field and growth of the Internet during the 1980s.

During the 1960s, a number of researchers began to investigate the technologies that would form the basis for computer networking. Most of this early networking research concentrated on packet switching, a technique of breaking up a conversation into small, independent units, each of which carries the address of its destination and is routed through the network independently. Specialized computers at the branching points in the network can vary the route taken by packets on a moment-to-moment basis in response to network congestion or link failure.

One of the earliest pioneers of packet switching was Paul Baran of the RAND Corporation, who was interested in methods of organizing networks to withstand nuclear attack. (His research interest is the likely source of a widespread myth concerning the ARPANET's original purpose [Hafner and Lyon, 1996]). Baran proposed a richly interconnected set of network nodes, with no centralized control system—both properties of today's Internet. Similar work was under way in the United Kingdom, where Donald Davies and Roger Scantlebury of the National Physical Laboratory (NPL) coined the term "packet."

Of course, the United States already had an extensive communications network, the public switched telephone network (PSTN), in which digital switches and transmission lines were deployed as early as 1962.

But the telephone network did not figure prominently in early computer networking. Computer scientists working to interconnect their systems spoke a different language than did the engineers and scientists working in traditional voice telecommunications. They read different journals, attended different conferences, and used different terminology. Moreover, data traffic was (and is) substantially different from voice traffic. In the PSTN, a continuous connection, or circuit, is set up at the beginning of a call and maintained for the duration. Computers, on the other hand, communicate in bursts, and unless a number of "calls" can be combined on a single transmission path, line and switching capacity is wasted. Telecommunications engineers were primarily interested in improving the voice network and were skeptical of alternative technologies. As a result, although telephone lines were used to provide point-to-point communication in the ARPANET, the switching infrastructure of the PSTN was not used. According to Taylor, some Bell Laboratories engineers stated flatly in 1967 that "packet switching wouldn't work."[2]

At the first Association for Computing Machinery (ACM) Symposium on Operating System Principles in 1967, Lawrence Roberts, then an IPTO program manager, presented an initial design for the packet-switched network that was to become the ARPANET (Davies et al., 1967). In addition, Roger Scantlebury presented the NPL work (Roberts, 1967), citing Baran's earlier RAND report. The reaction was positive, and Roberts issued a request for quotation (RFQ) for the construction of a four-node network.

From the more than 100 respondents to the RFQ, Roberts selected Bolt, Beranek, and Newman (BBN) of Cambridge, Massachusetts; familiar names such as IBM Corporation and Control Data Corporation chose not to bid. The contract to produce the hardware and software was issued in December 1968. The BBN group was led by Frank Heart, and many of the scientists and engineers who would make major contributions to networking in future years participated. Robert Kahn, who with Vinton Cerf would later develop the Transmission Control Protocol/Internet Protocol (TCP/IP) suite used to control the transmission of packets in the network, helped develop the network architecture. The network hardware consisted of a rugged military version of a Honeywell Corporation minicomputer that connected a site's computers to the communication lines. These interface message processors (IMPs)—each the size of a large refrigerator and painted battleship gray—were highly sought after by DARPA-sponsored researchers, who viewed possession of an IMP as evidence they had joined the inner circle of networking research.

The first ARPANET node was installed in September 1969 at Leonard Kleinrock's Network Measurement Center at the University of California at Los Angeles (UCLA). Kleinrock (1964) had published some of the earliest theoretical work on packet switching, and so this site was an appropriate choice. The second node was installed a month later at Stanford Research Institute (SRI) in Menlo Park, California, using Douglas Engelbart's On Line System (known as NLS) as the host. SRI also operated the Network Information Center (NIC), which maintained operational and standards information for the network. Two more nodes were soon installed at the University of California at Santa Barbara, where Glen Culler and Burton Fried had developed an interactive system for mathematics education, and the University of Utah, which had one of the first computer graphics groups.

Initially, the ARPANET was primarily a vehicle for experimentation rather than a service, because the protocols for host-to-host communication were still being developed. The first such protocol, the Network Control Protocol (NCP), was completed by the Network Working Group (NWG) led by Stephen Crocker in December 1970 and remained in use until 1983, when it was replaced by TCP/IP.

EXPANSION OF THE ARPANET: 1970-1980

Initially conceived as a means of sharing expensive computing resources among ARPA research contractors, the ARPANET evolved in a number of unanticipated directions during the 1970s. Although a few experiments in resource sharing were carried out, and the Telnet protocol was developed to allow a user on one machine to log onto another machine over the network, other applications became more popular.

The first of these applications was enabled by the File Transfer Protocol (FTP), developed in 1971 by a group led by Abhay Bhushan of MIT (Bhushan, 1972). This protocol enabled a user on one system to connect to another system for the purpose of either sending or retrieving a particular file. The concept of an anonymous user was quickly added, with constrained access privileges, to allow users to connect to a system and browse the available files. Using Telnet, a user could read the remote files but could not do anything with them. With FTP, users could now move files to their own machines and work with them as local files. This capability spawned several new areas of activity, including distributed client-server computing and network-connected file systems.

Occasionally in computing, a "killer application" appears that becomes far more popular than its developers expected. When personal computers (PCs) became available in the 1980s, the spreadsheet (initially VisiCalc) was the application that accelerated the adoption of the new hardware by businesses. For the newly minted ARPANET, the killer application was electronic mail, or e-mail. The first e-mail program was developed in 1972 by Ray Tomlinson of BBN. Tomlinson had built an earlier e-mail system for communication between users on BBN's Tenex time-sharing system, and it was a simple exercise to modify this system to work over the network. By combining the immediacy of the telephone with the precision of written communication, e-mail became an instant hit. Tomlinson's syntax (*user@domain*) remains in use today.

Telnet, FTP, and e-mail were examples of the leverage that research typically provided in early network development. As each new capability was added, the efficiency and speed with which knowledge could be disseminated improved. E-mail and FTP made it possible for geographically distributed researchers to collaborate and share results much more effectively. These programs were also among the first networking applications that were valuable not only to computer scientists, but also to scholars in other disciplines.

From ARPANET to Internet

Although the ARPANET was ARPA's largest networking effort, it was by no means the only one. The agency also supported research on terrestrial packet radio and packet satellite networks. In 1973, Robert Kahn and Vinton Cerf began to consider ways to interconnect these networks, which had quite different bandwidth, delay, and error properties than did the telephone lines of the ARPANET. The result was TCP/IP, first described in 1973 at an International Network Working Group meeting in England. Unlike NCP, which enabled the hosts of a single network to communicate, TCP/IP was designed to interconnect multiple networks to form an Internet. This protocol suite defined the packet format and a flow-control and error-recovery mechanism to allow the hosts to recover gracefully from network errors. It also specified an addressing mechanism that could support an Internet comprising up to 4 billion hosts.

The work necessary to transform TCP/IP from a concept into a useful system was performed under ARPA contract by groups at Stanford University, BBN, and University College London. Although TCP/IP has evolved over the years, it is still in use today as the Internet's basic packet transport protocol.

By 1975, the ARPANET had grown from its original four nodes to nearly 100 nodes. Around this time, two phenomena—the development of local area networks (LANs) and the integration of networking into operating systems—contributed to a rapid increase in the size of the network.

Local Area Networks

While ARPANET researchers were experimenting with dedicated telephone lines for packet transmission, researchers at the University of

Hawaii, led by Norman Abramson, were trying a different approach, also with ARPA funding. Like the ARPANET group, they wanted to provide remote access to their main computer system, but instead of a network of telephone lines, they used a shared radio network. It was shared in the sense that all stations used the same channel to reach the central station. This approach had a potential drawback: if two stations attempted to transmit at the same time, then their transmissions would interfere with each other, and neither one would be received. But such interruptions were unlikely because the data were typed on keyboards, which sent very short pulses to the computer, leaving ample time between pulses during which the channel was clear to receive keystrokes from a different user.

Abramson's system, known as Aloha, generated considerable interest in using a shared transmission medium, and several projects were initiated to build on the idea. Two of the best-known projects were the Atlantic Packet Satellite Experiment and Ethernet. The packet satellite network demonstrated that the protocols developed in Aloha for handling contention between simultaneous users, combined with more traditional reservation schemes, resulted in efficient use of the available bandwidth. However, the long latency inherent in satellite communications limited the usefulness of this approach.

Ethernet, developed by a group led by Robert Metcalfe at Xerox Corporation's Palo Alto Research Center (PARC), is one of the few examples of a networking technology that was *not* directly funded by the government. This experiment demonstrated that using coaxial cable as a shared medium resulted in an efficient network. Unlike the Aloha system, in which transmitters could not receive any signals, Ethernet stations could detect that collisions had occurred, stop transmitting immediately, and retry a short time later (at random). This approach improved the efficiency of the Aloha technique and made it practical for actual use. Shared-media LANs became the dominant form of computer-to-computer communication within a building or local area, although variations from IBM (Token Ring) and others also captured part of this emerging market.

Ethernet was initially used to connect a network of approximately 100 of PARC's Alto PCs, using the center's time-sharing system as a gateway to the ARPANET. Initially, many believed that the small size and limited performance of PCs would preclude their use as network hosts, but, with DARPA funding, David Clark's group at MIT, which had received several Altos from PARC, built an efficient TCP implementation for that system and, later, for the IBM PC. The proliferation of PCs connected by LANs in the 1980s dramatically increased the size of the Internet.

Integrated Networking

Until the 1970s, academic computer science research groups used a variety of computers and operating systems, many of them constructed by the researchers themselves. Most were time-sharing systems that supported a number of simultaneous users. By 1970, many groups had settled on the Digital Equipment Corporation (DEC) PDP-10 computer and the Tenex operating system developed at BBN. This standardization enabled researchers at different sites to share software, including networking software.

By the late 1970s, the Unix operating system, originally developed at Bell Labs, had become the system of choice for researchers, because it ran on DEC's inexpensive (relative to other systems) VAX line of computers. During the late 1970s and early 1980s, an ARPA-funded project at the University of California at Berkeley (UC-Berkeley) produced a version of Unix (the Berkeley System Distribution, or BSD) that included tightly integrated networking capabilities. The BSD was rapidly adopted by the research community because the availability of source code made it a useful experimental tool. In addition, it ran on both VAX machines and the personal workstations provided by the fledgling Sun Microsystems, Inc., several of whose founders came from the Berkeley group. The TCP/IP suite was now available on most of the computing platforms used by the research community.

Standards and Management

Unlike the various telecommunications networks, the Internet has no owner. It is a federation of commercial service providers, local educational networks, and private corporate networks, exchanging packets using TCP/IP and other, more specialized protocols. To become part of the Internet, a user need only connect a computer to a port on a service provider's router, obtain an IP address, and begin communicating. To add an entire network to the Internet is a bit trickier, but not extraordinarily so, as demonstrated by the tens of thousands of networks with tens of millions of hosts that constitute the Internet today.

The primary technical problem in the Internet is the standardization of its protocols. Today, this is accomplished by the Internet Engineering Task Force (IETF), a voluntary group interested in maintaining and expanding the scope of the Internet. Although this group has undergone many changes in name and makeup over the years, it traces its roots directly to Stephen Crocker's NWG, which defined the first ARPANET protocol in 1969. The NWG defined the system of requests for comments (RFCs) that are still used to specify protocols and discuss other engineering issues. Today's RFCs are still formatted as they were in 1969, eschewing the decorative fonts and styles that pervade today's Web.

Joining the IETF is a simple matter of asking to be placed on its mailing list, attending thrice-yearly meetings, and participating in the work. This grassroots group is far less formal than organizations such as the International Telecommunications Union, which defines telephony standards through the work of members who are essentially representatives of various governments. The open approach to Internet standards reflects the academic roots of the network.

Closing the Decade

The 1970s were a time of intensive research in networking. Much of the technology used today was developed during this period. Several networks other than ARPANET were assembled, primarily for use by computer scientists in support of their own research. Most of the work was funded by ARPA, although the NSF provided educational support for many researchers and was beginning to consider establishing a large-scale academic network.

During this period, ARPA pursued high-risk research with the potential for high payoffs. Its work was largely ignored by AT&T, and the major computer companies, notably IBM and DEC, began to offer proprietary networking solutions that competed with, rather than applied, the ARPA-developed technologies.[3] Yet the technologies developed under ARPA contract ultimately resulted in today's Internet. It is debatable whether a more risk-averse organization lacking the hands-on program management style of ARPA could have produced the same result.

Operation of the ARPANET was transferred to the Defense Communication Agency in 1975. By the end of the decade, the ARPANET had matured sufficiently to provide services. It remained in operation until 1989, when it was superseded by subsequent networks. The stage was now set for the Internet, which was first used by scientists, then by academics in many disciplines, and finally by the world at large.

THE NSFNET YEARS: 1980-1990

During the late 1970s, several networks were constructed to serve the needs of particular research communities. These networks—typically funded by the federal agency that was the primary supporter of the research area—included MFENet, which the Department of Energy established to give its magnetic fusion energy researchers access to supercomputers, and NASA's Space Physics Analysis Network (SPAN). The NSF began supporting network infrastructure with the establishment of CSNET, which was intended to link university computer science departments with the ARPANET. The CSNET had one notable property that the ARPANET lacked: it was open to all computer science researchers, whereas only ARPA contractors could use the ARPANET. An NSF grant to plan the CSNET was issued to Larry Landweber at the University of Wisconsin in 1980.

The CSNET was used throughout the 1980s, but as it and other regional networks began to demonstrate their usefulness, the NSF launched a much more ambitious effort, the NSFNET. From the start, the NSFNET was designed to be a network of networks—an "internet"—with a high-speed backbone connecting NSF's five supercomputer centers and the National Center for Atmospheric Research. To oversee the new network, the NSF hired Dennis Jennings from Trinity College, Dublin. In the early 1980s, Jennings had been responsible for the Irish Higher Education Authority network (HEANet), and so he was well-qualified for the task. One of Jennings' first decisions was to select TCP/IP as the primary protocol suite for the NFSNET.

Because the NSFNET was to be an internet (the beginning of today's Internet), specialized computers called routers were needed to pass traffic between networks at the points where the networks met. Today, routers are the primary products of multibillion-dollar companies (e.g., Cisco Systems Incorporated, Bay Networks), but in 1985, few commercial products were available. The NSF chose the "Fuzzball" router designed by David Mills at the University of Delaware (Mills, 1988). Working with ARPA support, Mills improved the protocols used by the routers to communicate the network topology among themselves, a critical function in a large-scale network.

Another technology required for the rapidly growing Internet was the Domain Name Service (DNS). Developed by Paul Mockapetris at the University of Southern California's Information Sciences Institute, the DNS provides for hierarchical naming of hosts. An administrative entity, such as a university department, can assign host names as it wishes. It also has a domain name, issued by the higher-level authority of which it is a part. (Thus, a host named *xyz* in the computer science department at UC-Berkeley would be named *xyz.cs.berkeley.edu*.) Servers located throughout the Internet provide translation between the host names used by human users and the IP addresses used by the Internet protocols. The name-distribution scheme has allowed the Internet to grow much more rapidly than would be possible with centralized administration.

Jennings left the NSF in 1986. He was succeeded by Stephen Wolff, who oversaw the deployment and growth of the NSFNET. During Wolff's tenure, the speed of the backbone, originally 56 kilobits per second, was increased 1,000-fold, and a large number of academic and regional networks were connected to the NSFNET. The NSF also began to expand the reach of the NSFNET beyond its supercomputing centers through its Connections program, which targeted the research and education community. In response to the Connections solicitation, the NSF received innovative proposals from what would become two of the major regional networks: SURANET and NYSERNET. These groups proposed to develop regional networks with a single connection to the NSFNET, instead of connecting each institution independently.

Hence, the NSFNET evolved into a three-tiered structure in which individual institutions connected to regional networks that were, in turn, connected to the backbone of the NSFNET. The NSF agreed to provide seed funding for connecting regional networks to the NSFNET, with the expectation that, as a critical mass was reached, the private sector would take over the management and operating costs of the Internet. This decision helped guide the Internet toward self-sufficiency and eventual commercialization (Computer Science and Telecommunications Board, 1994).

As the NSFNET expanded, opportunities for privatization grew. Wolff saw that commercial interests had to participate and provide financial support if the network were to continue to expand and evolve into a large, single internet. The NSF had already (in 1987) contracted with Merit Computer Network Incorporated at the University of Michigan to manage the backbone. Merit later formed a consortium with IBM and MCI Communications Corporation called Advanced Network and Services (ANS) to oversee upgrades to the NSFNET. Instead of reworking the existing backbone, ANS added a new, privately owned backbone for commercial services in 1991.[4]

EMERGENCE OF THE WEB: 1990 TO THE PRESENT

By the early 1990s, the Internet was international in scope, and its operation had largely been transferred from the NSF to commercial providers. Public access to the Internet expanded rapidly thanks to the ubiquitous nature of the analog telephone network and the availability of modems for connecting computers to this network. Digital transmission became possible throughout the telephone network with the deployment of optical fiber, and the telephone companies leased their broadband digital facilities for connecting routers and regional networks to the developers of the computer network. In April 1995, all commercialization restrictions on the Internet were lifted. Although still primarily used by academics and businesses, the Internet was growing, with the number of hosts reaching 250,000. Then the invention of the Web catapulted the Internet to mass popularity almost overnight.

The idea for the Web was simple: provide a common format for documents stored on server computers, and give each document a unique name that can be used by a browser program to locate and retrieve the document. Because the unique names (called universal resource locators, or URLs) are long, including the DNS name of the host on which they are stored, URLs would be represented as shorter hypertext links in other documents. When the user of a browser clicks a mouse on a link, the browser retrieves and displays the document named by the URL.

This idea was implemented by Timothy Berners-Lee and Robert Cailliau at CERN, the high-energy physics laboratory in Geneva, Switzerland, funded by the governments of participating European nations. Berners-Lee and Cailliau proposed to develop a system of links between different sources of information. Certain parts of a file would be made into nodes, which, when called up, would link the user to other, related files. The pair devised a document format called Hypertext Markup Language (HTML), a variant of the Standard Generalized Markup Language used in the publishing industry since the 1950s. It was released at CERN in May 1991. In July 1992, a new Internet protocol, the Hypertext Transfer Protocol (HTTP), was introduced to improve the efficiency of document retrieval. Although the Web was originally intended to improve communications within the physics community at CERN, it—like e-mail 20 years earlier—rapidly became the new killer application for the Internet.

The idea of hypertext was not new. One of the first demonstrations of a hypertext system, in which a user could click a mouse on a highlighted word in a document and immediately access a different part of the document (or, in fact, another document entirely), occurred at the 1967 Fall Joint Computer Conference in San Francisco. At this conference, Douglas Engelbart of SRI gave a stunning demonstration of his NLS (Engelbart, 1986), which provided many of the capabilities of today's Web browsers, albeit limited to a single computer. Engelbart's Augment project was supported by funding from NASA and ARPA. Engelbart was awarded the Association for Computing Machinery's 1997 A. M. Turing Award for this work. Although it never became commercially successful, the mouse-driven user interface inspired researchers at Xerox PARC, who were developing personal computing technology.

Widespread use of the Web, which now accounts for the largest volume of Internet traffic, was accelerated by the development in 1993 of the Mosaic graphical browser. This innovation, by Marc Andreessen at the NSF-funded National Center for Supercomputer Applications, enabled the use of hyperlinks to video, audio, and graphics, as well as text. More important, it provided an effective interface that allowed users to point-and-click on a menu or fill in a blank to search for information.

The development of the Internet and the World Wide Web has had a tremendous impact on the U.S. economy and society more broadly. By

January 1998, almost 30 million host computers were connected to the Internet (Zakon, 1998), and more than 58 million users in the United States and Canada were estimated to be online (Nielsen Media Research, 1997). Numerous companies now sell Internet products worth billions of dollars. Cisco Systems, a leader in network routing technology, for example, reported sales of $8.5 billion in 1998. Netscape Communications Corporation, which commercialized the Mosaic browser, had sales exceeding $530 million in 1997.[5] Microsoft Corporation also entered the market for Web browsers and now competes head-to-head with Netscape. A multitude of other companies offer hardware and software for Internet based systems.

The Internet has also paved the way for a host of services. Companies like Yahoo! and InfoSeek provide portals to the Internet and have attracted considerable attention from Wall Street investors. Other companies, like Amazon.com and Barnes & Noble, have established online stores. Amazon had online sales of almost $150 million for books in 1997.[6] Electronic commerce, more broadly, is taking hold in many types of organizations, from PC manufacturers to retailers to travel agencies. Although estimates of the value of these services vary widely, they all reflect a growing sector of the economy that is wholly dependent on the Internet. Internet retailing could reach $7 billion by the year 2000, and online sales of travel services are expected to approach $8 billion around the turn of the century. Forrester Research estimates that businesses will buy and sell $327 billion worth of goods over the Internet by the year 2002 (Blane, 1997).

The Web has been likened to the world's largest library—with the books piled in the middle of the floor. Search engines, which are programs that follow the Web's hypertext links and index the material they discover, have improved the organization somewhat but are difficult to use, frequently deluging the user with irrelevant information. Although developments in computing and networking over the last 40 years have realized some of the potential described by visionaries such as Licklider and Engelbart, the field continues to offer many opportunities for innovation.

LESSONS FROM HISTORY

The development of the Internet demonstrates that federal support for research, applied at the right place and right time, can be extremely effective. DARPA's support gave visibility to the work of individual researchers on packet switching and resulted in the development of the first large-scale packet-switched network. Continued support for experimentation led to the development of networking protocols and applications, such as e-mail, that were used on the ARPANET and, subsequently, the Internet.

By bringing together a diverse mix of researchers from different institutions, such federal programs helped the Internet gain widespread acceptance and established it as a dominant mode of internetworking. Government programs such as ARPANET and NSFNET created a large enough base of users to make the Internet more attractive in many applications than proprietary networking systems being offered by a number of vendors. Though a number of companies continue to sell proprietary systems for wide area networking, some of which are based on packet-switched technology, these systems have not achieved the ubiquity of the Internet and are used mainly within private industry.

Research in packet switching evolved in unexpected directions and had unanticipated consequences. It was originally pursued to make more-efficient use of limited computing capabilities and later seen as a means of linking the research and education communities. The most notable result, however, was the Internet, which has dramatically improved communication across society, changing the way people work, play, and shop. Although DARPA and the NSF were successful in creating an expansive packet-switched network to facilitate communication among researchers, it took the invention of the Web and its browsers to make the Internet more broadly accessible and useful to society.

The widespread adoption of Internet technology has created a number of new companies in industries that did not exist 20 years ago, and most companies that *did* exist 20 years ago are incorporating Internet technology into their business operations. Companies such as Cisco Systems, Netscape Communications, Yahoo!, and Amazon.com are built on Internet technologies and their applications and generate billions of dollars annually in combined sales revenues. Electronic commerce is also maturing into an established means of conducting business.

The complementary missions and operating styles of federal agencies are important to the development and implementation of new technologies. Whereas DARPA supported early research on packet switching and development of the ARPANET, it was not prepared to support an operational network, nor did it expand its network beyond DARPA-supported research institutions. With its charter to support research and education, the NSF both supported an operational network and greatly expanded its reach, effectively building the infrastructure for the Internet.

NOTES

1. Several other case studies of the Internet have also been written in recent years. In addition to the references cited in the text, see Leiner et al. (1998) and SRI International (1997).

2. Personal communication from Robert W. Taylor, former director of the

Information Processing Techniques Office, Defense Advanced Research Projects Agency, August 1988.

3. IBM and AT&T did support some in-house research on packet switching, but at the level of individual researchers. This work did not figure prominently in AT&T's plans for network deployment, nor did it receive significant attention at IBM, though researchers in both organizations published important papers.

4. Ferreiro, Mirna. 1996. "The Past and Future History of the Internet," research paper for International 610. George Mason University, Fairfax, Va., November.

5. Sales figures in this paragraph derive from annual reports filed by the companies cited.

6. Sales revenues as reported in Amazon.com's 1997 Annual Report available online at <http://www.amazon.com/exec/obidos/subst/misc/investor-relations/1997annual_report.html/>.

8

Theoretical Research: Intangible
Cornerstone of Computer Science

The theory and vocabulary of computing did not appear ready-made. Some important concepts, such as operating systems and compilers, had to be invented de novo. Others, such as recursion and invariance, can be traced to earlier work in mathematics. They became part of the evolving computer science lexicon as they helped to stimulate or clarify the design and conceptualization of computing artifacts. Many of these theoretical concepts from different sources have now become so embedded in computing and communications that they pervade the thinking of all computer scientists. Most of these notions, only vaguely perceived in the computing community of 1960, have since become ingrained in the practice of computing professionals and even made their way into high-school curricula.

Although developments in computing theory are intangible, theory underlies many aspects of the construction, explanation, and understanding of computers, as this chapter demonstrates. For example, the concept of state machines (described below) contributed to the development of compilers and communications protocols, insights into computational complexity have been applied to improve the efficiency of industrial processes and information systems, formal verification methods have provided a tool for improving the reliability of programs, and advances in number theory resulted in the development of new encryption methods. By serving as practical tools for use in reasoning and description, such theoretical notions have informed progress in all corners of computing. Although most of these ideas have a basis in mathematics, they have become so firmly fixed in the instincts of computer scientists and engineers that they are likely to be used as naturally as a cashier uses arithmetic, with little attention to the origins of the process. In this way, theory pervades the daily practice of computer science and lends legitimacy to the very identity of the field.

This chapter reviews the history and the funding sources of four areas of theoretical computer science: state machines, computational complexity, program correctness, and cryptography. A final section summarizes the lessons to be learned from history. Although by no means a comprehensive overview of theoretical computer science, the discussion focuses on topics that are representative of the evolution in the field and can be encapsulated fairly, without favoring any particular thesis. State machines, computational complexity, and verification can be traced to the work of logicians in the late 1800s and early 1900s. Cryptography dates back even further. The evolution of these subfields reflects the interplay of mathematics and computer science and the ways in which research questions changed as computer hardware placed practical constraints on theoretical constructs. Each of the four areas is now ubiquitous in the basic conceptual toolkit of computer scientists as well as in undergraduate curricula and textbooks. Each area also continues to evolve and pose additional challenging questions.

Because it tracks the rise of ideas into the general consciousness of the computer science community, this case study is concerned less with issues of ultimate priority than with crystallizing events. In combination, the history of the four topics addressed in this chapter illustrates the complex fabric of a dynamic field. Ideas flowed in all directions, geographically and organizationally. Breakthroughs were achieved in many places, including a variety of North American and European universities and a few industrial research laboratories. Soviet theoreticians also made a number of important advances, although they are not emphasized in this chapter. Federal funding has been important, mostly from the National Science Foundation (NSF), which began supporting work in theoretical computer science shortly after its founding in 1950. The low cost of theoretical research fit the NSF paradigm of single-investigator research. Originally, such work was funded through the division of mathematical sciences, but with the establishment of the Office of Computing Activities in 1970, the NSF initiated a theoretical computer science program that continues to this day. As Thomas Keenan, an NSF staffer, put it:

> Computer science had achieved the title "computer science" without much science in it, [so we] decided that to be a science you had to have theory, and not just theory itself as a separate program, but everything had to have a theoretical basis. And so, whenever we had a proposal . . .

we encouraged, as much as we could, some kind of theoretical background for this proposal. (Aspray et al., 1996)

The NSF ended up funding the bulk of theoretical work in the field (by 1980 it had supported nearly 400 projects in computational theory), much of it with great success. Although funding for theoretical computer science has declined as a percentage of the NSF budget for computing research (it constituted 7 percent of the budget in 1996, down from 20 percent in 1973), it has grown slightly in real dollars.[1] Mission-oriented agencies, such as the National Aeronautics and Space Administration or the Defense Advanced Research Projects Agency, tend not to fund theoretical work directly because of their emphasis on advancing computing technology, but some advances in theory were made as part of their larger research agendas.

MACHINE MODELS: STATE MACHINES

State machine are ubiquitous models for describing and implementing various aspects of computing. The body of theory and implementation techniques that has grown up around state machines fosters the rapid and accurate construction and analysis of applications, including compilers, text-search engines, operating systems, communication protocols, and graphical user interfaces.

The idea of a state machine is simple. A system (or subsystem) is characterized by a set of states (or conditions) that it may assume. The system receives a series of inputs that may cause the machine to produce an output or enter a different state, depending on its current state. For example, a simplified state diagram of a telephone activity might identify states such as idle, dial tone, dialing, ringing, and talking, as well as events that cause a shift from one state to another, such as lifting the handset, touching a digit, answering, or hanging up (see Figure 8.1). A finite state machine, such as a telephone, can be in only one of a limited number of states. More powerful state machine models admit a larger, theoretically infinite, number of states.

The notion of the state machine as a model of all computing was described in Alan Turing's celebrated paper on computability in 1936, before any general-purpose computers had been built. Turing, of Cambridge University, proposed a model that comprised an infinitely long tape and a device that could read from or write to that tape (Turing, 1936). He demonstrated that such a machine could serve as a general-purpose computer. In both academia and industry, related models were proposed and studied during the following two decades, resulting in a definitive 1959 paper by Michael Rabin and Dana Scott of IBM Corporation (Rabin

and Scott, 1959). Whereas Turing elucidated the undecidability[2] inherent in the most general model, Rabin and Scott demonstrated the tractability of limited models. This work enabled the finite state machine to reach maturity as a theoretical model.

Meanwhile, state machines and their equivalents were investigated in connection with a variety of applications: neural networks (Kleene, 1936; McCulloch and Pitts, 1943); language (Chomsky, 1956); communications systems (Shannon, 1948), and digital circuitry (Mealey, 1955; Moore, 1956). A new level of practicality was demonstrated in a method of deriving efficient sequential circuits from state machines (Huffman, 1954).

When formal languages—a means of implementing state machines in software—emerged as an academic research area in the 1960s, machines of intermediate power (i.e., between finite-state and Turing machines) became a focus of research. Most notable was the "pushdown automata," or state machine with an auxiliary memory stack, which is central to the mechanical parsing performed to interpret sentences (usually programs) in high-level languages. As researchers came to understand parsing, the work of mechanizing a programming language was formalized into a routine task. In fact, not only parsing but also the building of parsers was automated, facilitating the first of many steps in converting compiler writing from a craft into a science. In this way, state machines were added to the everyday toolkit of computing. At the same time, the use of state machines to model communication systems—as pioneered by Claude Shannon—became commonplace among electrical and communications engineers. These two threads eventually coalesced in the study of communications protocols, which are now almost universally specified in terms of cooperating state machines (as discussed below in the section dealing with correctness).

The development of formal language theory was spurred by the construction of compilers and invention of programming languages. Compilers came to the world's attention through the Fortran project (Backus, 1979), but they could not become a discipline until the programming language Algol 60 was written. In the defining report, the syntax of Algol 60 was described in a novel formalism that became known as Backus-Naur form. The crisp, mechanical appearance of the formalism inspired Edward Irons, a graduate student at Yale University, to try to build compilers directly from the formalism. Thereafter, compiler automation became commonplace, as noted above. A task that once required a large team could now be assigned as homework. Not only did parsers become easy to make; they also became more reliable. Doing the bulk of the construction automatically reduced the chance of bugs in the final product, which might be anything from a compiler for Fortran to an interpreter for Hypertext Markup Language (HTML).

State machines were developed by a mix of academic and industrial researchers. The idea began as a theoretical construct but is now fully naturalized throughout computer science as an organizing principle and specification tool, independent of any analytical considerations. Introductory texts describe certain programming patterns as state driven (Garland, 1986) or state based (Clancy and Linn, 1995). An archetypal state-based program is a menu-driven telephone-inquiry system. Based on their familiarity with the paradigm, software engineers instinctively know how to build such programs. The ubiquity of the paradigm has led to the development of special tools for describing and building state-based systems, just as for parsers. Work continues to devise machine models to describe different types of systems.

COMPUTATIONAL COMPLEXITY

The theory of computability preceded the advent of general-purpose computers and can be traced to work by Turing, Kurt Godel, Alonzo Church, and others (Davis, 1965). Computability theory concentrated on a single question: Do effective procedures exist for deciding mathematical questions? The requirements of computing have raised more detailed questions about the intrinsic complexity of digital calculation, and these questions have raised new issues in mathematics.

Algorithms devised for manual computing often were characterized by operation counts. For example, various schemes were proposed for carrying out Gaussian elimination or finite Fourier transforms using such counts. This approach became more common with the advent of computers, particularly in connection with algorithms for sorting (Friend, 1956). However, the inherent degree of difficulty of computing problems did not become a discrete research topic until the 1960s. By 1970, the analysis of algorithms had become an established aspect of computer science, and Knuth (1968) had published the first volume of a treatise on the subject that remains an indispensable reference today. Over time, work on complexity theory has evolved just as practical considerations have evolved: from concerns regarding the time needed to complete a calculation, to concerns about the space required to perform it, to issues such as the number of random bits needed to encrypt a message so that the code cannot be broken.

In the early 1960s, Hao Wang[3] noted distinctions of form that rendered some problems in mathematical logic decidable, whereas logical problems as a class are undecidable. There also emerged a robust classification of problems based on the machine capabilities required to attack them. The classification was dramatically refined by Juris Hartmanis and Richard Stearns at General Electric Company (GE), who showed that within a single machine model, a hierarchy of complexity classes exists, stratified by space or time requirements. Hartmanis then left GE to found the computer science department at Cornell University. With NSF support, Hartmanis continued to study computational complexity, a field widely supported by NSF.

Hartmanis and Stearns developed a "speed-up" theorem, which said essentially that the complexity hierarchy is unaffected by the underlying speed of computing. What distinguishes levels of the hierarchy is the way that solution time varies with problem size—and not the scale at which time is measured. Thus, it is useful to talk of complexity in terms of order-of-growth. To that end, the "big-oh" notation, of the form $O(n)$, was imported from algorithm analysis to computing (most notably by Knuth [1976]), where it has taken on a life of its own. The notation is used to describe the rate at which the time needed to generate a solution varies with the size of the problem. Problems in which there is a linear relationship between problem size and time to solution are $O(n)$; those in which the time to solution varies as the square of the problem size are $O(n^2)$.[4] Big-oh estimates soon pervaded algorithm courses and have since been included in curricula for computer science in high schools.

The quantitative approach to complexity pioneered by Hartmanis and Stearns spread rapidly in the academic community. Applying this sharpened viewpoint to decision problems in logic, Stephen Cook at the University of Toronto proposed the most celebrated theoretical notion in computing—NP completeness. His "P versus NP" conjecture is now counted among the important open problems of mathematics. It states that there is a sharp distinction between problems that can be computed deterministically or nondeterministically in a tractable amount of time.[5] Cook's theory, and previous work by Hartmanis and Stearns, helps categorize problems as either deterministic or nondeterministic. The practical importance of Cook's work was vivified by Richard Karp, at the University of California at Berkeley (UC-Berkeley), who demonstrated that a collection of nondeterministically tractable problems, including the famous traveling-salesman problem,[6] are interchangeable ("NP complete") in the sense that, if any one of them is deterministically tractable, then all of them are. A torrent of other NP-complete problems followed, unleashed by a seminal book by Michael Garey and David Johnson at Bell Laboratories (Garey and Johnson, 1979).

Cook's conjecture, if true, implies that there is no hope for precisely solving any of these problems on a real computer without incurring an exponential time penalty. As a result, software designers, knowing that particular applications (e.g., integrated-circuit layout) are intrinsically difficult, can opt for "good enough" solutions, rather than seeking "best possible" solutions. This leads to another question: How good a solution can be obtained for a given amount of effort? A more refined theory about approximate solutions to difficult problems has been developed (Hochbaum, 1997), but, given that approximations are not widely used by computer scientists, this theory is not addressed in detail here. Fortunately, good approximation methods do exist for some NP-complete problems. For example, huge "traveling salesman routes" are routinely used to minimize the travel of an automated drill over a circuit board in which thousands of holes must be bored. These approximation methods are good enough to guarantee that certain easy solutions will come very close to (i.e., within 1 percent of) the best possible solution.

VERIFYING PROGRAM CORRECTNESS

Although the earliest computer algorithms were written largely to solve mathematical problems, only a tenuous and informal connection existed between computer programs and the mathematical ideas they were intended to implement. The gap between programs and mathematics widened with the rise of system programming, which concentrated on the mechanics of interacting with a computer's environment rather than on mathematics.

The possibility of treating the behavior of programs as the subject of a mathematical argument was advanced in a compelling way by Robert Floyd at UC-Berkeley and later amplified by Anthony Hoare at The Queen's University of Belfast. The academic movement toward program verification was paralleled by a movement toward structured programming, christened by Edsger Dijkstra at Technische Universiteit Eindhoven and vigorously promoted by Harlan Mills at IBM and many others. A basic tenet of the latter movement was that good program structure fosters the ability to reason about programs and thereby assure their correctness.[7] Moreover, analogous structuring was to inform the design process itself, leading to higher productivity as well as better products. Structured programming became an obligatory slogan in programming texts and a mandated practice in many major software firms.

In the full verification approach, a program's specifications are described mathematically, and a formal proof that the program realizes the specifications is carried through. To assure the validity of the (exhaustingly long) proof, it would be carried out or checked mechanically. To date, this approach has been too onerous to contemplate for routine programming. Nevertheless, advocates of structured programming promoted some of its key ideas, namely precondition, postcondition, and invariant (see Box 8.1). These terms have found their way into every computer science curriculum, even at the high school level. Whether or

---

BOX 8.1
The Formal Verification Process

In formal verification, computer programs become objects of mathematical study. A program is seen as affecting the state of the data with which it interacts. The purpose of the program is to transform a state with known properties (the precondition) into a state with initially unknown, but desired properties (the postcondition). A program is composed of elementary operations, such as adding or comparing quantities. The transforming effect of each elementary operation is known. Verification consists of proving, by logical deduction, that the sequence of program steps starting from the precondition must inexorably lead to the desired postcondition.

When programs involve many repetitions of the same elementary steps, applied to many different data elements or many transformational stages starting from some initial data, verification involves showing once and for all that, no matter what the data are or how many steps it takes, a program eventually will achieve the postcondition. Such an argument takes the form of a mathematical induction, which asserts that the state after each repetition is a suitable starting state for the next repetition. The assertion that the state remains suitable from repetition to repetition is called an "invariant" assertion.

An invariant assertion is not enough, by itself, to assure a solution. To rule out the possibility of a program running forever without giving an answer, one must also show that the postcondition will eventually be reached. This can be done by showing that each repetition makes a definite increment of progress toward the postcondition, and that only a finite number of such increments are possible.

Although notionally straightforward, the formal verification of everyday programs poses a daunting challenge. Familiar programs repeat thousands of elementary steps millions of times. Moreover, it is a forbidding task to define precise preconditions and postconditions for a program (e.g., spreadsheet or word processor) with an informal manual running into the hundreds of pages. To carry mathematical arguments through on this scale requires automation in the form of verification tools. To date, such tools can handle only problems with short descriptions—a few dozen pages, at most. Nevertheless, it is possible for these few pages to describe complex or subtle behavior. In these cases, verification tools come in handy.

---

not logic is overtly asserted in code written by everyday programmers, these ideas inform their work.

The structured programming perspective led to a more advanced discipline, promulgated by David Gries at Cornell University and Edsger Dijkstra at Eindhoven, which is beginning to enter curricula. In this approach, programs are derived from specifications by algebraic calculation. In the most advanced manifestation, formulated by Eric Hehner, programming is identified with mathematical logic. Although it remains to be seen whether this degree of mathematicization will eventually become common practice, the history of engineering analysis suggests that this outcome is likely.

In one area, the design of distributed systems, mathematicization is spreading in the field perhaps faster than in the classroom. The initial impetus was West's validation of a proposed international standard protocol. The subject quickly matured, both in practice (Holzmann, 1991) and in theory (Vardi and Wolper, 1986). By now, engineers have harnessed a plethora of algebras (e.g., temporal logic, process algebra) in practical tools for analyzing protocols used in applications ranging from hardware buses to Internet communications.

It is particularly difficult to foresee the effects of abnormal events on the behavior of communications applications. Loss or garbling of messages between computers, or conflicts between concurrent events, such as two travel agents booking the same airline seat, can cause inconvenience or even catastrophe, as noted by Neumann (1995). These real-life difficulties have encouraged research in protocol analysis, which makes it possible to predict behavior under a full range of conditions and events, not just a few simple scenarios. A body of theory and practice has emerged in the past decade to make automatic analysis of protocols a practical reality.

CRYPTOGRAPHY

Cryptography is now more important than ever. Although the military has a long history of supporting research on encryption techniques to maintain the security of data transmissions, it is only recently that cryptography has come into widespread use in business and personal applications. It is an increasingly important component of systems that secure online business transactions or maintain the privacy of personal communications.[8] Cryptography is a field in which theoretical work has clear implications for practice, and vice versa. The field has also been controversial, in that federal agencies have sometimes opposed, and at other times supported, publicly accessible research. Here again, the NSF supported work for which no funding could be obtained from other agencies.

The scientific study of cryptography matured in conjunction with information theory, in which coding and decoding are central concerns, albeit typically in connection with compression and robust transmission of data as opposed to security or privacy concerns. Although Claude Shannon's seminal treatment of cryptography (Shannon, 1949) followed his founding paper on information theory, it was actually written earlier under conditions of wartime security. Undoubtedly, Shannon's involvement with cryptography on government projects helped shape his thinking about information theory.

Through the 1970s, research in cryptography was pursued mainly under the aegis of government agencies. Although impressive accomplishments, such as Great Britain's Ultra code-breaking enterprise in World War II, were known by reputation, the methods were largely kept secret. The National Security Agency (NSA) was for many years the leader in cryptographic work, but few of the results were published or found their way into the civilian community. However, an independent movement of cryptographic discovery developed, driven by the availability and needs of computing. Ready access to computing power made cryptographic experimentation feasible, just as opportunities for remote intrusion made it necessary and the mystery surrounding the field made it intriguing.

In 1977, the Data Encryption Standard (DES) developed at IBM for use in the private sector received federal endorsement (National Bureau of Standards, 1977). The mechanism of DES was disclosed, although a pivotal aspect of its scientific justification remained classified. Speculation about the strength of the system spurred research just as effectively as if a formal request for proposals had been issued.

On the heels of DES came the novel proposal for public-key cryptography by Whitfield Diffie and Martin Hellman at Stanford University, and, independently, by R.C. Merkle. Hellman had been interested in cryptography since the early 1970s and eventually convinced the NSF to support it (Diffie and Hellman, 1976). The notion of public-key cryptography was soon made fully practical by Ronald Rivest, Adi Shamir, and Leonard Adleman at the Massachusetts Institute of Technology, who, with funding from the NSF and Office of Naval Research (ONR), devised a public-key method based on number theory (Rivest et al., 1978) (see Box 8.2). Their method won instant acclaim and catapulted number theory into the realm of applied mathematics. Each of the cited works has become bedrock for the practice and study of computer security. The NSF support was critical, as it allowed the ideas to be developed and published in the open, despite pressure from the NSA to keep them secret.

The potential entanglement with International Traffic in Arms Regulations is always apparent in the cryptography arena (Computer Science and Telecommunications Board, 1996). Official and semiofficial attempts to suppress publication have often drawn extra notice to the field (Diffie, 1996). This unsolicited attention has evoked a notable level of independence among investigators. Most, however, have achieved a satisfactory modus vivendi with the concerned agencies, as evidenced by the seminal papers cited in this chapter that report on important cryptographic research performed under unclassified grants.

BOX 8.2
Rivest-Shamir-Adleman Cryptography

Before public-key cryptography was invented, cipher systems required two communicating parties to agree in advance on a secret key to be used in encrypting and decrypting messages between them. To assure privacy for every communication, a separate arrangement had to be made between each pair who might one day wish to communicate. Parties who did not know each other in advance of the need to communicate were out of luck.

By contrast, public-key cryptography requires merely that an individual announce a single (public) encryption key that can be used by everyone who wishes to send that individual a message. To decode any of the messages, this individual uses a different but mathematically related key, which is private. The security of the system depends on its being prohibitively difficult for anyone to discover the private key if only the public key is known. The practicality of the system depends on there being a feasible way to produce pairs of public and private keys.

The first proposals for public-key cryptography appealed to complexity theory for problems that are difficult to solve. The practical method proposed by Rivest, Shamir, and Adleman (RSA) depends on a problem believed to be of this type from number theory. The problem is factoring. The recipient chooses two huge prime numbers and announces only their product. The product is used in the encryption process, whereas decryption requires knowledge of the primes. To break the code, one must factor the product, a task that can be made arbitrarily hard by picking large enough numbers; hundred-digit primes are enough to seriously challenge a stable of supercomputers.

The RSA method nicely illustrates how theory and practice evolved together. Complexity theory was motivated by computation and the desire to understand whether the difficulty of some problems was inherent or only a symptom of inadequate understanding. When it became clear that inherently difficult problems exist, the stage was set for public-key cryptography. This was not sufficient to advance the state of practice, however. Theory also came to the fore in suggesting problems with structures that could be adapted to cryptography.

It took the combination of computers, complexity theory, and number theory to make public-key cryptography a reality, or even conceivable. Once the idea was proposed, remarkable advances in practical technique followed quickly. So did advances in number theory and logic, spurred by cryptographic needs. The general area of protection of communication now covers a range of topics, including codebreaking (even the "good guys" must try to break codes to confirm security); authentication (i.e., preventing imposters in communications); checks and balances (i.e., forestalling rogue actions, such as embezzlement or missile launches, by nominally trusted people); and protection of intellectual property (e.g., by making information theft-proof or providing evidence that knowledge exists without revealing the knowledge).

LESSONS FROM HISTORY

Research in theoretical computer science has been supported by both the federal government and industry. Almost without exception in the cases discussed, contributions from U.S. academia acknowledge the support of federal agencies, most notably the NSF and ONR. Nevertheless, many advances in theoretical computer science have emerged from major industrial research laboratories, such as IBM, AT&T (Bell Laboratories), and GE. This is partly because some of the areas examined developed before the NSF was established, but also because some large corporate laboratories have provided an environment that allows industry researchers to produce directly relevant results while also carrying on long-term, theoretical investigations in the background. Shannon, for example, apparently worked on information theory for a decade before he told the world about it.

Theoretical computer science has made important contributions to computing practice while, conversely, also being informed by that practice. Work on the theory of one-way functions, for example, led to the development of public-key cryptography, and the development of complexity theory, such as Cook's conjecture, sparked efforts to improve methods for approximating solutions to nondeterministically tractable problems. Similarly, the theoretical work in complexity and program correctness (or verification) has been redirected by the advancing needs of computing systems.

Academia has played a key role in propagating computing theory. By teaching and writing textbooks, academic researchers naturally influenced the subjects taught, especially during the formative years of computer science departments. However, some important synthesizing books have come from industrial research laboratories, where management has seen fit to support such writing to enhance prestige, attract candidates, and foster the competence on which research depends.

Foreign nations have contributed to theoretical computer science. Although the United States has been the center of systems-related research, a considerable share of the mathematical underpinnings for computer science can be attributed to British, Canadian, and European academics. (The wider practical implementation of this work in the United States may be explained by a historically greater availability of computers.) The major foreign contributions examined in this case were all supported by governments; none came from foreign industry.

Personal and personnel dynamics have also played important roles. Several of the papers cited in this chapter deal with work that originated during the authors' visiting or short-term appointments, when they were free of the ancillary burdens associated with permanent positions. Researchers in theoretical computer science have often migrated between industry and academia, and researchers in these sectors have often collaborated. Such mixing and travel helped infuse computing theory with an understanding of the practical problems faced by computer designers and helped establish a community of researchers with a common vocabulary.

NOTES

1.   Between 1973 and 1996, NSF funding for theoretical computer science grew from less than $2 million to almost $7 million dollars. In 1996 dollars (i.e., taking inflation into account), the NSF spent the equivalent of $6.1 million on theory in 1973, versus $6.9 million in 1996. Thus, the real increase in funding over 23 years was just 13 percent, or about 0.5 percent a year, on average.

2.   A class of mathematical problems, usually with yes or no answers, is called "decidable" if there is an algorithm that will produce a definite answer for every problem in the class. Otherwise, the class of problems is undecidable. Turing demonstrated that no algorithm exists for answering the question of whether a Turing-machine calculation will terminate. The question might be answered for many particular machines, even mechanically. But no algorithm will answer it for all machines: there must be some machine about which the algorithm will never come to a conclusion.

3.   Hao Wang, who began his work at Oxford University and later moved to Bell Laboratories and IBM, elucidated the sources of undecidability.

4.   As an example of big-oh notation, the number of identical fixed-size solid objects that can be fit into a cube with sides of length L is O(L3), regardless of the size or shape of the objects. This means that for L arbitrarily large, at most L3 objects will fit (scaled by some constant).

5.   A class of problems is said to be "tractable" when the time necessary to solve problems of the class varies at most as a power of problem size.

6.   This problem involves figuring out the most efficient route for a salesperson to follow in visiting a list of cities. Each additional city added to the list creates a whole series of additional possible routes that must be evaluated to identify the shortest one. Thus, the complexity of the problem grows much faster than does the list of cities.

7.   Correctness is defined as the property of being consistent with a specification.

8.   For a more complete discussion of cryptography's growing importance, see Computer Science and Telecommunications Board (1996).

9

Developments in Artificial Intelligence

Artificial intelligence (AI) has been one of the most controversial domains of inquiry in computer science since it was first proposed in the 1950s. Defined as the part of computer science concerned with designing systems that exhibit the characteristics associated with human intelligence—understanding language, learning, reasoning, solving problems, and so on (Barr and Feigenbaum, 1981)—the field has attracted researchers because of its ambitious goals and enormous underlying intellectual challenges. The field has been controversial because of its social, ethical, and philosophical implications. Such controversy has affected the funding environment for AI and the objectives of many research programs.

AI research is conducted by a range of scientists and technologists with varying perspectives, interests, and motivations. Scientists tend to be interested in understanding the underlying basis of intelligence and cognition, some with an emphasis on unraveling the mysteries of human thought and others examining intelligence more broadly. Engineering-oriented researchers, by contrast, are interested in building systems that behave intelligently. Some attempt to build systems using techniques analogous to those used by humans, whereas others apply a range of techniques adopted from fields such as information theory, electrical engineering, statistics, and pattern recognition. Those in the latter category often do not necessarily consider themselves AI researchers, but rather fall into a broader category of researchers interested in machine intelligence.

The concept of AI originated in the private sector, but the growth of the field, both intellectually and in the size of the research community, has depended largely on public investments. Public monies have been invested in a range of AI programs, from fundamental, long-term research into cognition to shorter-term efforts to develop operational systems. Most of the federal support has come from the Defense Advanced Research Projects Agency (DARPA, known during certain periods as ARPA) and other units of the Department of Defense (DOD). Other funding agencies have included the National Institutes of Health, National Science Foundation, and National Aeronautics and Space Administration (NASA), which have pursued AI applications of particular relevance to their missions—health care, scientific research, and space exploration.

This chapter highlights key trends in the development of the field of AI and the important role of federal investments. The sections of this chapter, presented in roughly chronological order, cover the launching of the AI field, the government's initial participation, the pivotal role played by DARPA, the success of speech recognition research, the shift from basic to applied research, and AI in the 1990s. The final section summarizes the lessons to be learned from history. This case study is based largely on published accounts, the scientific and technical literature, reports by the major AI research centers, and interviews conducted with several leaders of AI research centers. (Little information was drawn from the records of the participants in the field, funding agencies, editors and publishers, and other primary sources most valued by professional historians.)[1]

THE PRIVATE SECTOR LAUNCHES THE FIELD

The origins of AI research are intimately linked with two landmark papers on chess playing by machine.[2] They were written in 1950 by Claude E. Shannon, a mathematician at Bell Laboratories who is widely acknowledged as a principal creator of information theory. In the late 1930s, while still a graduate student, he developed a method for symbolic analysis of switching systems and networks (Shannon, 1938), which provided scientists and engineers with much-improved analytical and conceptual tools. After working at Bell Labs for half a decade, Shannon published a paper on information theory (Shannon, 1948). Shortly thereafter, he published two articles outlining the construction or programming of a computer for playing chess (Shannon, 1950a,b).

Shannon's work inspired a young mathematician, John McCarthy, who, while a research instructor in mathematics at Princeton University, joined Shannon in 1952 in organizing a conference on automata studies, largely to promote symbolic modeling and work on the theory of machine intelligence.[3] A year later, Shannon arranged for McCarthy and another future pioneer in AI, Marvin Minsky, then a graduate student in mathematics at Princeton and a participant in the 1952 conference, to work with him at Bell Laboratories during 1953.[4]

By 1955, McCarthy believed that the theory of machine intelligence was sufficiently advanced, and that related work involved such a critical mass of researchers, that rapid progress could be promoted by a concentrated summer seminar at Dartmouth University, where he was then an assistant professor of mathematics. He approached the Rockefeller Foundation's Warren Weaver, also a mathematician and a promoter of cutting-edge science, as well as Shannon's collaborator on information theory. Weaver and his colleague Robert S. Morison, director for Biological and Medical Research, were initially skeptical (Weaver, 1955). Morison pushed McCarthy and Shannon to widen the range of participants and made other suggestions. McCarthy and Shannon responded with a widened proposal that heeded much of Morison's advice. They brought in Minsky and a well-known industrial researcher, Nathaniel Rochester[5] of IBM, as co-principal investigators for the proposal, submitted in September 1955.[6]

In the proposal, the four researchers declared that the summer study was "to proceed on the basis of the conjecture that every aspect of learning or any other feature of intelligence can in principle be so precisely described that a machine can be made to simulate it." They sought to bring a number of U.S. scholars to Dartmouth to create a research agenda for AI and begin actual work on it. In spite of Morison's skepticism, the Rockefeller Foundation agreed to fund this summer project with a grant of $7,500 (Rhind, 1955), primarily to cover summer salaries and expenses of the academic participants. Researchers from industry would be compensated by their respective firms.

Although most accounts of AI history focus on McCarthy's entrepreneurship, the role of Shannon—an intellectual leader from industry—is also critical. Without his participation, McCarthy would not have commanded the attention he received from the Rockefeller Foundation. Shannon also had considerable influence on Marvin Minsky. The title of Minsky's 1954 doctoral dissertation was "Neural Nets and the Brain Model Problem."

The role of IBM is similarly important. Nathan Rochester was a strong supporter of the AI concept, and he and his IBM colleagues who attended the 1956 Dartmouth workshop contributed to the early research in the field. After the workshop IBM welcomed McCarthy to its research laboratories, in large part because of IBM's previous work in AI and because "IBM looked like a good bet to pursue artificial intelligence research vigorously" in the future.[7] Rochester was a visiting professor at the Massachusetts Institute of Technology (MIT) during 1958-1959, and he unquestionably helped McCarthy with the development of LISP, an important list-processing language (see Box 9.1).[8] Rochester also apparently lent his support to the creation in 1958 of the MIT Artificial Intelligence Project (Rochester and Gelertner, 1958).[9] Yet, in spite of the early activity of Rochester and other IBM researchers, the corporation's interest in AI cooled. Although work continued on computer-based checkers and chess, an internal report prepared about 1960 took a strong position against broad support for AI.

Thus, the activities surrounding the Dartmouth workshop were, at the outset, linked with the cutting-edge research at a leading private research laboratory (AT&T Bell Laboratories) and a rapidly emerging industrial giant (IBM). Researchers at Bell Laboratories and IBM nurtured the earliest work in AI and gave young academic researchers like McCarthy and Minsky credibility that might otherwise have been lacking. Moreover, the Dartmouth summer research project in AI was funded by private philanthropy and by industry, not by government. The same is true for much of the research that led up to the summer project.

THE GOVERNMENT STEPS IN

The federal government's initial involvement in AI research was manifested in the work of Herbert Simon and Allen Newell, who attended the 1956 Dartmouth workshop to report on "complex information processing." Trained in political science and economics at the University of Chicago, Simon had moved to Carnegie Institute of Technology in 1946 and was instrumental in the founding and early research of the Graduate School of Industrial Administration (GSIA). Funded heavily by the Ford Foundation and the Office of Naval Research (ONR), and the Air Force, GSIA was the pioneer in bringing quantitative behavioral social sciences research (including operations research) into graduate management education.[10] Because of his innovative work in human decision making, Simon became, in March 1951, a consultant to the RAND Corporation, the pioneering think tank established by the Air Force shortly after World War II.[11]

At RAND, where he spent several summers carrying out collaborative research, Simon encountered Newell, a mathematician who helped to conceive and develop the Systems Research Laboratory, which was spun out of RAND as the System Development Corporation in 1957. In 1955, Simon and Newell began a long collaboration on the simulation of human thought, which by the summer of 1956 had resulted in their fundamental work (with RAND computer programmer J.C. Shaw) on the Logic Theorist, a computer program capable of proving theorems found in the

---

BOX 9.1
The Development and Influence of LISP

LISP has been an important programming language in AI research, and its history demonstrates the more general benefits resulting from the efforts of AI researchers to tackle exceptionally difficult problems. As with other developments in AI, LISP demonstrates how, in addressing problems in the representation and computational treatment of knowledge, AI researchers often stretched the limits of computing technology and were forced to invent new techniques that found their way into mainstream application.

Early AI researchers interested in logical reasoning and problem solving needed tools to represent logical formulas, proofs, plans, and computations on such objects. Existing programming techniques were very awkward for this purpose, inspiring the development of specialized programming languages, such as list-processing languages. List structures provide a simple and universal encoding of the expressions that arise in symbolic logic, formal language theory, and their applications to the formalization of reasoning and natural language understanding. Among early list-processing languages (the name is based on that phrase), LISP was the most effective tool for representing both symbolic expressions and manipulations of them. It was also an object of study in itself. LISP can readily operate on other LISP programs that are represented as list structures, and it thus can be used for symbolic reasoning on programs. LISP is also notable because it is based on ideas of mathematical logic that are of great importance in the study of computability and formal systems (see Chapter 8).

LISP was successful in niche commercial applications. For instance, LISP is the scripting language in AutoCAD, the widely used computer-aided design (CAD) program from AutoDesk. But it had much broader implications for other languages. Effective implementation of LISP demanded some form of automatic memory management. Thus, LISP had critical influence far beyond AI in the theory and design of programming languages, including all functional programming languages as well as object-oriented languages such as Simula-67, SmallTalk, and, most notably, Java. This is not just a happy accident, but rather a consequence of the conceptual breakthroughs arising from the effort to develop computational models of reasoning. Other examples include frame-based knowledge representations, which strongly influenced the development of object-oriented programming and object databases; rule-based and logic-programming language ideas, which found practical applications in expert systems, databases, and optimization techniques; and CAD representations for reasoning with uncertainty, which have found their way into manufacturing control, medical and equipment diagnosis, and human-computer interfaces.

Principia of Bertrand Russell and Alfred North Whitehead (Newell and Simon, 1956).[12]

This program is regarded by many as the first successful AI program, and the language it used, IPL2, is recognized as the first significant list-processing language. As programmed by Simon, Newell, and Shaw, a computer simulated human intelligence, solving a problem in logic in much the same way as would a skilled logician. In this sense, the machine demonstrated artificial intelligence. The project was funded almost entirely by the Air Force through Project RAND, and much of the computer programming was done at RAND on an Air Force-funded computer (the Johnniac, named after RAND consultant John von Neumann, the creator of the basic architecture for digital electronic computers).[13]

Newell's collaboration with Simon took him to Carnegie Tech, where, in 1957, he completed the institution's first doctoral dissertation in AI, "Information Processing: A New Technique for the Behavioral Sciences." Its thrust was clearly driven by the agenda laid out by the architects of GSIA. As Newell later stressed, his work with Simon (and that of Simon's several other AI students at GSIA) reflected the larger agenda of GSIA, even though most of this work was funded by the Air Force and ONR until the early 1960s. All of this work concentrated on the formal modeling of decision making and problem solving.

Simon and Newell developed another well-known AI program as a sequel to Logic Theorist—the General Problem Solver (GPS), first run in 1957 and developed further in subsequent years. Their work on GPS, like that on Logic Theorist, was characterized by its use of heuristics (i.e., efficient but fallible rules of thumb) as the means to simulate human cognitive processes (Newell et al., 1959). The GPS was capable of solving an array of problems that challenge human intelligence (an important accomplishment in and of itself), but, most significantly, it solved these problems by simulating the way a human being would solve them. These overall research efforts at GSIA, including the doctoral research of Simon's students—all funded principally by Air Force and ONR money—remained modest in scale compared to those at Carnegie Tech after 1962.[14]

Also modest were the efforts at MIT, where McCarthy and Minsky established the Artificial Intelligence Project in September 1957. This effort was funded principally through a word-of-mouth agreement with Jerome Wiesner, then director of MIT's military-funded Research Laboratory in Electronics (RLE). In exchange for "a room, two programmers, a secretary and a keypunch [machine]," the two assistant professors of mathematics agreed, according to McCarthy, to "undertake the supervision of some of the six mathematics graduate students that RLE had undertaken to support."[15]

The research efforts at Carnegie Tech (which became Carnegie Mellon University [CMU] in 1967), RAND, and MIT, although limited, yielded outstanding results in a short time. Simon and Newell showed that computers could demonstrate human-like behavior in certain well-defined tasks.[16] Substantial progress was also made by McCarthy, with his pioneering development of LISP, and Minsky, who formalized heuristic processes and other means of reasoning, including pattern recognition.

Previously, computers had been used principally to crunch numbers, and the tools for such tasks were primitive. The AI researchers found ways to represent logical formulas, carry out proofs, conduct plans, and manipulate such objects. Buoyed by their successes, researchers at both institutions projected bold visions—which, as the research was communicated to the public, became magnified into excessive claims—about the future of the new field of AI and what computers might ultimately achieve.[17]

DARPA'S PIVOTAL ROLE

The establishment in 1962 of ARPA's Information Processing Techniques Office (IPTO) radically changed the scale of research in AI, propelling it from a collection of small projects into a large-scale, high-profile domain. From the 1960s through the 1990s, DARPA provided the bulk of the nation's support for AI research and thus helped to legitimize AI as an important field of inquiry and influence the scope of related research. Over time, the nature of DARPA's support changed radically—from an emphasis on fundamental research at a limited number of centers of excellence to more broad-based support for applied research tied to military applications—both reflecting and motivating changes in the field of AI itself.

The early academic centers were MIT and Carnegie Tech. Following John McCarthy's move to Stanford in 1963 to create the Stanford Artificial Intelligence Laboratory (SAIL), IPTO worked a similar transformation of AI research at Stanford by making it the third center of excellence in AI. Indeed, the IPTO increased Stanford's allocation in 1965, allowing it to upgrade its computing capabilities and to launch five major team projects in AI research. Commenting in 1984 about how AI-related research at Carnegie Tech migrated out of GSIA into what became an autonomous department (and later a college) of CMU, Newell (1984) captured the transformation wrought by IPTO:

> . . . the DARPA support of AI and computer science is a remarkable story of the nurturing of a new scientific field. Not only with MIT, Stanford and CMU, which are now seen as the main DARPA-supported university computer-science research environments, but with other universities as well . . . DARPA began to build excellence in information processing in whatever fashion we thought best. . . . The DARPA effort, or anything similar, had not been in our wildest imaginings. . . .

Another center of excellence—the Stanford Research Institute's (SRI's) Artificial Intelligence Center—emerged a bit later (in 1966), with Charles Rosen at the command. It focused on developing "automatons capable of gathering, processing, and transmitting information in a hostile environment" (Nilsson, 1984). Soon, SRI committed itself to the development of an AI-driven robot, Shakey, as a means to achieve its objective. Shakey's development necessitated extensive basic research in several domains, including planning, natural-language processing, and machine vision. SRI's achievements in these areas (e.g., the STRIPS planning system and work in machine vision) have endured, but changes in the funder's expectations for this research exposed SRI's AI program to substantial criticism in spite of these real achievements.

Under J.C.R. Licklider, Ivan Sutherland, and Robert Taylor, DARPA continued to invest in AI research at CMU, MIT, Stanford, and SRI and, to a lesser extent, other institutions.[18] Licklider (1964) asserted that AI was central to DARPA's mission because it was a key to the development of advanced command-and-control systems. Artificial intelligence was a broad category for Licklider (and his immediate successors), who "supported work in problem solving, natural language processing, pattern recognition, heuristic programming, automatic theorem proving, graphics, and intelligent automata. Various problems relating to human-machine communication—tablets, graphic systems, hand-eye coordination—were all pursued with IPTO support" (Norberg and O'Neill, 1996).

These categories were sufficiently broad that researchers like McCarthy, Minsky, and Newell could view their institutions' research, during the first 10 to 15 years of DARPA's AI funding, as essentially unfettered by immediate applications. Moreover, as work in one problem domain spilled over into others easily and naturally, researchers could attack problems from multiple perspectives. Thus, AI was ideally suited to graduate education, and enrollments at each of the AI centers grew rapidly during the first decade of DARPA funding.

DARPA's early support launched a golden age of AI research and rapidly advanced the emergence of a formal discipline. Much of DARPA's funding for AI was contained in larger program initiatives. Licklider considered AI a part of his general charter of Computers, Command, and Control. Project MAC (see Box 4.2), a project on time-shared computing at MIT, allocated roughly one-third of its $2.3 million annual budget to AI research, with few specific objectives.

SUCCESS IN SPEECH RECOGNITION

The history of speech recognition systems illustrates several themes common to AI research more generally: the long time periods between the initial research and development of successful products, and the interactions between AI researchers and the broader community of researchers in machine intelligence. Many capabilities of today's speech-recognition systems derive from the early work of statisticians, electrical engineers, information theorists, and pattern-recognition researchers. Another key theme is the complementary nature of government and industry funding. Industry supported work in speech recognition at least as far back as the 1950s, when researchers at Bell Laboratories worked on systems for recognizing individual spoken digits "zero" through "nine." Research in the area was boosted tremendously by DARPA in the 1970s.

DARPA established the Speech Understanding Research (SUR) program to develop a computer system that could understand continuous speech. Lawrence Roberts initiated this project in 1971 while he was director of IPTO, against the advice of a National Academy of Sciences committee.[19] Roberts wanted a system that could handle a vocabulary of 10,000 English words spoken by anyone. His advisory board, which included Allen Newell and J.C.R. Licklider, issued a report calling for an objective of 1,000 words spoken in a quiet room by a limited number of people, using a restricted subject vocabulary (Newell et al., 1971).

Roberts committed $3 million per year for 5 years, with the intention of pursuing a 5-year follow-on project. Major SUR project groups were established at CMU, SRI, MIT's Lincoln Laboratory, Systems Development Corporation (SDC), and Bolt, Beranek, and Newman (BBN). Smaller contracts were awarded to a few other institutions. Five years later, SUR products were demonstrated. CMU researchers demonstrated two systems, HARPY and HEARSAY-I, and BBN developed Hear What I Mean (HWIM). The system developed cooperatively by SRI and SDC was never tested (Green, 1988). The system that came the closest to satisfying the original project goals—and may have exceeded the benchmarks—was HARPY, but controversy arose within DARPA and the AI community about the way the tests were handled. Full details regarding the testing of system performance had not been worked out at the outset of the SUR program.[20] As a result, some researchers—including DARPA research managers—believed that the SUR program had failed to meet its objectives. DARPA terminated the program without funding the follow-on.[21] Nevertheless, industry groups, including those at IBM, continued to invest in this research area and made important contributions to the development of continuous speech recognition methods.[22]

DARPA began funding speech recognition research on a large scale again in 1984 as part of the Strategic Computing Program (discussed later in this chapter) and continued funding research in this area well into the late 1990s. Many of the same institutions that had been part of the SUR program, including CMU, BBN, SRI, and MIT, participated in the new initiatives. Firms such as IBM and Dragon Systems also participated. As a result of the controversy over SUR testing, evaluation methods and criteria for these programs were carefully prescribed though mutual agreements between DARPA managers and the funded researchers. Some researchers have hailed this development and praised DARPA's role in benchmarking speech-recognition technology, not only for research purposes but also for the commercial market.

By holding annual system evaluations on carefully designed tasks and test materials, DARPA and the National Bureau of Standards (later the National Institute of Standards and Technology) led the standards-definition process, drawing the participation of not only government contractors but also industry and university groups from around the world, such as AT&T, Cambridge University (of the United Kingdom), and LIMSI (of France). The overall effect was the rapid adoption of the most successful techniques by every participant and quick migration of those techniques into products and services. Although it resulted in quick diffusion of successful techniques, this approach may also have narrowed the scope of approaches taken. Critics have seen this as symptomatic of a profound change in DARPA's philosophy that has reduced the emphasis on basic research.

DARPA's funding of research on understanding speech has been extremely important. First, it pushed the research frontiers of speech recognition and AI more generally. HEARSAY-II is particularly notable for the way it parsed information into independent knowledge sources, which in turn interacted with each other through a common database that CMU researchers labeled a "blackboard" (Englemore et al., 1988). This blackboard method of information processing proved to be a significant advance in AI. Moreover, although early speech-recognition researchers appeared overly ambitious in incorporating syntax and semantics into their systems, others have recently begun to adopt this approach to improve statistically based speech-recognition technology.

Perhaps more important, the results of this research have been incorporated into the products of established companies, such as IBM and BBN, as well as start-ups such as Nuance Communications (an SRI spinoff) and Dragon Systems. Microsoft Corporation, too, is incorporating speech recognition technology into its operating system (DARPA, 1997; McClain, 1998). The leading commercial speech-recognition program on the market today, the Dragon Systems software, traces its roots directly back to the work done at CMU between 1971 and 1975 as part of SUR (see Box 9.2). The DRAGON program developed in CMU's SUR project (the predecessor of the HARPY program) pioneered the use of techniques borrowed from mathematics and statistics (hidden Markov models) to recognize continuous speech (Baker, 1975). According to some scholars, the adoption of hidden Markov models by CMU's research team owes much to activities outside the AI field, such as research by engineers and statisticians with an interest in machine intelligence.[23]

Other examples of commercial success abound. Charles Schwab and

BOX 9.2
Dragon Systems Profits from Success in Speech Recognition

Dragon Systems was founded in 1982 by James and Janet Baker to commercialize speech recognition technology. As graduate students at Rockefeller University in 1970, they became interested in speech recognition while observing waveforms of speech on an oscilloscope. At the time, systems were in place for recognizing a few hundred words of discrete speech, provided the system was trained on the speaker and the speaker paused between words. There were not yet techniques that could sort through naturally spoken sentences. James Baker saw the waveforms—and the problem of natural speech recognition—as an interesting pattern-recognition problem.

Rockefeller had neither experts in speech understanding nor suitable computing power, and so the Bakers moved to Carnegie Mellon University (CMU), a prime contractor for DARPA's Speech Understanding Research program. There they began to work on natural speech recognition capabilities. Their approach differed from that of other speech researchers, most of whom were attempting to recognize spoken language by providing contextual information, such as the speaker's identity, what the speaker knew, and what the speaker might be trying to say, in addition to rules of English. The Bakers' approach was based purely on statistical relationships, such as the probability that any two or three words would appear one after another in spoken English. They created a phonetic dictionary with the sounds of different word groups and then set to work on an algorithm to decipher a string of spoken words based on phonetic sound matches and the probability that someone would speak the words in that order. Their approach soon began outperforming competing systems.

After receiving their doctorates from CMU in 1975, the Bakers joined IBM's T.J. Watson Research Center, one of the only organizations at the time working on large-vocabulary, continuous speech recognition. The Bakers developed a program that could recognize speech from a 1,000-word vocabulary, but it could not do so in real time. Running on an IBM System 370 computer, it took roughly an hour to decode a single spoken sentence. Nevertheless, the Bakers grew impatient with what they saw as IBM's reluctance to develop simpler systems that could be more rapidly put to commercial use. They left in 1979 to join Verbex Voice Systems, a subsidiary of Exxon Enterprises that had built a system for collecting data over the telephone using spoken digits. Less than 3 years later, however, Exxon exited the speech recognition business.

With few alternatives, the Bakers decided to start their own company, Dragon Systems. The company survived its early years through a mix of custom projects, government research contracts, and new products that relied on the more mature discrete speech recognition technology. In 1984, they provided Apricot Computer, a British company, with the first speech recognition capability for a personal computer (PC). It allowed users to open files and run programs using spoken commands. But Apricot folded shortly thereafter. In 1986, Dragon Systems was awarded the first of a series of contracts from DARPA to advance large-vocabulary, speaker-independent continuous speech recognition, and by 1988, Dragon conducted the first public demonstration of a PC-based discrete speech recognition system, boasting an 8,000-word vocabulary.

In 1990, Dragon demonstrated a 5,000-word continuous speech system for PCs and introduced DragonDictate 30K, the first large-vocabulary, speech-to-text system for general-purpose dictation. It allowed control of a PC using voice commands only and found acceptance among the disabled. The system had limited appeal in the broader marketplace because it required users to pause between words. Other federal contracts enabled Dragon to improve its technology. In 1991, Dragon received a contract from DARPA for work on machine-assisted translation systems, and in 1993, Dragon received a federal Technology Reinvestment Project award to develop, in collaboration with Analog Devices Corporation, continuous speech recognition systems for desktop and hand-held personal digital assistants (PDAs). Dragon demonstrated PDA speech recognition in the Apple Newton MessagePad 2000 in 1997.

Late in 1993, the Bakers realized that improvements in desktop computers would soon allow continuous voice recognition. They quickly began setting up a new development team to build such a product. To finance the needed expansion of its engineering, marketing, and sales staff, Dragon brokered a deal whereby Seagate Technologies bought 25 percent of Dragon's stock. By July 1997, Dragon had launched Dragon NaturallySpeaking, a continuous speech recognition program for general-purpose use with a vocabulary of 23,000 words. The package won rave reviews and numerous awards. IBM quickly followed suit, offering its own continuous speech recognition program, ViaVoice, in August after a crash development program. By the end of the year, the two companies combined had sold more than 75,000 copies of their software. Other companies, such as Microsoft Corporation and Lucent Technologies, are expected to introduce products in the near future, and analysts expect a $4 billion worldwide market by 2001.

SOURCE: The primary source for this history is Garfinkel (1998). A corporate history is available on the company's Web site at <http://www.dragonsys.com>.

Company adopted DARPA technology to develop its VoiceBroker system, which provides stock quotes over the telephone. The system can recognize the names of 13,000 different securities as well as major regional U.S. accents. On the military side, DARPA provided translingual communication devices for use in Bosnia. These devices translated spoken English phrases into corresponding Serbo-Croatian or Russian phrases. The total market for these new personal-use voice recognition technologies is expected to reach about $4 billion in 2001 (Garfinkel, 1998).

SHIFT TO APPLIED RESEARCH INCREASES INVESTMENT

Although most founders of the AI field continued to pursue basic questions of human and machine intelligence, some of their students and other second-generation researchers began to seek ways to use AI methods and approaches to tackle real-world problems. Their initiatives were important, not only in their own right, but also because they were indicative of a gradual but significant change in the funding environment toward more applied realms of research. The development of expert systems, such as DENDRAL at SAIL, provides but one example of this trend (see Box 9.3).

BOX 9.3
Pioneering Expert Systems

The DENDRAL Project was initiated in 1965 by Edward Feigenbaum (one of Herbert Simon's doctoral students in AI); Nobel Prize-winning geneticist and biochemist Joshua Lederberg; and Bruce Buchanan, a recent recipient of a doctorate in philosophy from Michigan State University.[1] DENDRAL began as an effort to explore the mechanization of scientific reasoning and the formalization of scientific knowledge by working within a specific domain of science, organic chemistry. Developed in part with an initial research grant from the National Aeronautics and Space Administration (in anticipation of landing unmanned spacecraft on other planets), but also picked up under DARPA funding, DENDRAL used a set of knowledge- or rule-based reasoning commands to deduce the likely molecular structure of organic chemical compounds from known chemical analyses and mass spectrometry data. The program took almost 10 years to develop, combining the talents of chemists, geneticists, and computer scientists. In addition to rivaling the skill of expert organic chemists in predicting the structures of molecules in certain classes of compounds, DENDRAL proved to be fundamentally important in demonstrating how rule-based reasoning could be developed into powerful knowledge engineering tools. Its use resulted in a number of papers published in the chemistry literature. Although it is no longer a topic of academic research, the most recent version of the interactive structure generator, GENOA, has been licensed by Stanford University for commercial use.

DENDRAL led to the development of other rule-based reasoning programs at the Stanford Artificial Intelligence Laboratory (SAIL), the most important of which was MYCIN, which helped physicians diagnose a range of infectious blood diseases based on sets of clinical symptoms.[2] Begun in 1972 and completed in 1980, the MYCIN project went further than DENDRAL in that it kept the rules (or embodied knowledge) separate from the inference engine that applied the rules. This latter part of the MYCIN project was essentially the first expert-system shell (Buchanan and Shortliffe, 1984).[3]

The development of these pioneering expert systems not only constituted major achievements in AI but also gave both researchers and research funders a glimpse of the ultimate power of computers as a tool for reasoning and decision making. Moreover, the apparent success of these projects helped to touch off the rapid development of expert systems. Promoted by SAIL's Edward Feigenbaum, expert systems became the rage in AI research in the late 1970s and early 1980s and a commercial tool in the 1980s, when corporations were seeking to embody the knowledge of their skilled employees who were facing either retirement or downsizing (Feigenbaum et al., 1988). Expert-system shells, based in large part on the "Empty MYCIN" (EMYCIN) shell, moved on to the commercial software market.

Starting in the mid-1980s, numerous start-up AI companies began to appear, many with products akin to expert systems. Many such companies came and went, but some flourished. For example, Gensym Corporation, founded in 1986 by an alumnus of the Massachusetts Institute of Technology's Artificial Intelligence Laboratory, built a substantial business based on its G2 product for development of intelligent systems. More recently, Trilogy Development Group, Inc., went public, selling both software and services that apply rule-based reasoning and other AI methods to marketing operations. One of Trilogy's founders (a Stanford University graduate) learned about the expert system that Carnegie Mellon University (CMU) had developed for Digital Equipment Corporation to configure its VAX computers (XCON).[4] Basing their work in part on the systems that had emerged from DENDRAL and MYCIN and what they learned about XCON, Trilogy's founders also used constraint-based equations and object-oriented programming methods, derived in part from AI research.[5] Another of Trilogy's founders applied the company's methods to the marketing of personal computers (PCs) over the Internet. This new firm, pcOrder.com.Inc., promises to simplify the configuration of PCs and drastically lower the cost of buying (or selling) one (McHugh, 1996).

Many corporations committed substantial capital and human resources to the development of expert systems, and many reported substantial returns on these investments. Others found that, as AI pioneer McCarthy (1990) had argued, these expert systems were extremely "brittle" in that a small development in knowledge or change in practice rendered such programs obsolete or too narrow to use. In one study of AI (Office of Technology Assessment, 1985), expert systems were singled out as evidence of "the first real commercial products of about 25 years of AI research" but were also criticized for "several serious weaknesses" that demanded "fundamental breakthroughs" to overcome. But expert systems represented a failure to meet expectations as much as a failure of technology. They provided valuable help for users who understand the limitations of a system that embodied narrow domains of knowledge. One of the biggest problems with expert systems was the term itself, which implied a certain level of capability; a number of users started calling them *knowledge-based systems* to refer to the technology instead of the goal.

Despite these criticisms, work on expert systems continues to be published; some corporations with strong knowledge-engineering capabilities continue to report substantial savings from expert systems and have demonstrated a continued commitment to expanding their use. Expert-system shell programs continue to be developed, improved, and sold. By 1992, some 11 shell programs were available for the Macintosh platform, 29 for IBM-DOS platforms, 4 for Unix platforms, and 12 for dedicated mainframe applications.[6] A recent review of expert systems reported that the North American market for expert systems is roughly $250 million (representing about 70 percent of the total commercial AI market). Estimates suggest that more than 12,000 stand-alone expert systems are in use (Liebowitz, 1997). Moreover, small expert systems are being incorporated into other types of computer software, most of it proprietary.

continued on next page

BOX 9.3 continued

---

[1]The literature on DENDRAL is extensive. For the most recent participants' account, see Lindsay et al. (1993).

[2]Another important program, carried out in the early 1970s, was META-DENDRAL. This inductive program automatically formulates new rules for DENDRAL to use in explaining data about unknown chemical compounds. Using the plan-generate-test paradigm, META-DENDRAL has successfully formulated rules of mass spectrometry, both by rediscovering existing rules and by proposing entirely new rules. Although META-DENDRAL is no longer an active program, its contributions to ideas about learning and discovery are being applied to new domains. These ideas suggest, for example, that induction can be automated as a heuristic search; that, for efficiency, search can be broken into two steps—approximate and refined; that learning must be able to cope with noisy and incomplete data; and that learning multiple concepts at the same time is sometimes inescapable. More information is available online at <http://www-camis.stanford.edu/research/history.html#DENDRAL>.

[3]The MYCIN team also developed an important program known as TEIRESIAS, which made the basis of MYCIN's reasoning transparent to its users and allowed MYCIN's knowledge base to be changed or upgraded more easily. The literature on these programs is extensive.

[4]XCON (for eXpert Configurer) has been widely hailed as one of the first successful expert systems programs. It was the work of John McDermott and his team at CMU. See Crevier (1994).

[5]Trilogy's history is discussed by McHugh (1996).

[6]These data were compiled from R.R. Bowker Company (1992) and Table 3 in Pickett and Case (1991).

The promotion in 1969 of Lawrence Roberts to director of IPTO also contributed to a perceived tightening of AI research. Under Roberts, IPTO developed a formal AI program, which in turn was divided into formal subprograms (Norberg and O'Neill, 1996). The line-item budget of AI research inevitably led to greater scrutiny owing to reporting mechanisms and the need to justify programs to the DOD, the Administration, and the U.S. Congress. Consequently, researchers began to believe that they were being boxed in by IPTO and DARPA, and to a certain extent they were. The flow of DARPA's AI research money to CMU, MIT, and Stanford University did not cease or even diminish much, but the demand grew for interim reports and more tangible results.

External developments reinforced this shift. The most important was the passage of the Mansfield Amendment in 1969.[24] Passed during the Vietnam War amid growing public concern about the "military-industrial complex" and the domination of U.S. academic science by the military, the Mansfield Amendment restricted the DOD to supporting basic research that was of "direct and apparent" utility to specific military functions and operations. It brought about a swift decline in some of the military's support for basic research, often driving it toward the applied realm.[25]   Roberts and his successors now had to justify AI research programs on the basis of immediate utility to the military mission. The move toward relevance spawned dissatisfaction among both the established pioneers of the AI field and its outside skeptics.[26]

Another external development provided further impetus for change. In 1973, at the request of the British Scientific Research Council, Sir James Lighthill, the Lucasian Professor of Applied Mathematics at Cambridge University and a Fellow of the Royal Society of London, produced a survey that expressed considerable skepticism about AI in general and research domains in particular. Despite having no expertise in AI himself, Lighthill suggested that any particular successes in AI had stemmed from modeling efforts in more traditional disciplines, not from AI per se. He singled out robotics research for especially sharp criticism. The Lighthill report raised questions about AI research funding in the United States and led DOD to establish a panel to assess DARPA's AI program.

Known as the American Study Group, the panel (which included some of AI's major research figures) raised some of the same questions as did Lighthill's report and served to inform George Heilmeier, a former research manager from RCA Corporation who was then assistant director of Defense R&D and later became director of DARPA. The Lighthill report and its U.S. equivalent led to a shifting of DARPA funds out of robotics research (hurting institutions such as SRI that had committed heavily to the area) and toward "mission-oriented direct research, rather than basic undirected research" (Fleck, 1982).[27]

As a result of these forces, DARPA's emphasis on relevance in AI research grew during the late 1970s and 1980s. Despite the disgruntlement among some scientists, the changes led to increased funding—although not directly to widespread commercial success—for AI research. A magnet for these monies was the Strategic Computing Program (SCP), announced in 1983 (DARPA, 1983). DARPA committed $1 billion over the planned 10-year course of the program. The four main goals of the SCP were as follows:

1. Advance machine intelligence technology and high-performance computing, including speech recognition and understanding, natural-language computer interfaces, vision comprehension systems, and advanced expert systems development, and to do so by providing significant increases in computer performance, through parallel-computer architectures, software, and supporting microelectronics;

2. Transfer technology from DARPA-sponsored university research

efforts to the defense industry through competitive research contracts, with industry and universities jointly participating;

3. Develop more new scientists in AI and high-performance computing through increased funding of graduate student research in these areas; and

4. Provide the supporting research infrastructure for AI research through advanced networking, new microcircuit fabrication facilities, advanced emulation facilities, and advanced symbolic processors (Kahn, 1988).

To achieve these goals, DARPA established three specific applications as R&D objectives: a pilot's associate for the Air Force, an autonomous land vehicle for the Army, and an aircraft battle management system for the Navy. The applications were intended to spark the military services' interest in developing AI technology based on fundamental research. The SCP differed from some other large-scale national efforts in that its goals were extremely ambitious, requiring fundamental advances in the underlying technology. (By contrast, efforts such as the Apollo space program were principally engineering projects drawing from an established scientific base [Office of Technology Assessment, 1985]). The SCP also differed from earlier large AI programs in that some 60 percent of its funds were committed to industry. However, of the 30 prime contractors for the SCP involved in software or AI research, more than 20 were established defense contractors (Goldstein, 1992).

The SCP significantly boosted overall federal funding for AI research but also altered its character. Between 1984 and 1988, total federal funding for AI research, excluding the SCP, tripled from $57 million to $159 million (see Table 9.1). With support for the SCP included, federal funding increased from $106 million to $274 million. Because the SCP was budgeted as an applied program, it tipped the balance of federal funding toward applied research. Although DARPA's funding for basic AI research doubled from roughly $20 million to $40 million during this same period, the DOD's overall role in basic AI research declined (see Table 9.2). Meanwhile, it continued to play the dominant role in supporting applied research in AI (see Table 9.3). Although budget categorizations for programs such as the SCP are somewhat arbitrary and subject to political influence, researchers noted a change in DARPA's funding style.

The SCP also attracted a tremendous amount of industry investment and venture capital to AI research and development. Firms developing and selling expert systems entered the market, often basing their systems on the LISP machines developed by the AI community. Several new firms entered the market to design, make, and sell the very expensive LISP machines. Yet the rapid development of engineering workstations, especially those of Sun Microsystems, Inc., soon undermined the LISP machine industry. This segment of the market, which was clearly tied to

TABLE 9.1 Total Federal Funding for Artificial Intelligence Research (in millions of dollars), 1984-1988

	1984	1985	1986	1987	1988
Excluding Strategic Computing					
Basic	44.1	63.1	81.5	85.5	86
Applied	12.5	31	54.5	79.5	73
TOTAL	56.6	94.1	136	165	159
Percent Applied	22	33	40	48	46
Including Strategic Computing					
Basic	44.1	63.1	81.5	85.5	86
Applied	61.5	94	170.5	171.5	188
TOTAL	105.6	157.1	252	257	274
Percent Applied	58	60	68	67	69

SOURCE: Goldstein (1992).

TABLE 9.2 Federal Funding for Basic Research in Artificial Intelligence by Agency (in millions of dollars), 1984-1988

Year	1984	1985	1986	1987	1988
DARPA	21.6	34.1	41	44	36
Other DOD	10.5	12.5	17	15	15
Non-DOD	12	16.5	23.5	26.5	35
TOTAL	44.1	63.1	81.5	85.5	86
Percent DOD	73	74	71	69	59

SOURCE: Goldstein (1992).

TABLE 9.3 Federal Funding for Applied Research in Artificial Intelligence by Agency (in millions of dollars), 1984-1988

	1984	1985	1986	1987	1988
DARPA	56	78	138	135.5	151
Other DOD	0.5	8	21.5	26	27
Non-DOD	5	8	11	10	10
TOTAL	61.5	94	170.5	171.5	188
Percent DOD	92	91	94	94	95

SOURCE: Goldstein (1992).

the SCP, collapsed. Even with the development of expert-system shells to run on less-costly machines, doubts began to arise about the capabilities and flexibility of expert systems; this doubt hampered the commercialization of AI. In addition, commercial contractors had difficulty meeting the high-profile milestones of the major SCP projects because of difficulties with either the AI technologies themselves or their incorporation into larger systems. Such problems undermined the emergence of a clearly identifiable AI industry and contributed to a shift in emphasis in high-performance computing, away from AI and toward other grand challenges, such as weather modeling and prediction and scientific visualization.

ARTIFICIAL INTELLIGENCE IN THE 1990s

Despite the commercial difficulties associated with the Strategic Computing Program, the AI-driven advances in rule-based reasoning systems (i.e., expert systems) and their successors—many of which were initiated with DARPA funding in the 1960s and 1970s—proved to be extremely valuable for the emerging national information infrastructure and electronic commerce. These advances, including probabilistic reasoning systems and Bayesian networks, natural language processing, and knowledge representation, brought AI out of the laboratory and into the marketplace. Paradoxically, the major commercial successes of AI research applications are mostly hidden from view today because they are embedded in larger software systems. None of these systems has demonstrated general human intelligence, but many have contributed to commercial and military objectives.

An example is the Lumiere project initiated at Microsoft Research in 1993. Lumiere monitors a computer user's actions to determine when assistance may be needed. It continuously follows the user's goals and tasks as software programs run, using Bayesian networks to generate a probability distribution over topic areas that might pose difficulties and calculating the probability that the user will not mind being bothered with assistance. Lumiere forms the basis of the "office assistant" that monitors the behavior of users of Microsoft's Office 97 and assists them with applications. Lumiere is based on earlier work on probabilistic models of user goals to support the display of customized information to pilots of commercial aircraft, as well as user modeling for display control for flight engineers at NASA's Mission Control Center. These earlier projects, sponsored by the NASA-Ames Research Center and NASA's Johnson Space Center, were undertaken while some of the Lumiere researchers were students at Stanford University.[28]

Patent trends suggest that AI technology is being incorporated into growing numbers of commercial products. The number of patents in AI, expert systems, and neural networks jumped from fewer than 20 in 1988 to more than 120 in 1996, and the number of patents citing patents in these areas grew from about 140 to almost 800.[29] The number of AI-related patents (including patents in AI, expert systems, neural networks, intelligent systems, adaptive agents, and adaptive systems) issued annually in the United States increased exponentially from approximately 100 in 1985 to more than 900 in 1996 (see Figure 9.1). Changes in the U.S. Patent and Trademark Office's rules on the patentability of algorithms have no doubt contributed to this growth, as has the increased commercial value of AI technology. The vast majority of these patents are held by private firms, including large manufacturers of electronics and computers, as well as major users of information technology (see Table 9.4). These data indicate that AI technology is likely to be embedded in larger systems, from computers to cars to manufacturing lines, rather than used as stand-alone products.

A central problem confronting the wider commercialization of AI today revolves around integration. Both the software and the hardware developed by the AI research community were so advanced that their integration into older, more conservative computer and organizational

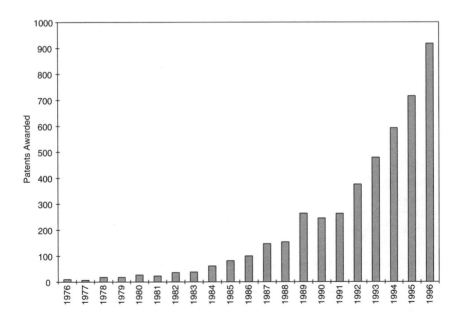

FIGURE 9.1 Artificial-intelligence-related patents awarded per year, 1976-1996. SOURCE: Compiled from data in the U.S. Patent and Trademark Office's U.S. Patent Bibliographic Database, available online at <http://patents.uspto.gov>; and the IBM Patent Server, available online at <http://patent.womplex.ibm.com>.

TABLE 9.4 Leading Holders of Patents Related to
Artificial Intelligence, 1976-1997

Assignee	Number of Patents
IBM	297
Hitachi	192
Motorola	114
Mitsubishi	94
Toshiba	92
General Electric	91
NEC Corp.	73
Taligent	67
Toyota	60
U.S. Phillips Corp.	59
Fujitsu Ltd	58
Lucent Technologies	57
Ford Motor Co.	53
Digital Equipment Corp.	53
Westinghouse Electric	48
Eastman-Kodak	44
AT&T	44
Hughes Aircraft Co.	42
Matsushita	42
Texas Instruments	42

NOTE: The patents included artificial intelligence, expert systems,
neural networks, intelligent systems, adaptive agents, and adaptive
systems.
SOURCES: U.S. Patent and Trademark Office database, available
online at <http://patents.uspto.gov>; IBM Corp. patent database,
available online at <http://patent.womplex.ibm.com>.

systems proved to be an enormous challenge. As one observer has noted,
"Because AI was a leading-edge technology, it arrived in this world too
early. As a consequence, the AI application community had to ride many
waves of technological quick fixes and fads. . . . Many of these integration
problems are now being addressed head on by a broad community of
information technologists using Internet-based frameworks such as
CORBA [common object request broker architecture] and the World Wide
Web" (Shrobe, 1996).

The rapid development of computer hardware and software, the networking of information systems, and the need to make these systems
function smoothly and intelligently are leading to wide diffusion of AI
knowledge and technology across the infrastructure of the information
age. Federal funding reflects these changes (see Box 9.4). Meanwhile,
much of the knowledge acquired through AI research over the years is

now being brought to bear on real-world problems and applications while also being deepened and broadened. The economic and social benefits are enormous. Technologies such as expert systems, natural-language processing, and computer vision are now used in a range of applications, such as decision aids, planning tools, speech-recognition systems, pattern recognition, knowledge representation, and computer-controlled robots.[30]

BOX 9.4
DARPA's Current Artificial Intelligence Program

At DARPA, funding for AI research is spread among a number of program areas, each with a specific application focus. For example, funding for AI is included in the Intelligent Systems and Software program, which received roughly $60 million in 1995. This applied research program is intended to leverage work in intelligent systems and software that supports military objectives, enabling information systems to assist in decision-making tasks in stressful, time-sensitive situations. Areas of emphasis include intelligent systems, software development technology, and manufacturing automation and design engineering. Intelligent systems encompass autonomous systems, interactive problem solving, and intelligent integration of information.[1]

Additional DARPA funding for AI is contained in the Intelligent Integration of Information (I3) program, which is intended to improve commanders' awareness of battlefield conditions by developing and demonstrating technology that integrates data from heterogeneous sources. Specific goals include a 100-fold reduction in the time needed to retrieve information from large, dynamically changing databases, as well as the development, demonstration, and transition to the services of tools that will reduce the time needed to develop, maintain, and evolve large-scale integrated data systems.[2] The program supports basic computer sciences, specifically in AI relevant to integration, technology development, prototyping, demonstrations, and early phases of technology transfer.

DARPA continues to fund some basic research in AI as well. Such funding is included in its information sciences budget, which declined from $35 million to $22 million annually between 1991 and 1996. The AI funding supports work in software technology development, human-computer interfaces, microelectronics, and speech recognition and understanding, in addition to intelligent systems. The work on intelligent systems focuses on advanced techniques for knowledge representation, reasoning, and machine learning, which enable computer understanding of spoken and written language and images. Also included are advanced methods for planning, scheduling, and resource allocation.

---

[1]This definition was obtained from the *FY 97 Implementation Plan* on the Web site of the National Science and Technology Council's Committee on Computing, Information, and Communications at <http://www.ccic.gov/pubs/imp97/14.html>.
[2]This information was obtained from the project description ("Intelligent Integration of Information") on DARPA's Web site at <http://web-ext2.darpa.mil/iso/i3/about/main.html>.

AI technologies help industry diagnose machine failures, design new products, and plan, simulate, and schedule production. They help scientists search large databases and decode DNA sequences, and they help doctors make more-informed decisions about diagnosis and treatment of particular ailments. AI technologies also make the larger systems into which they are incorporated easier to use and more productive. These benefits are relatively easy to identify, but measuring them is difficult.

Federal investments in AI have produced a number of notable results, some envisioned by the founders of the field and others probably not even imagined. Without question, DARPA's generous, enduring funding of various aspects of AI research created a scientific research discipline that meets the standard criteria of discipline formation laid out by sociologists of science.[31] At least three major academic centers of excellence and several other significant centers were established, and they produced a large number of graduates with Ph.D.s who diffused AI research to other research universities, cross-pollinated the major research centers, and moved AI methods into commercial markets. (Figure 9.2 shows the production of Ph.D. degrees in AI and related fields at U.S. universities.

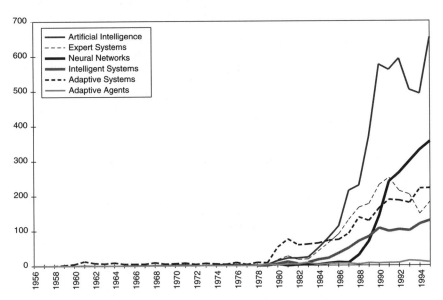

FIGURE 9.2 Ph.D. dissertations submitted annually in artificial intelligence and related fields, 1956-1995.
SOURCE: Data from Dissertation Abstracts Online, which is available through subscription to the OCLC Firstsearch database from UMI Company.

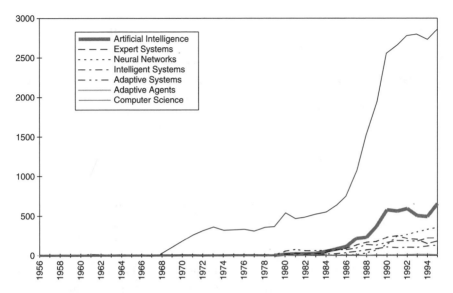

FIGURE 9.3 Number of Ph.D. dissertations submitted annually in AI and related fields and in computer science, 1956-1995.
SOURCE: Data from Dissertation Abstracts Online, which is available through subscription to the OCLC Firstsearch database from UMI Company.

Figure 9.3 compares Ph.D. production in AI and related disciplines to degree production in computer science more broadly.) In sum, the returns on the public investment are clearly enormous, both in matters of national security (which are beyond the scope of this study)[32] and in contributions to the U.S. economy.

LESSONS FROM HISTORY

As this case study demonstrates, federal funding is critical in establishing new disciplines because it can sustain long-term, high-risk research areas and nurture a critical mass of technical and human resources. DARPA helped legitimize the AI field and served as the major source of research funds beginning in the 1960s. It created centers of excellence that evolved into today's major computer science research centers. This support was particularly critical given that some objectives took much longer to realize than was originally anticipated.

A diversity of approaches to research problems can be critical to the development of practical tools. A prime example is the field of speech recognition, in which the most effective products to date have used techniques borrowed from the mathematics and statistics communities rather than more traditional AI techniques. This outcome could not have been predicted and demonstrates the importance of supporting competing approaches, even those outside the mainstream.

Federal funding has promoted innovation in commercial products such as expert systems, the establishment of new companies, the growth of billion-dollar markets for technologies such as speech recognition, and the development of valuable military applications. AI technologies often enhance the performance of the larger systems into which they are increasingly incorporated.

There is a creative tension between fundamental research and attempts to create functional devices. Original attempts to design intelligent, thinking machines motivated fundamental work that created a base of knowledge. Initial advances achieved through research were not sufficient to produce, by themselves, commercial products, but they could be integrated with other components and exploited in different applications. Efforts to apply AI technology often failed initally because they uncovered technical problems that had not yet been adequately addressed. Applications were fed back into the research process, thus motivating inquiries into new areas.

NOTES

1. Several histories of AI research have appeared over the last 25 years, some written by members of the AI community, some published by those outside the field, and still others produced by science journalists. These histories have been based largely on the published scientific literature, journalistic accounts of work in the field, published accounts of participants in the field, and interviews with participants. With some notable exceptions, few of these histories have relied on original source materials, such as manuscript records of participants or their funding agencies or editors.

2. The 1997 victory of IBM Corporation's Deep Blue Computer over world chess champion Gary Kasparov demonstrates the public's interest in AI. In the days leading up to the match and throughout the match itself, almost every major U.S. newspaper, news magazine, and television news or magazine program carried news and feature articles about the match and AI research in general.

3. Papers presented at the conference were published by Shannon and McCarthy (1956).

4. Minsky had an impressive background: a bachelor's degree in mathematics from Harvard University (1950); a doctorate in mathematics from Princeton University (1954); and the title of junior fellow, Harvard Society of Fellows (1954-1957). His 1954 dissertation was entitled "Neural Nets and the Brain Model Problem." The paper he presented at the 1952 conference was entitled "Some Universal Elements for Finite Automata." His early work at Lincoln Laboratory (Minsky, 1956) dealt with AI.

5. Rochester was the chief designer of IBM's 701 computer.

6. Dated August 31, 1955, "A Proposal for the Dartmouth Summer Research Project on Artificial Intelligence" was actually submitted, along with a cover letter to Morison, on September 2, 1955, according to the Rockefeller Foundation Archives grant files. An edited and lightly annotated version of this proposal can be found online at <http://www-formal.stanford.edu/jmc/history/dartmouth/dartmouth.html>.

7. This quote comes from an article entitled "LISP Prehistory—Summer 1956 through Summer 1958," which can be found online at <http://www-formal.stanford.edu/jmc/history/lisp/node2.html#SECTION00020000000000000000>. See also McCarthy (1981).

8. Indeed, McCarthy's first memorandum on LISP (dated September 16, 1958) survives only because Rochester saved and annotated it. Rochester was the author of at least one of the foundational LISP memoranda; his Memo 5, November 18, 1958, provides clear evidence of Rochester's intellectual contributions to LISP. For an interesting treatment of LISP's history, see "Early LISP History (1956-1959)" by Herbert Stoyan, available online at <http://www8.informatik.uni-erlangen.de/html/lisp/histlit1.html>.

9. Rochester also published papers on AI (e.g., Rochester and Gelernter, 1958).

10. The founding of GSIA and its "new look" are described by Gleeson and Schlossman (1994).

11. The early history of RAND is described by Smith (1966), Jardini (1996), Hounshell (1997), and Collins (1998).

12. This report describes the Logic Theorist and the IPL2 list processing language (developed with J.C. Shaw) for the Johnniac. See also Newell, Simon, and Shaw (1957).

13. The history of the Johnniac is recounted by Gruenberger (1979).

14. Another of Simon's doctoral students, Edward Feigenbaum, as part of his 1960 doctoral dissertation developed a theory of human perception, memory, and learning and then modeled these processes successfully in his EPAM program. This program is still regarded as a major contribution both to theories of human intelligence and to AI research.

15. This quote comes from an article entitled "The Implementation of LISP" available online at <http://www-formal.stanford.edu/jmc/history/lisp/node3.html#SECTION00030000000000000000>.

16. The history and design of both the Logic Theorist and GPS are described by Newell and Simon (1972).

17. For example, bold predictions about the future of AI were made by Simon and Newell (1958); Simon, Newell, and Shaw (1958); Simon (1965); Minsky (1956, 1979).

18. DARPA definitely created a two-tier system in AI research, with CMU, MIT, Stanford University, and SRI occupying the top tier. The second tier included the University of Massachusetts, University of Maryland, Brown University, University of Pennsylvania, New York University, Columbia University, Rutgers University, University of Texas, and University of Illinois.

19. This was the so-called Pierce Committee, named after its chairperson J.R. Pierce, who, according to Roberts, said it would be impossible to make a com-

puter understand human speech (Roberts, "Expanding AI Research"). A researcher at Bell Laboratories (where important speech recognition research had been done for decades), Pierce published an infamous letter to the editor of the *Journal of the Acoustical Society of America* in 1969 in which he railed against the "mad scientist and untrustworthy engineers" who believed that the development of a flexible, continuous speech recognition system was possible (Pierce, 1969).

20.   One of the characteristics of AI that sets it apart from many other research domains of computer science is the degree to which the objectives can be described in general, nontechnical language that makes measuring performance difficult (e.g., an objective might be to make a machine that thinks or learns). Although specific metrics often can be developed, this may require a conscious effort by program managers and researchers.

21.   Considerable controversy surrounded this decision and its motivations. J.C.R. Licklider claimed the project was turned off because "it didn't really prove itself by coming up with a conspicuously good demonstrable device. There was a lot of feeling that speech understanding was a bit ahead of its time, and DARPA did a good thing by stimulating the field but it wasn't really time yet to drive for a workable system. In this case, the speech project met its main objectives, but that wasn't enough to save it" (Licklider, 1988a). Some observers suggest that the demise of the SUR program illustrates "the dangers of prematurely imposing short-term goals and milestones on an underdeveloped field of research" such as speech recognition (Stefik, 1985). Marvin Denicoff, then at ONR, believed so strongly in the speech program and what it could do for future researchers that he convinced Robert Kahn, director of IPTO from 1979 to 1985, to fund a project to study SUR—to "take a year or two out, visit all the sites and create a document of everything that had been accomplished and what the issues were, what the failures were, and what the positives were" (Denicoff, 1988). The results were the ONR reports by W. Lea and J. Shoup (1979) and W. Lea (1980).

22.   Here the allusion is to the work of Frederick Jelinek and the speech research group at IBM, which contributed enormously to the technology through statistical language modeling (e.g., N-gram models). Other firms that not only pursued speech recognition research but also entered commercial markets with related products included Verbex Voice Systems and Texas Instruments.

23.   For example, L.E. Baum and J.A. Eagon of the Institute for Defense Analyses have been credited with introducing HMM theory (Makhoul and Schwartz, 1994). See also Baum and Eagon (1967). Moreover, even within CMU, the decision to use HMMs in speech recognition was, according to a recent analysis, "[w]ay out of step with the mainstream [of AI thought at CMU]. . . . The system had no knowledge of English grammar, no knowledge base, no rule-based expert system, no intelligence. Nothing but numbers" (Garfinkel, 1998).

24.   The Mansfield Amendment was passed as part of the Defense Authorization Act of 1970 (Public Law 91-121) on November 19, 1969.

25.   As noted in Chapter 4, several of the DOD's basic research programs in computer science were transferred to the National Science Foundation as a result of the Mansfield Amendment.

26.   The Mansfield Amendment and the spirit of the times in which it was passed also established the conditions under which some members of the Con-

gress would raise questions about AI research, particularly with regard to its focus on the playing of games such as chess and checkers but extending to the research on speech understanding, which is discussed in Box 9.2.

27. Fleck (1982) also said the Lighthill report "led to a considerable sharpening of the focus of AI research." Not all leaders in AI research agree with Fleck's assessment of the impact of the report. Amarel (1988), for example, maintained that "it didn't affect this country."

28. For more information, see Microsoft's home page at <www.research. microsoft.com/research/dtg/horovitz/lum.htm>.

29. These data were obtained from the U.S. Patent and Trademark Office database, available online at <http://patents.uspto.gov>, and IBM's patent database, also available online at <http://patent.womplex.ibm.com>.

30. These technologies are the results of the efforts of AI researchers as well as researchers in other, related fields.

31. See, for example, Fleck (1982).

32. A report by the American Association for Artificial Intelligence (1994) paraphrased a former director of ARPA in saying that DART (the intelligent system used for troop and materiel deployment for Operation Desert Shield and Operation Desert Storm in 1990 and 1991) "justified ARPA's entire investment in artificial-intelligence technology." (The report is also available on the association's Web site at <http://www.aaai.org/Policy/Papers/arpa-report.html>).

10

Virtual Reality Comes of Age

Virtual reality (VR) is a highly multidisciplinary field of computing that emerged from research on three-dimensional interactive graphics and vehicle simulation in the late 1960s and early 1970s.[1] For much of its early development, VR often seemed more like science fiction than science, but it is now transforming fields such as military training, entertainment, and medicine. Applications range from navigation systems that enable pilots and air traffic controllers to operate in dense fog[2] to fully digital design environments for creating new car models[3] (see Box 10.1).

This chapter focuses on research and development (R&D) in computer graphics and related technologies that contributed to the emergence of VR as a practical technology. In particular, it examines the diversity of funding agencies, missions, and environments, as well as the strong interactions between public and private research and personnel, that have promoted advances in the field. The analysis is not intended to be comprehensive but rather concentrates on selected topics that illuminate the R&D process. It highlights medical and entertainment applications of VR because they demonstrate interesting aspects of the innovation process. The emphasis on head-mounted displays is not meant to downplay the significance of other VR technologies that are not addressed, such as the large projection environments at the National Center for Supercomputing Applications at the University of Illinois at Urbana-Champaign.[4] The research on head-mounted displays is but one illustration of the many ways in which federally sponsored research programs have influenced the VR field.

BOX 10.1
What Is Virtual Reality?

Virtual reality (VR) refers to a set of techniques for creating synthetic, computer-generated environments in which human operators can become immersed. In VR systems, human operators are connected to computers that can simulate a wide variety of worlds, both real and imaginary, and can interact with those worlds through a variety of sensory channels and manipulators (National Research Council, 1995, pp. 247-303). Simple VR systems include home video games that produce three-dimensional (3D) graphical displays and stereo sound and are controlled by an operator using a joystick or computer keyboard. More sophisticated systems—such as those used for pilot training and immersive entertainment experiences—can include head-mounted displays or large projection screens for displaying images, 3D sound, and treadmills that allow operators to walk through the virtual environment.

Such systems are increasingly being used in a variety of applications, from telecommunications and information visualization to health care, education and training, product design, manufacturing, marketing, and entertainment. Among other things, they enable operators to explore foreign cities from the comfort of their own homes, train for hazardous missions, develop new surgical procedures, and test new product designs.

VR is the outcome of a complex alignment of research fields that include computer graphics, image processing, computer vision, computer-aided design, geometric modeling, user-interface design, and physiological psychology. It also incorporates robotics; haptics and force feedback; computer architectures and systems development; entire new generations of processors, graphics boards, and accelerators; and a host of software applications converted to firmware in computers for rendering data visually. Finally, VR also involves work on high-speed data transmission and networks.

This case history demonstrates that federal support has been the single most important source of sustained funding for innovative research in both computer graphics and VR. Beginning in the 1960s with its investments in computer modeling, flight simulators, and visualization techniques, and continuing through current developments in virtual worlds, the federal government has made significant investments in military, civilian, and university research that laid the groundwork for one of today's most dynamic technologies. The commercial payoffs have included numerous companies formed around federally funded research in graphics and VR.

The first section of the chapter briefly outlines the origins of VR. The next seven sections, which are organized in roughly chronological order, discuss early development of the academic talent pool, the private sector's cautious initial approach, the role of synergy in launching visionary VR research, a breakthrough that provided initial building blocks for a commercial VR infrastructure, the mixture of research projects that led to biomedical applications, the role of entertainment applications in expanding use of VR, and the growing role of military R&D in producing commercial spin-offs. The last section of the chapter summarizes the lessons learned from history.

LAUNCHING THE GRAPHICS AND
VIRTUAL REALITY REVOLUTION

The earliest use of a computer-generated graphical display on a cathode ray tube (CRT) was in Project Whirlwind, a project sponsored by the U.S. Navy to develop a general-purpose flight simulator (see Chapter 4). By the late 1940s, Robert Everett at the Massachusetts Institute of Technology (MIT) had developed a light gun that could cause the CRT to react. Researchers on SAGE, the successor to Whirlwind, made extensive use of interactive graphics consoles with displays equipped with a light gun capable of sending signals coordinated with the display. By 1955, U.S. Air Force personnel working on SAGE were using light guns for data manipulation.

These and other early projects convinced a number of researchers that the capability to interact with a computer in real time through a graphical representation was a powerful tool for making complex information understandable. In the late 1950s and early 1960s, several government agencies, including the National Science Foundation (NSF), National Institutes of Health (NIH), National Aeronautics and Space Administration (NASA), and various divisions within the Department of Defense (DOD), began funding research to address an array of computer graphics problems, including the development of input/output devices and programming.

The total funding for these early programs was comparatively small. For example, the NSF allocated about 8 percent of its annual computing research budget to computer graphics between 1966 and 1985. Its graphics-related expenditures rose from $93,000 to $1.8 million annually during this period.[5] Another source of funding for computer graphics research during these years was the Information Processing Techniques Office (IPTO) of the DOD's Defense Advanced Research Projects Agency (DARPA, known at times as ARPA). The IPTO support for the development of interactive graphics was concentrated at MIT, Carnegie Mellon University, and especially the University of Utah, which received $10 million in IPTO support for interactive graphics research between 1968 and 1975 (Stockham and Newell, 1975; Van Atta et al., 1991a,b). University programs were only loosely coupled to deliverable systems but supported visionary ideas and the training of students to pursue them.

The eventual payoffs from these small initial investments were enormous. The government support established an infrastructure for the computer graphics field through university-based research and training in fundamental science. These centers identified key research and technical problems, developed sample solutions, created tools and methods, and, above all, produced cadres of students, researchers, and teachers who became the leading practitioners in the field. The graduates of the federally supported academic programs have made substantial contributions not only to many areas of science, technology, and medicine, but also to the intellectual and artistic culture of the late 20th century. They have also launched companies that laid the foundations for a worldwide market for computer graphics worth $40 billion in 1997.

SEEDING THE ACADEMIC TALENT POOL

Among the greatest contributions of the federal government has been support for the development of human resources. (Associations also played a role in building the graphics community, as illustrated in Box 10.2). An early pioneer, Steven Coons, benefited from federal support of research at MIT that helped realize his vision of interactive computer graphics as a powerful design tool. During World War II, Coons worked on the design of aircraft surfaces, developing the mathematics to describe generalized surface patches. An early advocate of the use of computers in mechanical engineering, Coons taught in the Mechanical Engineering Department at MIT during the 1950s and 1960s, where he inspired his students with the vision of creating interactive computer graphics to assist design (Coons, 1967). Among the students he inspired were Ivan Sutherland and Lawrence Roberts, both of whom went on to make numerous contributions to computer graphics and (in Roberts' case) to computer networks. Both men also served as directors of IPTO.

Working in the early 1960s on the TX-2 at MIT's Lincoln Laboratory, which was equipped with an interactive display tube, Sutherland developed a graphics system called Sketchpad as his dissertation in 1963. Sketchpad was an interactive design tool for the creation, manipulation, and display of geometric objects in two-dimensional (2D) or three-dimensional (3D) space. The system could sketch with a light pen on the face of the CRT, position objects, change their size, square up corners, create multiple copies of objects, and paste them into an evolving design. Sketchpad was the first system to explore the data management techniques required for interactive graphics.

Roberts, meanwhile, wrote the first algorithm to eliminate hidden or obscured surfaces from a perspective picture (Roberts, 1963). In 1965, Roberts implemented a homogeneous coordinate scheme for transforma-

---

BOX 10.2
Community Building

Many researchers credit the group SIGGRAPH with helping to build a strong community of graphics researchers that propelled the field forward rapidly. SIG-GRAPH, which is the Association for Computing Machinery's Special Interest Group on Graphics, facilitates the exchange of ideas among researchers and technology developers through conferences and publications in an attempt to advance the technology of computer graphics and interactive techniques. It introduces the latest topics in computer graphics through conference courses and other educational activities, including development and distribution of curriculum materials.

SIGGRAPH attracts a diverse range of members, from computer scientists specializing in computer graphics and visualization, to business leaders and artists who use graphics as a means to further their craft. Interaction among such diverse members can help technology developers better understand the needs of users and promote advances in the capabilities of graphics technology. An annual conference has become a central location for the exchange of ideas and demonstration of developmental systems. Numerous academic and industry researchers publish papers in SIG-GRAPH journals and conference proceedings. Edwin Catmull has called SIGGRAPH a "tremendous community" and credits its collaborative spirit and broad-based constituency with helping to accelerate the development of computer graphics. [1]

---

[1]Presentation by Edwin Catmull, chief technical officer, Pixar Animation Studios, at the Computer Science and Telecommunications Board workshop, "Modeling and Simulation: Competitiveness Through Collaboration," October 19, 1996, Irvine, CA.

---

tions and perspective. His solutions to these problems prompted attempts over the next decade to find faster algorithms for generating hidden surfaces (Roberts, 1965).

Sutherland expanded the talent pool everywhere he went. First MIT, then Harvard University (especially after Sutherland's return from his stint as IPTO director in 1966), and, following Sutherland's move there in 1968, the University of Utah became the major academic centers of early work in interactive graphics. In particular, the period from the late 1960s through the late 1970s was a golden era of computer graphics at Utah. Students and faculty in Utah's ARPA-funded program contributed to the growth of a number of exploratory systems in computer graphics and the identification of key problems for future work (Table 10.1).

Among their notable activities were efforts to develop fast algorithms for removing hidden surfaces from 3D graphics images, a problem identified as a key computational bottleneck (Sutherland et al., 1974). Students of the Utah program made two important contributions in this field, in-

TABLE 10.1 Select Alumni of the University of Utah's Computer Graphics Program

Name	Affiliation	Accomplishments
Alan Kay	Ph.D. 1969	Developed the notion of a graphical user interface at Xerox PARC, which led to the design of Apple MacIntosh computers. Developed SmallTalk. Fellow at Apple Computer.
John Warnock	Ph.D. 1969	Worked on the ILLIAC 4 Project, a spaceflight simulator, and airplane simulators at Evans & Sutherland. Developed the Warnock recursive subdivision algorithm for hidden surface elimination. Founder of Adobe Systems, which developed the Postscript language for desktop publishing.
Nolan Bushnell	B.S. 1969	Developed the table tennis game Pong, which in 1972 launched the video game industry. Founder of Atari, which became the leading company in video games by 1982.
Charles Seitz	Faculty 1970-1973	Pioneer in asynchronous circuits. Co-designer of the first graphics machine, LDS-1 (Line Drawing System). Designed the Cosmic Cube machine as a research prototype that led to the design of the Intel iPSC. Founder of Myricom Corp.
Henri Gouraud	Ph.D. 1971	Developed the Gouraud shading method for polygon smoothing—a simple rendering method that dramatically improved the appearance of objects.
Edwin Catmull	Ph.D. 1974	Pioneer in computer animation. Developed the first computer animation course in the world. Co-founder of Pixar Animation Studios, a leading computer graphics company that has worked for LucasFilm and was recently involved in the production of the movie *Toy Story*. Received a technical Academy Award (with Tom Porter, Tom Duff, and Alvy Ray Smith) in 1996 for "pioneering inventions in Digital Image Compositing."
James Clark	Ph.D. 1974	Rebuilt the head-mounted display and 3D wand to see and interact with three-dimensional graphic spaces. Former faculty member at Stanford University. Founder of Silicon Graphics Incorporated and chairman of Netscape Communications Corporation.

TABLE 10.1 *Continued*

Name	Affiliation	Accomplishments
Bui Tuong-Phong	Ph.D. 1975	Invented the Phong shading method for capturing highlights in graphical images by modeling specular reflection. Phong's lighting model is still one of the most widely used methods for illumination in computer graphics.
Henry Fuchs	Ph.D. 1975	Federico Gil Professor, University of North Carolina at Chapel Hill. Research in high-performance graphics hardware; three-dimensional medical imaging; head-mounted display and virtual environments. Founder of Pixel Planes.
Martin Newell	Ph.D. 1975; Faculty 1977-1979	Developed procedural modeling for object rendering. Co-developed the Painter's algorithm for surface rendering. Founder of Ashlar Incorporated, which develops computer-assisted design software.
James Blinn	Ph.D. 1978	Invented the first method for representing surface textures in graphical images. Scientist at Jet Propulsion Laboratory, where he worked on computer animation of the Voyager flybys.
James Kajiya	Ph.D. 1979	Developed the frame buffer concept for storing and displaying single-raster images.

cluding an area search method by Warnock (1969) and a scan-line algorithm that was developed by Watkins (1970) and constructed into a hardware system. Perhaps the most important breakthrough was Henri Gouraud's development of a simple scheme for continuous shading (Gouraud, 1971). Unlike polygonal shading, in which an entire polygon (a standard surface representation) was a single level of gray, Gouraud's scheme involved interpolation between points on a surface to describe continuous shading across a single polygon, thus achieving a closer approximation of reality. The effect made a surface composed of discrete polygons appear to be continuous.

The work of these individuals alone reflects the high level of fundamental research performed under federal sponsorship in a variety of graphics fields, including surface rendering, simulations, computer animation, graphical user interface design, and early steps toward VR. No less than 11 commercial firms, several of which ship more than $100 million in products annually, trace their origins to the Utah program.[6]

VIRTUAL REALITY IN THE PRIVATE SECTOR: APPROACH WITH CAUTION

Industry and private research centers played an important role in the early development of interactive graphics. But an examination of several key players—Bell Laboratories, the Mathematical Applications Group Incorporated (MAGI), and General Electric Company (GE)—illustrates that the private sector, even when it has federal funding for isolated projects, cannot support development of nascent technologies requiring high-risk research with uncertain payoffs. Indeed, even when a company contributes lucrative new technologies to the field, the government is often the key to sustaining progress over time (see Box 10.3).

Bell Laboratories had one group of researchers, including Michael Noll, Bela Julesz, and C. Bosche, working on computer-animated stereo

---

BOX 10.3
The Rise and Fall of Atari

Atari, founded by University of Utah graduate Nolan Bushnell, was once the fastest-growing company in the United States. Started in 1972 with an initial investment of $500, Atari attained sales exceeding $500 million in 1980. During the late 1970s and early 1980s, Atari was a center for exciting developments in software and chip design for the home entertainment market. A joint venture with LucasFilm in 1982, in which Atari licensed and manufactured games designed by LucasFilm, established cross-pollination between video games and film studios.

Several pioneering figures in the VR field got their start at Atari. For instance, Warren Robinett, who has directed the head-mounted display and nano-manipulator projects at the University of North Carolina in Chapel Hill, developed the popular video game *Adventure* at Atari in the late 1970s. Jaron Lanier got his start by creating the video game *Moondust.* He used the profits to launch VPL-Research in 1984, the first commercial VR company. In 1980 Atari created its own research center, directed by Alan Kay, who came from Xerox PARC and assembled a team of the best and brightest in the field of interface design and VR research.

But Atari fell on hard times. Not long after its banner year in 1980, Atari registered $536 million in losses for 1983. The Atari Research Laboratory was a casualty of the economic crash in the video game industry (and computer industry more generally). Most of the people working in VR at Atari either migrated to work on VR projects in federal laboratories, or, like Jaron Lanier, landed government contracts. Lanier won a contract to build the DataGlove for NASA.

Industry was clearly not prepared, after sustaining such a big economic blow, to continue the development of VR technology on its own. Indeed Lanier's failed efforts to market a consumer entertainment version of the DataGlove, called Power-Glove, for Nintendo, demonstrated that the 1980s was not the right time for a sustained industry push. Federal support was crucial to building the array of hardware and software necessary for industry to step in and move VR forward.

movies, and another group, including Ken Knowlton, Leon Harmon, and Manfred Schroeder, working on pixel graphics methods for digitizing still images, gray-scale techniques, and rule-directed animation. Knowlton also produced an important animation language, called BEFLIX, which permitted the creation and modification of gray-scale pixel images.

MAGI, headed by Phillip Mittleman, was supported by military contracts for projects simulating equipment behavior. MAGI developed a hidden-surface algorithm along with a user language, Synthavision, which sent output to a specially built monitor for microfilming through color filters. The system provided a user-oriented syntax for making computer animation, and it was important for creating film footage for advertising.

The GE group built the first real-time, full-color, interactive flight simulator, a project funded by a NASA contract for the manned space program (Rouselot and Schumacker, 1967).[7] The simulator, completed in 1967, permitted up to 40 solid objects to be displayed in full color, with hidden surfaces removed and visible surfaces shaded to approximate reflected illumination. The entire display was updated in real time, depending on a trainee's actions on the controls. This GE system was the prototype for a new generation of training simulators that integrated computer-driven synthetic visual environments with interactive tactile feedback.

Although GE had a well-endowed in-house research infrastructure of venerable standing, the company took a cautious approach to this new area of research. GE Aerospace did not market its early image-generating systems to customers other than the federal government, nor did it initiate its own program to develop VR. GE did spin off a commercially successful system called Genigraphics, a full-color, interactive, 2D slide-generating system aimed at the commercial audiovisual market. And of course, GE did continue contract work on image generators for flight simulators, including its highly rated Compu-Scene IV system, which "practically stole the market in high-end military flight simulation and training in 1984 when [it] introduced photographic-quality texturing to real-time graphics."[8]

GE also pursued medical imaging. Its Medical Systems Laboratory has been a major manufacturer of medical imaging systems, from x-ray machines to ultrasound, computerized tomography (CT), magnetic resonance imaging (MRI), and positron emission tomography (PET) systems. In addition, GE scientists have made distinguished contributions to the published literature on scientific and medical visualization. For example, the "marching cubes" algorithm developed by William E. Lorensen and Harvey E. Cline of the Electronic Systems Laboratory at the GE Research and Development Center is one of the most fundamental algorithms for high-resolution, 3D surface reconstruction from CT, MRI, or SPECT data

(Lorensen and Cline, 1987).[9] Graphics work of this sort has been regarded by GE as central to the development of new imaging systems.

Significantly, GE's achievements in this area have benefited from university collaborations and federal support. An example is the recent arrangement between GE Medical Systems and the University of Chicago involving the GE digital detector system, a 10-year, $100 million R&D effort that has been the basis of a portfolio of medical imaging and computer-aided detection systems involving more than 100 scientists and resulting in 80 patents (General Electric, 1997). The GE technology will be used by the University of Chicago Medical Center in a long-term project supported by the National Cancer Institute, American Cancer Society, U.S. Army, and Whitaker Foundation to develop a platform for computer-aided diagnosis, which provides the radiologist with guidance for reading a mammographic image.[10]

The GE experience demonstrates the difficulty faced by private firms in funding long-term research that is not directly related to ongoing product development efforts. Industry seldom funds research that is expected to take more than 5 to 7 years to produce tangible results, although firms can misjudge how long it will take to develop a marketable product from new technology. And, some firms do support limited research with longer time horizons (see Chapter 5 for a discussion of long-term research). In its press releases on the Digital Detector System, GE emphasizes that this 10-year project is the largest development project in company history. Commercial VR, by comparison, has taken 30 years to mature.

None of the companies discussed in this section (Bell Laboratories, MAGI, or GE) pursued commercial applications of VR. MAGI left the graphics field completely, failing to sustain a research capability in computer animation and simulation even though it helped launch the field.[11] Both Bell Laboratories and GE abandoned work on commercial simulation systems in spite of commanding early positions in the field. It is not difficult to see why. VR is one of those fields that Ivan Sutherland would christen "holy grails"—fields involving the synthesis of many separate, expensive, and risky lines of innovation in a future too far distant and with returns too unpredictable to justify the long-term investment.

SYNERGY LAUNCHES THE QUEST FOR THE "HOLY GRAIL"

Work on head-mounted displays illustrates the synergy between the applications-focused environments of industry and government-funded (both military and civilian) projects and the fundamental research focus of university work that spills across disciplinary boundaries. Work on head-mounted displays benefited from extensive interaction and cross-fertilization of ideas among federally funded, mission-oriented military projects and contracts as well as private-sector initiatives. The players included NASA Ames, Armstrong Aerospace Medical Research Laboratory of the Air Force, Wright-Patterson Air Force Base, and, more recently, DOD programs on modeling and simulation, such as the Synthetic Theater of War program. Each of these projects generated a stream of published papers, technical reports, software (some of which became commercially available), computer-animated films, and even hardware that was accessible to other graphics researchers. Other important ideas for the head-mounted display came from Knowlton and Schroeder's work at Bell Laboratories, the approach to real-time hidden-line solutions by the MAGI group, and the GE simulator project (Sutherland, 1968).

Early work on head-mounted displays took place at Bell Helicopter Company. Designed to be worn by pilots, the Bell display received input from a servo-controlled infrared camera, which was mounted on the bottom of a helicopter. The camera moved as the pilot's head moved, and the pilot's field of view was the same as the camera's. This system was intended to give military helicopter pilots the capability to land at night in rough terrain. The helicopter experiments demonstrated that a human could become totally immersed in a remote environment through the eyes of a camera.

The power of this immersive technology was demonstrated in an example cited by Sutherland (1968). A camera was mounted on the roof of a building, with its field of view focused on two persons playing catch. The head-mounted display was worn by a viewer inside the building, who followed the motion of the ball, moving the camera by using head movements. Suddenly, the ball was thrown at the camera (on the roof), and the viewer (inside the building) ducked. When the camera panned the horizon, the viewer reported seeing a panoramic skyline. When the camera looked down to reveal that it was "standing" on a plank extended off the roof of the building, the viewer panicked!

In 1966, Ivan Sutherland moved from ARPA to Harvard University as an associate professor in applied mathematics. At ARPA, Sutherland had helped implement J.C.R. Licklider's vision of human-computer interaction, and he returned to academe to pursue his own efforts to extend human capabilities. Sutherland and a student, Robert Sproull, turned the "remote reality" vision systems of the Bell Helicopter project into VR by replacing the camera with computer-generated images.[12] The first such computer environment was no more than a wire-frame room with the cardinal directions—north, south, east, and west—initialed on the walls. The viewer could "enter" the room by way of the "west" door and turn to look out windows in the other three directions. What was then called the head-mounted display later became known as VR.

Sutherland's experiments built on the network of personal and professional contacts he had developed at MIT and ARPA. Funding for Sutherland's project came from a variety of military, academic, and industry sources. The Central Intelligence Agency provided $80,000, and additional funding was provided by ARPA, the Office of Naval Research, and Bell Laboratories. Equipment was provided by Bell Helicopter. A PDP-1 computer was provided by the Air Force and an ultrasonic head-position acoustic sensor was provided by MIT Lincoln Laboratory, also under an ARPA contract.

Sutherland outlined a number of forms of interactive graphics that later became popular, including augmented reality, in which synthetic, computer-generated images are superimposed on a realistic image of a scene. He used this form of VR in attempting a practical medical application of the head-mounted display. The first published research project deploying the 3D display addressed problems of representing hemodynamic flow in models of prosthetic heart valves. The idea was to generate the results of calculations involving physical laws of fluid mechanics and a variety of numerical analysis techniques to generate a synthetic object that one could walk toward and move into or around (Greenfield et al., 1971).

As Sutherland later recalled, there was clearly no chance of immediately realizing his initial vision for the head-mounted display. Still, he viewed the project as an important "attention focuser" that "defined a set of problems that motivated people for a number of years." Even though VR was impossible at the time, it provided "a reason to go forward and push the technology as hard as you could. Spin-offs from that kind of pursuit are its greatest value."[13]

In Sutherland's view, the most important spin-offs were the students and the personal and professional connections. Sociologists of science talk about the importance of "core sets" of individuals who define the intellectual and technological direction of a domain. Certainly the students trained by Sutherland and Dale Evans, who founded Utah's Computer Science Department, constitute one of the best examples of a core set in the history of computer science.

Sutherland knew Evans from his ARPA days, and in 1968 they cofounded Evans & Sutherland Computer Corporation, which manufactured graphical display systems and built military flight and tank simulators under government contract. Many commercial and military pilots were trained on Evans & Sutherland flight simulators. A number of their students worked on an ARPA-supported project on 3D graphics, and several worked at Evans & Sutherland on simulations. Several of the original Harvard group also helped form the corporation, including Charles Seitz, who joined the Utah faculty in 1970 and remained until 1973, when he moved to California Institute of Technology and founded

Myricom with Dan Cohen, another Harvard alumnus who contributed to the head-mounted display. The interaction between research on basic problems and development of hardware and software for military projects at Evans & Sutherland was an important feature of work at Utah.

GRAPHICS HARDWARE: RISC TECHNOLOGY

Central to advances in computer graphics and VR technology have been improvements in the underlying computer hardware that enhanced capabilities and reduced costs. A significant advance, derived from both industrial and academic research, was the development of reduced instruction set computing (RISC), starting in the mid-1980s. By eliminating certain instructions based on careful quantitative analysis and emulating those instructions in software, RISC processors can increase the performance of some computers. With RISC processors, the performance of graphics hardware grew at about 55 percent per year—resulting in a doubling of performance every 18 months.[14]

The roots of RISC lie in three research projects: the IBM Corporation's 801, the University of California at Berkeley's RISC processor, and Stanford University's million-instructions-per-second (MIPS) processor. These architectures promised two to five times the performance of traditional machines. The Berkeley and Stanford projects were funded by DARPA's highly ambitious Very Large Scale Integrated Circuits (VLSI) program, which envisioned that integrated circuit (or chip) technology could be made available to system designers, who had an overall view of the objectives and constraints of an entire hardware/software system. The VLSI program also developed the concept of the multichip wafer, which dramatically reduced costs. It expanded the availability of the metal oxide silicon implementation service, which created a multichip wafer from designs submitted electronically from multiple sites, allowing university system designers to access state-of-the-art silicon fabrication (see Chapter 4).

Begun in the late 1970s, the IBM machine was designed as a minicomputer made from hundreds of chips, whereas the university projects were both microprocessors. John Cocke, the father of the 801 design, received both the A.M. Turing Award, the highest award in computer science and engineering, and the Presidential Medal of Technology. The Berkeley project, headed by David A. Patterson, began in 1980. The Berkeley group built two machines, RISC-I and RISC-II. Because the IBM project was not widely known, the Berkeley group's role in promoting the RISC approach was critical to the acceptance of the technology. The Stanford MIPS project, begun in 1981, was led by John L. Hennessy. MIPS is a high-performance RISC, built in VLSI.[15]

Both the Stanford and the Berkeley groups were interested in designing a simple machine that could be built as a microchip within the university environment. Hennessy played a key role in transferring this technology to industry. During a sabbatical from Stanford in 1984-1985, he co-founded MIPS Computer Systems (acquired by Silicon Graphics Incorporated, in 1992), which specialized in the production of computers and chips based on these concepts.

In 1986 the computer industry began to announce commercial processors based on RISC technology. Hewlett-Packard Company (HP) converted its existing minicomputer line to RISC architectures. IBM never turned the 801 into a product but adapted the ideas for a new low-end architecture that was incorporated into the IBM RT-PC. This machine was a commercial failure, but subsequent RISC processors with which IBM has been involved (e.g., the Apple/IBM/Motorola PowerPC) have been highly successful. In 1987 Sun Microsystems, Inc. began delivering machines based on the SPARC architecture, a derivative of the Berkeley RISC-II machine. In the view of many, it was Sun's success with RISC-based workstations that convinced the remaining skeptics that RISC was significant commercially. Sun's success sparked renewed interest at IBM, which announced a new RISC architecture in 1990, as did Digital Equipment Corporation in 1993. By 1995, RISC had become the foundation of a $15 billion industry in computer workstations.

RISC computers advanced the field of interactive graphics and promoted the development of VR. Silicon Graphics Incorporated (SGI), co-founded by James Clark in 1982, was an early adopter of RISC processors and has been a leader in the recent development of high-end graphics, including VR. Clark joined the Stanford engineering faculty in 1979 after completing his doctorate with Ivan Sutherland on problems related to the head-mounted display. Clark worked with Hennessy and Forest Baskett in the Stanford VLSI program and was supported by DARPA in the Geometry Engine project, which attempted to harness the custom chip technology of MIPS to create cost-effective, high-performance graphics systems. In 1981, Clark received a patent for his Geometry Engine—the 3D algorithms built into the "firmware" that enable the unit to serve up real-time, interactive 3D graphics. The patent formed the basis of SGI. Clark also invented the GraphicsLibrary, the graphics interface language used to program SGI's computers.

Silicon Graphics is part of the commercial infrastructure for interactive graphics and VR that finally took root in the fertile ground laid by early federal funding initiatives. Companies such as SGI, Evans & Sutherland, HP, Sun Microsystems, and others have generated products that have enabled simulations of all sorts, scientific visualizations, and computer-aided design programs for engineering. They also helped create the film and video game industries, which have stimulated advances in graphics by providing jobs, markets, and substantial research advances.[16] In 1997, SGI reported revenues of $3.66 billion (McCracken, 1997).[17]

BIOMEDICAL APPLICATIONS

The basic technologies developed through VR research have been applied in a variety of ways over the last several decades. One line of work led to applications of VR in biochemistry and medicine. This work began in the 1960s at the University of North Carolina (UNC) at Chapel Hill. The effort was launched by Frederick Brooks, who was inspired by Sutherland's vision of the ultimate display as enabling a user to see, hear, and feel in the virtual world. Flight simulators had incorporated sound and haptic feedback for some time. Brooks selected molecular graphics as the principal driving problem of his program. The goal of Project GROPE, started by Brooks in 1967, was to develop a haptic interface for molecular forces (Brooks, 1990). The idea was that, if the force constraints on particular molecular combinations could be "felt," then the designer of molecules could more quickly identify combinations of structures that could dock with one another.

GROPE-I was a 2D system for continuous force fields. GROPE II was expanded to a full six-dimensional (6D) system with three forces and three torques. The computer available for GROPE II in 1976 could produce forces in real time only for very simple world models—a table top; seven child's blocks; and the tongs of the Argonne Remote Manipulator (ARM), a large mechanical device. For real-time evaluation of molecular forces, Brooks and his team estimated that 100 times more computing power would be necessary. After building and testing the GROPE II system, the ARM was mothballed and the project was put on hold for about a decade until 1986, when VAX computers became available. GROPE III, completed in 1988, was a full 6D system. Brooks and his students then went on to build a full-molecular-force-field evaluator and, with 12 experienced biochemists, tested it in GROPE IIIB experiments in 1990. In these experiments, the users changed the structure of a drug molecule to get the best fit to an active site by manipulating up to 12 twistable bonds.

The test results on haptic visualization were extremely promising (Ouh-Young et al., 1988, 1989; Minsky et al., 1990). The subjects saw the haptic display as a fast way to test many hypotheses in a short time and set up and guide batch computations. The greatest promise of the technique, however, was not in saving time but in improving situational awareness. Chemists using the method reported better comprehension of the force fields in the active site and of exactly why each particular candidate drug docked well or poorly. Based on this improved grasp of the problem, users could form new hypotheses and ideas for new candidate drugs.

The docking station is only one of the projects pursued by Brooks's group at the UNC Graphics Laboratory. The virtual world envisioned by Sutherland would enable scientists or engineers to become immersed in the world rather than simply view a mathematical abstraction through a window from outside. The UNC group has pursued this idea through the development of what Brooks calls "intelligence-amplifying systems." Virtual worlds are a subclass of intelligence-amplifying systems, which are expert systems that tie the mind in with the computer, rather than simply substitute a computer for a human.

In 1970, Brooks's laboratory was designated as an NIH Research Resource in Molecular Graphics, with the goal of developing virtual worlds of technology to help biochemists and molecular biologists visualize and understand their data and models. However, because of budget cutbacks and a reorientation of the program, support from the NIH National Center for Research Resources has declined by more than 50 percent since 1979. Fortunately, a variety of other federal agencies have continued to support the virtual worlds project since the early 1980s. These agencies include NIH's National Cancer Institute, DARPA, and the NSF. Collaboration with the Air Force Institute of Technology on image-delivery systems has also been an important part of the work at UNC since 1983 (U.S. Congress, 1991). During the 1990s, UNC has collaborated with industry sponsors such as HP to develop new architectures incorporating 3D graphics and volume-rendering capabilities into desktop computers (HP later decided not to commercialize the technology).[18]

Since 1985, NSF funding has enabled UNC to pursue the Pixel-Planes project, with the goal of constructing an image-generation system capable of rendering 1.8 million polygons per second and a head-mounted display system with a lagtime under 50 milliseconds. This project is connected with GROPE and a large software project for mathematical modeling of molecules, human anatomy, and architecture. It is also linked to VISTANET, in which UNC and several collaborators are testing high-speed network technology for joining a radiologist who is planning cancer therapy with a virtual world system in his clinic, a Cray supercomputer at the North Carolina Supercomputer Center, and the Pixel-Planes graphics engine in Brooks's laboratory.

With Pixel-Planes and the new generation of head-mounted displays, the UNC group has constructed a prototype system that enables the notions explored in GROPE to be transformed into a wearable virtual-world workstation. For example, instead of viewing a drug molecule through a window on a large screen, the chemist wearing a head-mounted display sits at a computer workstation with the molecule suspended in front of him in space. The chemist can pick it up, examine it from all sides, even zoom into remote interior dimensions of the molecule. Instead of an ARM gripper, the chemist wears a force-feedback exoskeleton that enables the right hand to "feel" the spring forces of the molecule being warped and shaped by the left hand.

In a similar use of this technology, a surgeon can work on a simulation of a delicate procedure to be performed remotely. A variation on and modification of the approach taken in the GROPE project is being pursued by UNC medical researcher James Chung, who is designing virtual-world interfaces for radiology. One approach is data fusion, in which a physician wearing a head-mounted display in an examination room could, for example, view a fetus by ultrasound imaging superimposed and projected in 3D by a workstation. The physician would see these data fused with the body of the patient. In related experiments with MRI and CT scan data fusion, a surgeon has been able to plan localized radiation treatment of a tumor.

In the UNC case, funding of VR research by several different agencies has sustained the laboratory through changing federal priorities and enabled it to pursue a complementary mix of alternative approaches, basic and applied research, and prototype development. Although federal agencies have different mission objectives, a synergy evolved between the various projects, and a common base of knowledge and personnel was established. Over the years, the government's investment has greatly expanded the range of tools available to both the research community and industry.

VIRTUAL REALITY AND ENTERTAINMENT: TOWARD A COMMERCIAL INDUSTRY

At a 1991 Senate hearing, several VR pioneers noted that commercial interests, with their need for quick returns, could not merge the substantially different technologies needed to create virtual worlds, particularly while the technologies remained at precompetitive stages for so many years (U.S. Congress, 1991). But a sustained mixture of government, industry, and university-based R&D and the synergistic development of several applications has helped bring VR to the marketplace. In particular, the nexus between public research and privately developed entertainment systems made VR technology more affordable and scaled it up for large consumer markets, thereby promoting the rapid adoption and widespread use of imaging technology in science and medicine.

An example is RenderMan, developed by Pixar Animation Studios. Edwin Catmull, an alumnus of the Utah graphics program, joined Alvy Ray Smith at LucasFilm in 1979. Catmull and Smith had worked together at the New York Institute of Technology (NYIT). To realize the dream of constructing an entire film from computer-generated material, Smith and Catmull recruited a number of young computer graphics talents to LucasFilm. Among them was Loren Carpenter from the Boeing Company, who had studied the research of Mandelbrot and then modified it to create realistic fractal images. In 1981, Carpenter wrote the first renderer for LucasFilm, REYES (Renders Everything You Ever Saw), which was the beginning of RenderMan.

In 1986, the computer graphics division of LucasFilm's Industrial Light and Magic was spun off as Pixar, with Catmull as president and Smith as vice president. Under their direction, Pixar worked on developing a rendering computer. Also joining the REYES machine group at Pixar in 1986 was Patrick Hanrahan, who worked with Robert Drebin and Loren Carpenter in developing the first volume-rendering algorithms for the Pixar image computer (Drebin et al., 1988). These algorithms created images directly from 3D arrays without the typical intermediate steps of converting to standard surface representations, such as polygons. Hanrahan was the principal architect of the interface and was responsible for the rendering software and the graphics architecture of RenderMan.

The rendering interface evolved into the RenderMan standard now widely used in the movie industry. This standard describes the information the computer needs to render a 3D scene—the objects, light sources, cameras, and atmospheric effects. Once a scene is converted to a RenderMan file, it can be rendered on a variety of systems, from Macintoshes to personal computers to SGI workstations. This opened up many possibilities for 3D computer graphics software developers. RenderMan was used in creating *Toy Story*, the first feature-length computer-animated film; the dinosaurs in *Jurassic Park*; and the cyborg in *Terminator 2*.

This powerful tool also has contributed to visualization and volume rendering in a number of fields of science, engineering, and medicine. In addition, the hardware and software components and the individuals involved have circulated between industry and academe. Pat Hanrahan, after moving from NYIT to Pixar, moved back to an academic laboratory, first as an associate professor at Princeton University, and more recently as a professor at Stanford University, where he has contributed to several areas of graphics. One was the development of applications for the Responsive Workbench, a 3D, interactive virtual environment workspace for scientific visualization, architecture, and medicine. The workbench has been a cooperative project between Stanford and the German Institute for Information Design, supported by grants from Interval Research Corporation, DARPA (for visualization of complex systems), and NASA Ames (for virtual windtunnel). Silicon Graphics and Fakespace Incorporated donated equipment.

THE RIGHT MIX: VIRTUAL REALITY IN THE 1990s

Continued improvements in computer graphics in processors and new chip architectures have stimulated the growth of commercial markets for VR technology, fueling the revenues of companies such as SGI and cutting the prices of graphics workstations drastically. The resulting improvements in the price-performance ratios for computer graphics technologies have, in turn, increased demand for these products. Furthermore, potential markets for multimedia products have driven the search for new architectures for image caching and compression techniques that greatly reduce bandwidth and memory requirements. This convergence of high-end computer architectures, graphics-rendering hardware, and software with low-end commercial markets for computer graphics expands the opportunities for the use of VR technologies in a variety of commercial applications. It also motivates further technical advances that benefit commercial and military customers alike. As SGI chief executive officer Ed McCracken once explained, "Our entertainment customers drive our technological innovation. And technological innovation is the foundation of Silicon Graphics."[19]

As civilian research has proceeded and the DOD has come under increasing pressure to operate effectively on reduced budgets, the traditional relationship between military and commercial VR research projects has changed. The DOD continues to be a major consumer of VR technology, but now it can draw increasingly on the commercial technologies. A number of reforms have been enacted to enable the DOD to procure products from the commercial industrial base more easily. A number of defense contractors have also diversified into commercial applications of VR technology (see Box 10.4). In 1998, the DOD expected to spend more than $2.5 billion on programs for modeling and simulation (U.S. Department of Defense, 1997). Such considerable resources will likely stimulate further development of graphics and VR technologies. Directive 5000.1 (U.S. Department of Defense, 1996) mandates that models and simulations be required of all proposed systems, and that "representations of proposed systems (virtual prototypes) shall be embedded in realistic, synthetic environments to support the various phases of the acquisition process, from requirements determination and initial concept exploration to the manufacturing and testing of new systems, and related training."

More interestingly, attempts have been made to better coordinate the efforts of military and commercial research programs in VR technologies. The Defense Modeling and Simulation Office, for example, asked the National Research Council to examine areas of mutual interest to the defense modeling and simulation community and the entertainment industry. The resulting report identified five broad areas of common inter-

BOX 10.4
Real3D Emerges from Military-Commercial Linkage

Real3D, one of several companies that offers real-time three-dimensional (3D) graphics products for commercial systems, traces its origins to the first GE Aerospace Visual Docking Simulator for the Apollo lunar landings. In 1991, GE Aerospace began exploring commercial applications of its real-time 3D graphics technology, which led to a contract with Sega Enterprises, Limited, of Japan, which was interested in improving its arcade graphics hardware so that the games would present more realistic images. GE Aerospace adapted a miniaturized version of its real-time 3D graphics technology specifically for Sega's Model 2 and Model 3 arcade systems, which incorporated new algorithms that provided a visual experience far exceeding expectations.[1] To date, Sega has shipped more than 200,000 systems that include what is today Real3D technology.

In 1993, GE Aerospace was acquired by Martin Marietta, another leader in the field of visual simulation. Martin Marietta not only advocated expanding the relationship with Sega but also encouraged further research and analysis to look at other commercial markets, such as personal computers (PCs) and graphics workstations. In 1995, Martin Marietta merged with Lockheed Corporation and shortly thereafter launched Real3D to focus solely on developing and producing 3D graphics products for commercial markets. To that end, in November 1996, a strategic alliance was formed between Real3D and Chips and Technologies Incorporated, aimed at selling Real3D R3D/100 two-chip graphics accelerators to the PC industry and bringing world-class 3D applications to professionals who use the Windows NT environment.[2] Finally, in December 1997, Lockheed Martin established Real3D Incorporated as an independent company and announced that Intel Corporation had purchased a 20 percent minority stake in Real3D.

Real3D thus builds on more than three decades of experience in real-time 3D graphics hardware and software going back to the Apollo Visual Docking Simulator. This experience has led to more than 40 key patents on 3D graphics hardware and software. Strategic relationships with various companies provide opportunities to transition high-end graphics technology from leading-edge research environments to the desktops of physicians, engineers, and scientists. Conversely, the company may also be able to transfer technology developed for video games to developers of military training simulators.

---

[1]See the discussion by Jeffrey Potter in CSTB (1997b), pp. 163-164. Additional information is available online at <http://www.real3d.com/sega.html>.

[2]The R3D/100 chipset directly interfaces with Microsoft-compliant application programming interfaces, such as OpenGL.

est: fundamental technologies for immersive environments, networked simulation, standards for interoperability across systems, computer-generated characters, and tools for creating simulated environments (Computer Science and Telecommunications Board, 1997b). Already, the DOD has work under way in many of these areas. It is exploring ways of improving representations of human behaviors in synthetic environments and has developed a High-Level Architecture (HLA) to facilitate interoperability of distributed simulation systems.[20] Commercial entertainment companies are also exploring related areas of research and may benefit from—and contribute to—defense-related activities.

The growing linkages between the commercial and military VR communities are also apparent in the movement of experts between the two sectors. For example, Robert Jacobs, director and president of Illusion Incorporated, a company that derives some 80 percent of its revenues from the commercial entertainment industry, is an inventor of DARPA's Defense Simulation Network (SIMNET) program and has been a technical contributor to most of the related training programs. Eric Haseltine, now vice-president and chief scientist of research and development at Walt Disney Imagineering, was previously an executive at Hughes Aircraft Company, a defense contractor he joined after completing a postdoctoral fellowship in neuroanatomy and a doctorate in physiological psychology. Real3D senior software engineer Steven Woodcock began his career developing game simulations for Martin Marietta, where he has been responsible for weapons code development, testing, integration, and documentation for the Advanced Real-time Gaming Universal Simulation (ARGUS).[21] ARGUS is a real-time, distributed, interactive command-and-control simulation focusing on ballistic missile defense and theater missile defense, running on a network consisting of a Cray-2 supercomputer and more than 50 SGI workstations. Woodcock has noted that his Martin Marietta experience in distributed applications, real-time simulations, and artificial intelligence has proven invaluable in the real-time, 3D, multiplayer environments of games he has been designing recently.

These examples demonstrate the complex and changing relationship between federally funded research and commercial innovation. Yet even as the commercial industry has grown, federal funding has played a critical role in advancing technologies to serve the government's own needs as well as supporting underlying fundamental technologies. Indeed, DARPA, the NSF, Department of Energy (DOE), and other federal agencies continue to invest in VR and graphics-related research. The NSF's funding of the Science and Technology Research Center in Computer Graphics and Scientific Visualization supports collaborative research on computer graphics among participants from five universities. The DOE's Advanced Strategic Computing Initiative, although aimed at supporting development of models of nuclear weapons, includes funding for university research on fundamental techniques for computer graphics and scientific visualization. Such programs may ultimately help build a self-sustaining technological infrastructure for VR.

LESSONS FROM HISTORY

Federal funding has played a critical role in developing VR technology. It funded early, precompetitive research on topics such as CRTs that industry had few incentives to support. As the technology advanced and practical applications emerged, federal funding continued to complement industry support, as illustrated by work in head-mounted displays and the continuing government support of the field after the collapse of Atari. Federal support has enabled universities to create and maintain leading-edge computer graphics and VR research centers, which have contributed to the information revolution. Industry sectors and companies that generate billions of dollars in annual revenues (SGI is but one example) trace their roots to federally funded research.

A primary benefit of federal funding, particularly of university research, has been the creation of human resources that have carried out, and driven advances in, VR research. A number of graduate students and academic researchers who received federal support have made significant contributions to the field and have established leading companies (see Table 10.1).

Research in computer graphics and VR has benefited from multiple sources of federal support, which have enabled the simultaneous pursuit of various approaches to technical problems, funded a complementary mix of basic and applied research, developed a range of applications, provided a funding safety net that has sustained emerging technology despite changes in federal mission priorities, and offered the flexibility needed to pursue promising new ideas. The success of this approach is evidenced by the rich selection of VR products now available across the aerospace, military, industrial, medical, education, and entertainment sectors.

Finally, this case study demonstrates that advances in computing and communications seldom proceed along a linear or predictable path. Progress in VR technologies has benefited from varied interactions among government, universities, and industry and from the fusion of ideas from different areas of research, such as computer graphics, computer architectures, and military simulation.

NOTES

1. Such statements are invariably subject to the "back to the ancients" process of identifying precursors, such as Edwin Link's work on vehicle simulation in the 1920s. See Ellis (1991, 1994).

2. This project and others are listed on the Advanced Displays and Spatial Perception Laboratory page on the NASA Ames Research Center Web site at <http://duchamp.arc.nasa.gov:80/adsp.html>.

3. See Rowell (1998) and an article posted on the Silicon Graphics Web site at <http://www.sgi.com/features/1998/aug/chrysler/>.

4. The contributions of this center to scientific visualization and work in VR are discussed by Cruz-Neira et al. (1992).

5. These estimates are based on data compiled from NSF's annual report *Summary of Grants and Awards* for the years cited.

6. Another noteworthy graduate of the Utah program in the late 1970s was Gary Demos, who started several major computer graphics production companies and had a big impact on the introduction of computer graphics technology in the film industry.

7. The equipment was installed at the Manned Spacecraft Center in Houston.

8. Jeffrey Potter, Intel Corporation, as quoted in CSTB (1997b). For an evaluation of one of the GE systems, see Brown et al. (1994). This document is also available online at <http://tspg.wpafb.af.mil/programs/documents/asctr94.htm>.

9. This algorithm could run on Sun, VAX, or IBM systems with conventional graphics displays, such as the GE Graphicon 700. Additional information about Lorensen's work is available online at <http://www.crd.ge.com/~lorensen/>, as is information about the GE Computer Graphics Systems Program at <http://www.crd.ge.com/esl/cgsp/index.html>.

10. Like the spellcheck program on a word processor, which helps writers avoid typographical errors, the aim of this project is to develop a CAD program that provides "another set of 'eyes' in reviewing images, alerting a radiologist to look closer at specific areas of an image," according to Dr. Martin J. Lipton, chairman of the Radiology Department at the University of Chicago Medical Center, where the CAD technology is being developed. "GE and EG&G Sign Collaboration Pact to Produce Digital X-Ray Detectors," 21 August, 1997, available online at <http://www.ge.com/medical/Media/msxrldd>.

11. Along with Triple I, MAGI was involved in making the film *Tron*.

12. Other head-mounted display projects using a television camera system were undertaken by Philco in the early 1960s, as discussed by Ellis (1996).

13. Ivan E. Sutherland in "Virtual Reality Before It Had That Name," a videotaped lecture before the Bay Area Computer History Association.

14. See National Research Council (1995), especially Figure 8.4, "The History of Workstation Computation and Memory."

15. Hennessy et al. (1981) published a description of the Stanford MIPS machine, also developed under DARPA sponsorship.

16. Scott Fisher, "Current Status of VR and Entertainment," presentation to the National Research Council's Committee on Virtual Reality Research and Development, Woods Hole, MA, August, 1993, as cited in National Research Council (1995).

17.   Also see the comparative financial data reported for 1993 through 1997 at <http://www.sgi.com/company_info/investors/annual_report/97/fin_sel_info.html>.

18.   This collaboration is described on the Web site of PixelFusion at <http://www.pixelfusion.com>.

19.   See McCracken (1997). McCracken also noted: "While there have been incredible advances across many areas of science and technology—the new Craylink architecture for supercomputers, new improvements on the space shuttle, sheep cloning—no advance has been more prolific, more ubiquitous, more wide-reaching than consumer-oriented entertainment developments."

20.   The program description is available online at <http://www.stricom.army.mil/STRICOM/PM-ADS/ADSTII/>.

21.   Steven Woodcock's biography is available online at <http://www.cris.com/~swoodcoc/stevegameresume.html>. Also see *Wall Street Journal Interactive Edition* (May 19, 1997). Also see Coco (1997), which is available online at <http://www.cgw.com/cgw/Archives/1997/07/07story1.html>.

Bibliography

Aho, A.V., and J.D. Ullman. 1992. *Foundations of Computer Science.* W.H. Freeman, San Francisco, Calif.

Aho, A.V., R. Sethi, and J.D. Ullman. 1986. *Compilers: Principles, Techniques, and Tools.* Addison-Wesley, Reading, Mass.

Aitken, Hugh G.J. 1985. *The Continuous Wave: Technology and American Radio, 1900-1932.* Princeton University Press, Princeton, N.J.

Akera, Atsushi. 1996. "Computers and Systems Analysis: Transforming Research Strategies at the National Bureau of Standards," Dibner Symposium on the Spread of the Systems Approach. Dibner Institute for the History of Science and Technology, Cambridge, Mass., April.

Alic, John, Lewis M. Branscomb, and Gerald L. Epstein. 1992. *Beyond Spinoff: Military and Commercial Technologies in a Changing World.* Harvard Business School Press, Boston, Mass.

Amarel, Saul. 1988. "Current AI Research," p. 268 in *Expert Systems and Artificial Intelligence: Applications and Management,* Thomas C. Bartee, ed. Howard W. Sams & Co., Indianapolis, Ind.

Amarel, Saul. 1989. Interview with Arthur Norberg, New Brunswick, N.J., Charles Babbage Institute Oral History Collection, University of Minnesota, Minneapolis, October 5.

American Association for Artificial Intelligence (AAAI). 1994. *A Report to ARPA on Twenty-First Century Intelligent Systems,* Barbara Grosz and Randall Davis, eds. AAAI, Menlo Park, Calif. Available online at <http://www.aaai.org/Policy/Papers/arpa-report.html>.

Anderson, Margo J. 1988. *The American Census: A Social History.* Yale University Press, New Haven, Conn.

Andrews, Gregory R. 1997. "1996 CRA Taulbee Survey: Grad, Undergrad Student Enrollments Up," *Computing Research News,* March, pp. 5-9.

Arrow, Kenneth. 1962. "Economic Welfare and the Allocation of Resources for Invention," *The Rate and Direction of Inventive Activity.* Princeton University Press, Princeton, N.J.

Aspray, William, and Bernard O. Williams. 1994. "Arming American Scientists: NSF and the Provision of Scientific Computing Facilities for Universities, 1950-1973," *Annals of the History of Computing* 16(4):60-74.

Aspray, William, Andrew Goldstein, and Bernard Williams. 1996. "The Social and Intellectual Shaping of a New Mathematical Discipline: The Role of the National Science Foundation in the Rise of Theoretical Computer Science," *Vita Mathematica*, MAA Notes No. 40, Ronald Calinger, ed. Mathematical Association of America, Washington, D.C.

Association for Computing Machinery (ACM) Sigplan. 1978. *A History of Programming Languages, Proceedings of the ACM Conference on Programming Languages.* Academic Press, Los Angeles, Calif.

Association for Computing Machinery (ACM) Curriculum Committee on Computer Science Curriculum. 1979. "Curriculum '78: Recommendations for the Undergraduate Program in Computer Science," *Communications of the ACM* 22:147-166.

Association for Computing Machinery (ACM). 1993. "Before the Altair: The History of Personal Computing," *Communications of the ACM* 36(9):27-33.

Astrahan, M.M., M.W. Blasgen, D.D. Chamberlin, K.P. Eswaran, J.N. Gray, P.P. Griffiths, W.F. King, R.A. Lorie, P.R. McJones, J.W. Mehl, G.R. Putzolu, I.L. Traiger, B.W. Wade, and V. Watson. 1976. "System R: Relational Approach to Database Management," *ACM Transactions on Database Systems* 1(2):97-137.

Bachman, C. 1973. "The Programmer as Navigator: 1973 ACM Turing Award Lecture," *Communications of the ACM* 16(11):653-658.

Backus, John. 1979. "The History of FORTRAN I, II, and III," *Annals of the History of Computing* 1(1):21-37.

Baker, James K. 1975. "The DRAGON System—An Overview," *IEEE Transactions on Acoustics, Speech, and Signal Processing* 23(1):24-29.

Barber Associates, Richard J. 1975. *The Advanced Research Projects Agency 1958-1974*, report prepared for the Advanced Projects Research Agency under contract MDA 903-74-C-0096. Defense Technical Information Center, Springfield, Va., December.

Barr, Avron, and Edward A. Feigenbaum, eds. 1981. *The Handbook of Artificial Intelligence, Vol. 1.* HeurisTech Press, Stanford, Calif.

Bashe, Charles J., Lyle R. Johnson, John H. Palmer, and Emerson W. Pugh. 1986. *IBM's Early Computers.* MIT Press, Cambridge, Mass.

Baum, Claude. 1981. *The System Builders: The Story of SDC.* System Development Corporation, Santa Monica, Calif.

Baum, L.E., and J.A. Eagon. 1967. "An Inequality with Applications to Statistical Estimation for Probabilistic Functions of Markov Processes and to a Model of Ecology," *Bulletin of the American Mathematical Society* 73:360-362.

Bhushan, Abhay. 1972. *File Transfer Protocol.* Internet Request for Comment 354. July. RFC Editor, Information Sciences Institute, University of Southern California, Los Angeles. Available online at <http://www.rfc-editor.org/rfc.html>.

Blane, Erwin, et al. 1997. *Sizing Intercompany Commerce.* Forrester Research, Cambridge, Mass., July.

Branscomb, Lewis, et al. 1997. *Investing in Innovation: Toward a Consensus Strategy for Federal Technology Policy*, April 24. Available online at <http://www.ksg.harvard.edu/iip/techproj/invest.html>.

Braudel, Fernand. 1972. *The Mediterranean and the Mediterranean World in the Age of Philip II.* Harper & Row, New York.

Brooks, Frederick P. 1990. "Project GROPE: Haptic Displays for Scientific Visualization," *ACM Computer Graphics* 24(4):177-185.

Brown, James E., Timothy J. Lincourt, Melissa J. Leos, et al. 1994. *Visual System Operational Evaluation,* ASC-TR-94-5030. Available online at <http://tspg.wpafb.af.mil/programs/documents/asctr94.htm>.

Brynjolfsson, Erik, and Lorin Hitt. 1996. "Paradox Lost? Firm-level Evidence of High Returns to Information Systems Spending," *Management Science* 42(4):541-558.

Buchanan, Bruce G., and Edward H. Shortliffe. 1984. *Rule-based Expert Systems: The MYCIN Experiments of the Stanford Heuristic Programming Project.* Addison-Wesley, Reading, Mass.

Buderi, Robert. 1998. "Bell Labs Is Dead. Long Live Bell Labs," *Technology Review* 101(5):50-57.

Bureau of the Census, U.S. Department of Commerce, Economics and Statistics Administration. 1997. *Current Industrial Reports: Communication Equipment Including Telephone, Telegraph, and Other Electronic Systems and Equipment—1996,* MA36P(96)-1. U.S. Government Printing Office, Washington, D.C.

Bush, Vannevar. 1945a. *Science, The Endless Frontier.* U.S. Government Printing Office, Washington, D.C.

Bush, Vannevar. 1945b. "As We May Think," *Atlantic Monthly* 176(July):101-108.

Campbell-Kelly, Martin, and William Aspray. 1996. *Computer: A History of the Information Machine.* Basic Books, New York.

Cardenas, A. 1979. *Database Management Systems.* Allyn and Bacon, Boston, Mass.

Chamberlin, D., et al. 1981. "A History and Evaluation of System R," *Communications of the ACM* 24(10):632-646.

Chomsky, Noam. 1956. "Three Models for the Description of Language," *IRE Transactions on Information Theory* 2(3):113-124.

Church, A. 1936. "An Unsolvable Problem of Elementary Number Theory," *American Journal of Mathematics* 58:345-363.

Clancy, M.J., and M.C. Linn. 1995. *Designing Pascal Solutions.* W.H. Freeman, San Francisco, Calif.

Coco, Donna. 1997. "Creating Intelligent Creatures: Game Developers Are Turning to AI to Give Their Characters Personalities and to Distinguish Their Titles from the Pack," *Computer Graphics World* 20(7):22-28. Available online at <http://www.cgw.com/cgw/Archives/1997/07/07story1.html>.

Codd, Edgar F. 1970. "A Relational Model of Data for Large Shared Data Banks," *Communications of the ACM* 13(6):377-387.

Codd, Edgar F. 1982. "Relational Database: A Practical Foundation for Productivity (1983 ACM Turing Award Lecture)," *Communications of the ACM* 25(2):109-117.

Cohen, Arnold. 1983. Interview with James Ross, Charles Babbage Institute Center for the History of Information Processing, University of Minnesota, Minneapolis, January-March.

Cohen, Arnold A., and Erwin Tomash. 1979. "The Birth of an Era: Engineering Research Associates Inc.," *Annals of the History of Computing* 1(October):83-100.

Collins, Martin J. 1998. "Planning for Modern War: RAND and the Air Force, 1945-1950," Ph.D. dissertation, University of Maryland, College Park.

Comer, D. 1984. *Operating System Design, the Xinu Approach.* Prentice-Hall, Englewood Cliffs, N.J.

Committee on Science, U.S. House of Representatives. 1998. *Unlocking Our Future: Toward a New National Science Policy,* a Report to Congress, September 24. Available online at <http://www.house.gov/science/science_policy_report.htm>.

Computer Science and Technology Board, National Research Council. 1982. Paper 8, "Research in Data Processing: The Primacy of Practice," pp. 67-70 in *Roles of Industry and the University in Computer Research and Development*. National Academy Press, Washington, D.C.

Computer Science and Telecommunications Board (CSTB), National Research Council. 1992. *Computing the Future: A Broader Research Agenda for Computer Science and Engineering*. National Academy Press, Washington, D.C.

Computer Science and Telecommunications Board (CSTB), National Research Council. 1994. *Realizing the Information Future: The Internet and Beyond*. National Academy Press, Washington, D.C.

Computer Science and Telecommunications Board (CSTB), National Research Council. 1995a. *Evolving the High-Performance Computing and Communications Initiative to Support the Nation's Information Infrastructure*. National Academy Press, Washington, D.C.

Computer Science and Telecommunications Board (CSTB), National Research Council. 1995b. *Information Technology in the Service Sector: A Twenty-first Century Lever*. National Academy Press, Washington, D.C.

Computer Science and Telecommunications Board (CSTB). National Research Council. 1996. *Cryptography's Role in Securing the Information Society*. National Academy Press, Washington, D.C.

Computer Science and Telecommunications Board (CSTB), National Research Council. 1997a. *Ada and Beyond: Software Policies for the Department of Defense*. National Academy Press, Washington, D.C.

Computer Science and Telecommunications Board (CSTB). National Research Council. 1997b. *Modeling and Simulation: Linking Entertainment and Defense*. National Academy Press, Washington, D.C.

Conway, Lynn. 1981. *The MPC Adventures: Experiences with the Generation of VLSI Design and Implementation Methodologies*, Technical Report VLSI-81-2. Xerox Palo Alto Research Center, Palo Alto, Calif.

Cook, S.A. 1971. "The Complexity of Theorem Proving Procedures," pp. 151-158 in *Proceedings of the Third Annual ACM Symposium on the Theory of Computing*. ACM Press, New York.

Coons, Steven A. 1967. *Surfaces for Computer-aided Design of Space Forms*, Project MAC Report MAC-TR-41. Massachusetts Institute of Technology, Cambridge, Mass.

Crevier, Daniel. 1994. *AI*. Basic Books, New York.

Crout, P.D. 1941. "A Short Method for Evaluating Determinants and Solving Systems of Linear Equations with Real or Complex Coefficients," *Transactions of the American Institute of Electrical Engineers* 60:1235-1240.

Cruz-Neira, C., D.J. Sandin, T.A. DeFanti, R.V. Kenyon, and J.C. Hart. 1992. "The CAVE: Audio Visual Experience Automatic Virtual Environment," *Communications of the ACM* 35(6):65-72.

Cutter, Mary E. 1997. "Approval of the 'Partnerships for Advanced Computational Infrastructure' Program Awards." Memorandum to the National Science Board, NSB 97-50. Available online at <http://www.cise.nsf.gov/acir/nsb_memo.html>.

Dahl, O.J., E.W. Dijkstra, and C.A.R. Hoare. 1972. *Structured Programming*. Academic Press, New York.

Dale, N.B., and C. Weems. 1992. *Introduction to Pascal and Structured Design*. D.C. Heath, Lexington, Mass.

Dasgupta, P., and P.A. David. 1987. "Information Disclosure and the Economics of Science and Technology," *Arrow and the Ascent of Modern Economic Theory*, G. Feiwel, ed. New York University Press, New York.

Dasgupta, P., and P.A. David. 1994. "Toward a New Economics of Science," *Research Policy* 23:487-521.

Date, C. 1986. *Relational Databases: Selected Writing.* Addison-Wesley, Reading, Mass.

David, P.A., and D. Foray. 1996. "Accessing and Expanding the Science and Technology Knowledge Base," *Science, Technology, Industry Review 16.* Organisation for Economic Cooperation and Development, Paris.

David, P.A., D.C. Mowery, and W.E. Steinmueller. 1992. "A Framework for Evaluating Economics Payoffs from Basic Research," *Economics of Innovation and New Technologies* 2(1):73-90.

Davies, D.W., K.A. Bartlett, R.A. Scantlebury, and P. T. Wilkinson. 1967. "A Digital Communication Network for Computers Giving Rapid Response at Remote Terminals," *Proceedings of the ACM Symposium on Operating System Principles.* Association for Computing Machinery, New York.

Davis, M. 1965. *The Undecidable.* Raven Press, Hewlett, N.Y.

de Forest, Lee. 1950. *Father of Radio: The Autobiography of Lee de Forest.* Wilcox & Follet Co., Chicago.

Defense Advanced Research Projects Agency (DARPA). 1983. *Strategic Computing—New Generation Technology: A Strategic Plan for Its Development and Application to Critical Problems in Defense.* DARPA, Arlington, Va., October 28.

Defense Advanced Research Projects Agency (DARPA). 1997. *DARPA Technology Transition.* DARPA, Arlington, Va., January.

Defense Advanced Research Projects Agency (DARPA). 1998. *FY 1999 DARPA Descriptive Summaries.* DARPA, Arlington, Va. Available online at <http://www.darpa.mil/budget.html>.

Denicoff, Marvin. 1988. "AI Development and the Office of Naval Research," p. 280 in *Expert Systems and Artificial Intelligence: Applications and Management,* Thomas C. Bartee, ed. Howard W. Sams & Co., Indianapolis, Ind.

Denning, D.E.R. 1982. *Cryptography and Data Security.* Addison-Wesley, Reading, Mass.

Diffie, W. 1996. Foreword in B. Schneier, *Applied Cryptography.* John Wiley & Sons, New York.

Diffie, W., and M.E. Hellman. 1976. "New Directions in Cryptography," *IEEE Transactions on Information Theory* 22:644-654.

Dijkstra, E.W. 1976. *A Discipline of Programming.* Prentice-Hall, Englewood Cliffs, N.J.

Drebin, R.A., L. Carpenter, and P. Hanrahan. 1988. "Volume Rendering," SIGGRAPH 88 Conference Proceedings, *Computer Graphics* 22(4):65-74.

Edwards, Paul. 1996. *The Closed World: Computers and the Politics of Discourse in Cold War America.* MIT Press, Cambridge, Mass.

Ehlers, Vernon. 1998. U.S. Representative Vern Ehlers as cited in *FYI: The American Institute of Physics Bulletin of Science Policy News* 32 (February 20). Available online at <http://www.aip.org/enews/fyi/1998/fyi98.032.htm>.

Ellis, Stephen R. 1991. "Nature and Origins of Virtual Environments: A Bibliographical Essay," *Computer Systems in Engineering* 2(4):321-347.

Ellis, Stephen R. 1994. "What Are Virtual Environments?" *IEEE Computer Graphics and Applications* 14(January):17-22.

Ellis, Stephen R. 1996. "Virtual Environments and Environmental Instruments," pp. 11-51 in *Simulated and Virtual Realities,* K. Carr and R. England, eds. Taylor & Francis, London.

Engelbart, Douglas C. 1986. "The Augmented Knowledge Workshop," *Proceedings of the ACM Conference on the History of Personal Workstations.* ACM Press, New York.

Engineering Research Associates (ERA). 1950. *High Speed Computing Devices,* W.W. Stifler, Jr., ed. McGraw-Hill, New York.

Englemore, R.S., et al. 1988. "Hearsay-II," p. 25 in *Blackboard Systems*, R. Englemore and T. Morgan, eds. Addison-Wesley, Boston. Cited in Reed, Sidney G., Richard H. Van Atta, and Seymour J. Deitchman, 1990, pp. 21-28 in *DARPA Technical Accomplishments, Volume 1*, IDA Paper P-2192, Institute for Defense Analyses, Alexandria, Va., February.

Fano, Robert M. 1979. "Project MAC," *Encyclopedia of Computer Science and Technology*, Vol. 12, Jack Belzer, Albert G. Holzman, and Allen Kent, eds. Marcel Dekker, New York.

Feigenbaum, Edward, Pamela McCorduck, and H. Penny Nii. 1988. *The Rise of the Expert Company: How Visionary Companies Are Using Artificial Intelligence to Achieve Higher Productivity and Profits*. Times Books, New York.

Flamm, Kenneth. 1987. *Targeting the Computer: Government Support and International Competition*. Brookings Institution, Washington, D.C.

Flamm, Kenneth. 1988. *Creating the Computer: Government, Industry, and High Technology*. Brookings Institution, Washington D.C.

Fleck, James. 1982. "Development and Establishment in Artificial Intelligence," pp. 169-217 in *Scientific Establishments and Hierarchies*, Vol. 6 of *Sociology of the Sciences*, Norbert Elias, ed. D. Reidel Publishing Company, Dordrecht, Holland.

Floyd, R.W. 1967. "Assigning Meanings to Programs," pp. 19-32 in *Mathematical Aspects of Computer Science*, J.T. Schwartz, ed., Vol. 19 of *American Mathematics Society Proceedings of Symposia in Applied Mathematics*. American Mathematical Society, Providence, R.I.

Freeman, Eva C., ed. 1995. *MIT Lincoln Laboratory: Technology in the National Interest*. Lincoln Laboratory, Massachusetts Institute of Technology, Lexington, Mass.

Friedel, Robert, and Paul Israel, with Bernard S. Finn. 1986. *Edison's Electric Light: Biography of an Invention*. Rutgers University Press, New Brunswick, N.J.

Friend, E.H. 1956. "Sorting on Electronic Computer Systems," *Journal of the Association for Computing Machinery* 3:134-163.

Fry, J.P., and E.H. Sibley. 1974. "Evolution of Data-base Management Systems," *Computing Surveys* 8(1):7-42. Reprinted in L. Laplante, ed., 1996, *Great Papers in Computer Science*, IEEE Press, New York.

Garey, M.R., and D.S. Johnson. 1979. *Computers and Intractability*. W.H. Freeman, San Francisco, Calif.

Garfinkel, Simpson L. 1998. "Enter the Dragon," *Technology Review* 101(5):58-64.

Garland, S.J. 1986. *Introduction to Computer Science with Applications in Pascal*. Addison-Wesley, Reading, Mass.

General Electric. 1997. "GE and EG&G Sign Collaboration Pact to Produce Digital X-Ray Detectors," August 21. Available online at <http://www.ge.com/medical/Media/msxrldd>.

Gleeson, Robert E., and Steven Schlossman. 1994. "The Many Faces of the New Look: The University of Virginia, Carnegie Tech, and the Reform of American Management Education in the Postwar Era," *The Beginnings of Graduate Management Education in the United States*. Graduate Management Admission Council, Santa Monica, Calif.

Godel, K. 1931. "Uber formal unentscheidbare Satze der Principia Mathematica und verwander Systeme," *Monatshefte fur Mathematik und Physik* 38:173-198.

Goldstein, Nance. 1992. "Defense Advanced Research Project Agency's Role in Artificial Intelligence R&D: Case Study of the Military as the National Agent for Technological and Industrial Change," *Defense Analysis* 8(1):61-80.

Goldstine, Herman H. 1972. *The Computer: From Pascal to von Neumann*. Princeton University Press, Princeton, N.J.

Goldstine, Herman. 1980. Interview with Nancy Stern, OH 18, Charles Babbage Institute Center for the History of Information Processing, University of Minnesota, Minneapolis, August 11.

Gouraud, H. 1971. "Continuous Shading of Curved Surfaces," *IEEE Transactions on Computers* C-20(6):623-629.

Green C. 1988. "AI During IPTO's Middle Years," p. 241 in *Expert Systems and Artificial Intelligence: Applications and Management,* Thomas C. Bartee, ed. Howard W. Sams & Co., Indianapolis, Ind.

Greenfield, Harvey, Donald Vickers, Ivan Sutherland, Willem Kolff, et al. 1971. "Moving Computer Graphic Images Seen from Inside the Vascular System," *Transactions of the American Society of Artificial Internal Organs* 17:381-385.

Gries, D. 1987. *The Science of Programming.* Springer-Verlag, New York.

Grossman, Gene M., and Elhanan Helpman. 1991. *Innovation and Growth in the Global Economy.* MIT Press. Cambridge, Mass.

Gruenberger, F.J. 1979. "History of the Johnniac," *Annals of the History of Computing* 1(1):49-64.

Hafner, Katie, and Matthew Lyon. 1996. *Where Wizards Stay Up Late: The Origins of the Internet.* Simon & Schuster, New York.

Hartmanis, J., and R.E. Stearns. 1964. "Computational Complexity of Recursive Sequences," pp. 82-90 in *Proceedings of the 5th Annual Symposium on Switching Theory and Logical Design.* IEEE Press, New York.

Hayes-Roth, Frederick. 1997. "Artificial Intelligence: What Works and What Doesn't?" *AI Magazine* 18(2):100.

Hehner, E.C. 1993. *A Practical Theory of Programming.* Springer-Verlag, New York.

Hennessy, John L., and D.A. Patterson. 1990. *Computer Architecture: A Quantitative Approach.* Morgan Kaufman Publishers, San Mateo, Calif.

Hennessy, John L., N. Jouppi, F. Baskett, and F. Gill. 1981. "MIPS: A VLSI Processor Architecture," in *Proceedings of Carnegie Mellon University (CMU).* Computer Science Press, Rockville, Md.

High Performance Computing Modernization Office, U.S. Department of Defense. 1995. *Contributions to DoD Mission Success from High Performance Computing—March 1995,* DOD HPCM Pub 95-001. Available from the Defense Technical Information Center, Springfield, Va.

Hoare, C.A.R. 1969. "An Axiomatic Basis for Computer Programming," *Communications of the ACM* 12:576-581.

Hochbaum, Dorit S., ed. 1997. *Approximation Algorithms for NP-Hard Problems.* PWS Publishing Company, Boston, Mass.

Holzmann, G.J. 1991. *The Design and Validation of Computer Protocols.* Prentice-Hall, Englewood Cliffs, N.J.

Hounshell, David A. 1997. "The Cold War, RAND, and the Generation of Knowledge, 1946-1962," *Historical Studies in the Physical Sciences* 27(2):1-31.

Huffman, D.A. 1954. "The Synthesis of Sequential Switching Machines," *Journal of the Franklin Institute* 257:161-190, 275-303.

Hughes, Thomas. 1990. *American Genesis: A Century of Invention and Technological Enthusiasm, 1870-1970.* Penguin, New York.

Hughes, Thomas. 1998. *Rescuing Prometheus.* Pantheon Books, New York.

Hurd, Cuthbert C. 1994. Interview with Robert Seidel, Palo Alto, Calif., Charles Babbage Institute Center for the History of Information Processing, University of Minnesota, Minneapolis, November 18.

Huskey, Harry D. 1980. "The Standards Western Automatic Computer," *Annals of the History of Computing* 2(2):111-121.

Information Technology Industry Council (ITI). 1997. *1996 ITI Information Technology Industry Databook.* ITI, Washington, D.C.

Intel Corporation. 1996. As cited in "Intel Shifts Its Focus to Long-Term, Original Research," *Wall Street Journal*, August 2, p. B3.

International Business Machines Corporation (IBM). 1997. *1997 IBM Annual Report*. IBM, Armonk, N.Y.

Jardini, David R. 1996. "Out of the Blue Yonder: The RAND Corporation's Diversification into Social Welfare Research, 1946-1968." Ph.D. dissertation, Carnegie Mellon University, Pittsburgh, Pa.

Jones, Charles I., and John C. Williams. 1996. *Too Much of a Good Thing? The Economics of Investment in R&D*, Working Paper in Economics 96-005. Stanford University, Department of Economics, Palo Alto, Calif., February 26.

Kahn, D. 1967. *The Codebreakers: The Story of Secret Writing*. Macmillan, New York.

Kahn, Robert. 1988. "Later Years at IPTO," p. 250 in *Expert Systems and Artificial Intelligence: Applications and Management*, Thomas C. Bartee, ed. Howard W. Sams & Co., Indianapolis, Ind.

Kahn, Robert. 1989. Interview with William Aspray, OH 158, Charles Babbage Institute Center for the History of Information Processing, University of Minnesota, Minneapolis, March 22.

Kahr, A.S., E.F. Moore, and Hao Wang. 1962. "Entsscheidungsproblem Reduced to the AEA Case," *Proceedings of the National Academy of Sciences USA* 48:365-377.

Karp, R.M. 1972. "Reducibility Among Combinatorial Problems," pp. 85-103 in *Complexity of Computer Computations*, R.E. Miller and J.W. Thatcher, eds. Plenum, New York.

King, P.J.H., ed. 1983. *Database Management Systems: A Technical Comparison*. Pergamon Infotech Ltd., Maidenhead, Berkshire, England.

Kleene, S. 1936. "General Recursive Functions of Natural Numbers," *Mathematische Annalen* 112:727-742.

Kleene, S.C. 1956. "Representation of Events in Nerve Nets and Finite Automata," pp. 3-40 in *Automata Studies*, C.E. Shannon and J. McCarthy, eds. Princeton University Press, Princeton, N.J.

Kleinrock, Leonard. 1964. *Communication Nets: Stochastic Flow and Delay*. McGraw-Hill, New York.

Knuth, D.E. 1968. *The Art of Computer Programming*, 4 vols. Addison-Wesley, Reading, Mass.

Knuth, D.E. 1976. "Big Omicron, Big Omega and Big Theta," *SIGACT News* 8:18-23.

Laplante, Phillip. 1966. *Great Papers in Computer Science*. West Publishing, St. Paul, Minn.

Lea, Wayne, ed. 1980. *Trends in Speech Recognition*. Prentice-Hall, Englewood Cliffs, N.J.

Lea, Wayne, and June Shoup. 1979. *Review of the ARPA SUR Project and Survey of Current Technology in Speech Understanding*. Office of Naval Research, Arlington, Va., January.

Leiner, Barry M., Vinton G. Cerf, David D. Clark, Robert E. Kahn, Leonard Kleinrock, Daniel C. Lynch, Jon Postel, Larry G. Roberts, and Stephen Wolff. 1998. *A Brief History of the Internet*. Available online at <http://www.isoc.org/internet/history/brief.html>, Version 3.1, February 20.

Lesk, Michael. 1995. "The Seven Ages of Information Retrieval." Available online at <http://community.bellcore.com/lesk>.

Licklider, J.C.R. 1960. "Man-Computer Symbiosis," *IRE Transactions on Human Factors in Electronics* 1(March):4-11.

Licklider, J.C.R. 1964. "Artificial Intelligence, Military Intelligence, and Command and Control," *Military Information Systems: The Design of Computer-Aided Systems for Command*, Edward Bennett, James Degan, and Joseph Spiegel, eds. F.A. Praeger, New York.

Licklider, J.C.R. 1988a. "The Early Years," p. 226 in *Expert Systems and Artificial Intelligence: Applications and Management*, Thomas C. Bartee, ed. Howard W. Sams & Co., Indianapolis, Ind.

Licklider, J.C.R. 1988b. Interview with William Aspray and Arthur L. Norberg, Cambridge, Mass., OH 150, Charles Babbage Institute Center for the History of Information Processing, University of Minnesota, Minneapolis, October 28.

Licklider, J.C.R., and R.W. Taylor. 1968. "The Computer as a Communications Device." *Science and Technology* 76(April):21-31.

Liebowitz, Jay. 1997. "Worldwide Perspectives and Trends in Expert Systems: An Analysis Based on the Three World Congresses on Expert Systems," *AI Magazine* 18(Summer):115-119.

Lindsay, Robert K., Bruce G. Buchanan, Edward A. Feigenbaum, and Joshua Lederberg. 1993. "DENDRAL—A Case Study of the First Expert System for Scientific Hypothesis Information," *Artificial Intelligence Journal* 61(2):209-261.

Lorensen, William E., and Harvey E. Cline. 1987. "Marching Cubes: A High Resolution 3D Surface Construction Algorithm," *Computer Graphics* 21(4):163-169.

Lorie, R.A., P.R. McJones, J.W. Mehl, G.R. Putzolu, I.L. Traiger, B.W. Wade, and V. Watson. 1976. "System R: Relational Approach to Database Management," *ACM Transactions on Database Systems* 1(2):97-137.

MacKenzie, Donald. 1991. "The Influence of the Los Alamos and Livermore National Labs on Supercomputing," *Annals of the History of Computing* 13(2):179-201.

Makhoul, John, and Richard Schwartz. 1994. "State of the Art in Continuous Speech Recognition," p. 175 in *Voice Communication Between Humans and Machines,* National Research Council, David B. Roe and Jay G. Wilpon, eds. National Academy Press, Washington, D.C.

Malone, Michael S. 1995. *The Microprocessor: A Biography.* Springer-Verlag, New York.

Mansfield, Edwin. 1988. "Industrial Innovation in Japan and the United States," *Science* 241(September 30):1769-1775.

Markov, John. 1996. "Microsoft Plans 300% Increase in Spending for Basic Research in 1997," *New York Times,* December 9, p. D1.

Marshall, Martin, Larry Waller, and Howard Wolff. 1981. "The 1981 Achievement Award: Lynn Conway and Carver Mead," *Electronics* 54(21):102-105.

May, Ernest R. 1972. *Lessons of the Past: The Use and Misuse of History in American Foreign Policy.* Oxford University Press, New York.

McCarthy, John. 1981. "History of Lisp," in Richard Wexelblat, ed., *History of Programming Languages.* Academic Press, New York. The paper is also available online at <http://www-formal.stanford.edu/jmc/history/lisp/lisp.html>.

McCarthy, John. 1990. "Some Expert Systems Need Commonsense," *Formalizing Common Sense: Papers by John McCarthy,* V. Lifschitz, ed. Ablex Publishing, Norwood, N.J.

McCarthy, John, et al. 1955. "A Proposal for the Dartmouth Summer Research Project on Artificial Intelligence." Available from the Rockefeller Foundation Archives grant files, "Dartmouth College—Artificial Intelligence," RG 1.2, series 200, box 26, folder 219. Rockefeller Archives Center, North Tarrytown, N.Y.

McClain, D. 1998. "Voice Technology Appears Ready to Recognize Bottom Line," *New York Times,* January 19, pp. C1-C2.

McCracken, Edward. 1997. "Inspired by Vision: A Letter from Ed McCracken," in *National Association of Broadcasters '97 & National Association of Broadcasters MultiMedia World.* NAB Office of Science and Technology, Washington, D.C.

McCulloch, Warren S., and Walter Pitts. 1943. "A Logical Calculus of the Ideas Immanent in Nervous Activity," *Bulletin of Mathematical Biophysics* 3:115-133. Reprinted in Warren S. McCulloch, 1965, *Embodiments of Mind,* MIT Press, Cambridge, Mass.

McHugh, Josh. 1996. "'Holy Cow, No One's Done This!'" *Forbes* 57(11):122-128.

McJones, Paul, ed. 1995. "The 1995 SQL Reunion: People, Projects, and Politics." Available online at <http://www.research.digital.com/SRC/personal/Paul_McJones/System_R>.

Mead, Carver, and Lynn Conway. 1980. *Introduction to VLSI Systems*, Addison-Wesley, New York.

Mealy, G.H. 1955. "A Method for Synthesizing Sequential Circuits." *Bell System Technical Journal* 34:1045-1079.

Merkle, R.C. 1978. "Secure Communication Over Insecure Channels," *Communications of the ACM* 21:294-299.

Mills, D.L. 1988. "The Fuzzball," *Proceedings of the ACM SIGCOMM Symposium* 18(4):115-122.

Mills, H.D., R.C. Linger, and A.R. Hevner. 1986. *Principles of Information Systems Analysis and Design*. Academic Press, New York.

Minsky, Margaret, M. Ouh-Young, O. Steele, F.P. Brooks, Jr., et al. 1990. "Feeling and Seeing: Issues in Force Display," *Computer Graphics* 24(2):235-244.

Minsky, Marvin. 1956. *Heuristic Aspects of the Artificial Intelligence Problem*, MIT Lincoln Laboratory Report 34-55, ASTIA Doc. No. AS236885. Massachusetts Institute of Technology, Cambridge, Mass., December.

Minsky, Marvin. 1979. "The Society Theory of Thinking," pp. 423-450 in *Artificial Intelligence: An MIT Perspective*, Patrick Henry Winston and Richard Henry Brown, eds. MIT Press, Cambridge, Mass.

Misa, Thomas J. 1985. "Military Needs, Commercial Realities, and the Development of the Transistor, 1948-1958," *Military Enterprise and Technological Change: Perspectives on the American Experience*, Merritt Roe Smith, ed. MIT Press, Cambridge, Mass.

Moore, E. 1956. "Gedanken Experiments on Sequential Machines," *Automata Studies*, Claude E. Shannon and J. McCarthy, eds. Princeton University Press, Princeton, N.J.

Narin, Francis, Kimberly S. Hamilton, Dominic Olivastro. 1997. "The Increasing Linkage Between U.S. Technology and Public Science," *Research Policy* 26(3):317-330.

National Academy of Public Administration (NAPA). 1995. *National Science Foundation's Science and Technology Centers*. NAPA, Washington, D.C., July.

National Bureau of Standards. 1977. *Data Encryption Standard*, NBS FIPS PUB 46. National Technical Information Service, Springfield, Va.

National Research Council. 1995. *Virtual Reality: Scientific and Technological Challenges*, Nathaniel I. Durlach and Anne S. Mavor, eds. National Academy Press, Washington, D.C.

National Research Council. 1996. *An Assessment of the National Science Foundation's Science and Technology Centers Program*. National Academy Press, Washington, D.C.

National Science and Technology Council (NSTC), Committee on Computing, Information, and Communications. 1997. *Computing, Information, and Communications Technologies for the 21st Century: Supplement to the President's FY 1998 Budget*. National Coordination Office for Computing, Information, and Communications, Arlington, Va.

National Science Board. 1996. *Science and Engineering Indicators—1996*, NSB 96-21. U.S. Government Printing Office, Washington, D.C.

National Science Foundation (NSF). 1956. *Sixth Annual Report*. NSF, Washington, D.C.

National Science Foundation (NSF). 1958. *Annual Budget Request to Congress*. NSF, Washington, D.C.

National Science Foundation (NSF). 1967. *Grants and Awards for the Fiscal Year Ended June 30, 1967*. NSF, Washington, D.C.

National Science Foundation (NSF). 1968. *Grants and Awards for the Fiscal Year Ended June 30, 1968*. NSF, Washington, D.C.

National Science Foundation (NSF). 1971. *Summary of Awards: Grants and Awards for the Fiscal Year Ended June 30, 1971*. NSF, Washington, D.C.

National Science Foundation (NSF). 1973. *Summary of Awards: Grants and Awards for the Fiscal Year Ended June 30, 1973*. NSF, Washington, D.C.

National Science Foundation (NSF). 1979. *Annual Budget Request to Congress 1979.* NSF, Washington, D.C.

National Science Foundation (NSF). 1981a. *Budget Request to Congress.* NSF, Washington, D.C.

National Science Foundation (NSF). 1981b. *Summary of Awards.* NSF, Washington, D.C.

National Science Foundation (NSF). 1988. *Profiles—Computer Sciences: Human Resources and Funding,* NSF 88-324. NSF, Washington, D.C.

National Science Foundation (NSF). 1991. *Academic Research Equipment in Computer Science, Central Computer Facilities, and Engineering: 1989,* NSF 91-304. NSF, Washington, D.C.

National Science Foundation (NSF), Division of Science Resources Studies. 1995. *Federal Funds for Research and Development: Fiscal Years 1993, 1994, and 1995,* Vol. 43, Detailed Statistical Tables, NSF 95-334. NSF, Arlington, Va.

National Science Foundation (NSF), Division of Science Resources Studies. 1997a. *Federal Funds for Research and Development: Fiscal Years 1995, 1996, and 1997,* Vol. 45, Detailed Statistical Tables, NSF 97-327, by Ronald Meeks. NSF, Arlington, Va.

National Science Foundation (NSF), Division of Science Resources Studies. 1997b. *Science and Engineering Degrees: 1966-95,* NSF 97-335, Susan T. Hill, ed. NSF, Arlington, Va.

National Science Foundation (NSF), Division of Science Resources Studies. 1998a. *Research and Development in Industry: 1996 (Early Release Tables),* by Raymond M. Wolfe. NSF, Arlington, Va.

National Science Foundation (NSF). 1998b. *Federal Funds Survey, Detailed Historical Tables, Fiscal Years 1951-1998,* NSF 98-328. NSF, Arlington, Va.

National Science Foundation (NSF). 1998c. *Federal Funds Survey, Fields of Science and Engineering Research, Historical Tables, Fiscal Years 1970-1998,* NSF 98-326. NSF, Arlington, Va.

National Science Foundation (NSF). 1998d. *Federal Funds Survey, Fields of Science and Engineering Research to Universities and Colleges, Historical Tables, Fiscal Years 1973-1998,* NSF 98-327. NSF, Arlington, Va.

Naur, P., et al. 1960. "Report on Algol 60," *Communications of the ACM* 3:299-314.

Nelson, Richard. 1959. "The Simple Economics of Basic Scientific Research," *Journal of Political Economy* 67(2):297-306.

Nelson, Richard, ed. 1982. *Government and Technical Progress: A Cross-Industry Analysis.* Pergamon Press, New York.

Nelson, Richard. 1990. "Why Do Firms Do Basic Research (with Their Own Money)?" *Research Policy* 19:165-174.

Neumann, P.G. 1995. *Computer-Related Risks.* Addison-Wesley, Reading, Mass.

Newell, Allen. 1984. "Reports on Artificial Intelligence from Carnegie-Mellon University: Introduction to the Comtex Microfiche Edition," *AI Magazine* 5(3):35-39.

Newell, Allen, and Herbert Simon. 1956. *Current Developments in Complex Information Processing,* RAND P-850. RAND Corporation, Santa Monica, Calif., May 1.

Newell, Allen, and Herbert Simon. 1972. *Human Problem Solving.* Prentice-Hall, Englewood Cliffs, N.J.

Newell, Allen, Herbert Simon, and J.C. Shaw. 1957. *Empirical Explorations of the Logic Theory Machine: A Case Study in Heuristics,* RAND P-951. RAND Corporation, Santa Monica, Calif., February 14.

Newell, Allen, J.C. Shaw, and Herbert A. Simon. 1959. *Report on a General Problem-Solving Program,* RAND P-1584. RAND Corporation, Santa Monica, Calif., February 9.

Newell, Allen, et al. 1971. *Speech-Understanding Systems: Final Report of a Study Group.* North-Holland, New York, May.

Nielsen Media Research. 1997. As cited in Christian G. Hill, "Technology: Adult Users of Net in US and Canada Put at 58 Million," *Wall Street Journal,* December 11, p. A11.

Nilsson, Nils J. 1984. "Introduction to the COMTEX Microfiche Edition of the SRI Artificial Intelligence Center Technical Notes," *AI Magazine* 5(1):42-43.

Norberg, Arthur L. 1996. "Changing Computing: The Computing Community and DARPA," *Annals of the History of Computing* 18(2):40-53.

Norberg, Arthur L., and Judy E. O'Neill. 1996. *Transforming Computer Technology: Information Processing for the Pentagon 1962-1986.* Johns Hopkins University Press, Baltimore, Md.

Office of Technology Assessment (OTA). 1985. *Information Technology R&D: Critical Trends and Issues,* OTA-CIT-268. U.S. Government Printing Office, Washington, D.C.

Office of Technology Assessment (OTA). 1991. *Miniaturization Technologies,* OTA-TCT-514. U.S. Government Printing Office, Washington, D.C.

Office of Technology Assessment (OTA). 1993. *Defense Conversion: Redirecting R&D,* OTA-ITE-552. U.S. Government Printing Office, Washington, D.C.

Office of Technology Assessment (OTA). 1995. *Innovation and Commercialization of Emerging Technologies,* OTA-BP-ITC 165. U.S. Government Printing Office, Washington, D.C., September.

Old Associates, Bruce S. Inc. 1981. *Return on Investment in Basic Research—Exploring a Methodology,* report to Office of Naval Research, Department of the Navy, prepared under contract N00014-79-C-0192, November. Available from Defense Technical Information Center, Springfield, Va.

Olle, T.W. 1978. *The Codasyl Approach to Database Management.* John Wiley & Sons, New York.

Ouh-Young, M., D.V. Beard, and F.P. Brooks, Jr. 1989. "Force Display Performs Better Than Visual Display in a Simple 6-D Docking Task," pp. 1462-1466 in *Proceedings of the IEEE International Conference on Robotics and Automation.* IEEE Computer Society Press, Scottsdale, Ariz.

Ouh-Young, M., M. Pique, J. Hughes, N. Srinivasan, et al. 1988. "Using a Manipulator for Force Display in Molecular Docking," *Proceedings of the IEEE Robotics and Automation Conference* 3(April):1824-1829.

Parker, John E. 1985, 1986. Interview with Arthur L. Norberg, Washington, D.C., OH 99, Charles Babbage Institute Center for the History of Information Processing, University of Minnesota, Minneapolis, December 13, 1985, and May 6, 1986.

Petska-Juliussen, Karen, and Egil Juliussen. 1996. *Eighth Annual Computer Industry Almanac.* Coriolis Group, Scottsdale, Ariz.

Pickett, John R., and Thomas L. Case. 1991. "Implementing Expert Systems in R&D," *Research, Technology, Management* 34(4):37-42.

Pierce, J.R. 1969. "Whither Speech Recognition?" *Journal of the Acoustical Society of America* 46:1049-1051.

President's Information Technology Advisory Committee (PITAC). 1998. *Interim Report to the President.* National Coordinating Office for Computing, Information, and Communications, Arlington, Va.

Pugh, Emerson W. 1995. *Building IBM: Shaping an Industry and Its Technology.* MIT Press, Cambridge, Mass.

Rabin, M.O., and D. Scott. 1959. "Finite Automata and Their Decision Problems," *IBM Journal of Research and Development* 3:114-125.

Redmond, Kent C., and Thomas M. Smith. 1980. *Project Whirlwind: The History of a Pioneer Computer.* Digital Press, Bedford, Mass.

Reed, Sidney G., Richard H. Van Atta, and Seymour J. Deitchman. 1990. *DARPA Technical Accomplishments: An Historical Review of Selected DARPA Projects,* IDA Paper P-2192. Institute for Defense Analyses, Alexandria, Va., February.

Rees, Mina. 1982. "The Computing Program of the Office of Naval Research, 1946-1953," *Annals of the History of Computing* 4(2):102-120.

Rhind, Flora M. 1955. Letter from Flora M. Rhind, secretary of the Rockefeller Foundation, to Donald H. Morrison, provost, Dartmouth College, December 23, 1955. Available in the records of the Rockefeller Foundation, Rockefeller Archives Center, North Tarrytown, N.Y.

Rivest, R.L., A. Shamir, and L.M. Adleman. 1978. "A Method for Obtaining Digital Signatures and Public-key Cryptosystems," *Communications of the ACM* 21:120-136.

Roberts, Lawrence G. 1963. *Machine Perception of Three Dimensional Solids*, TR-315. Lincoln Laboratory, Massachussetts Institute of Technology, Lexington, Mass., May. Cited in Tipper et al., eds., 1963. *Optical and Electro-Optical Information Processing*, MIT Press, Cambridge, Mass.

Roberts, Lawrence G. 1965. *Homogenous Matrix Representation and Manipulation of N-Dimensional Constructs*, MS-1505. MIT Lincoln Laboratory, Lexington, Mass.

Roberts, Lawrence G. 1967. "Multiple Computer Networks and Intercomputer Communication," *Proceedings of the ACM Symposium on Operating System Principles*. Association for Computing Machinery, New York.

Roberts, Lawrence G. 1988. "Expanding AI Research and Founding ARPANET," p. 234 in *Expert Systems and Artificial Intelligence: Applications and Management*, Thomas C. Bartee, ed. Howard W. Sams & Co., Indianapolis, Ind.

Rochester, Nathaniel. 1959. *Symbol Manipulation Language*, AI Memo No. 5, MIT Artificial Intelligence Laboratory, Cambridge, Mass., November 18.

Rochester, Nathaniel, and Herbert Gelernter. 1958. "Intelligent Behavior in Problem-Solving Machines," *IBM Journal of Research and Development* 2(October):336-345.

Rosenberg, Nathan. 1987. "Civilian 'Spillovers' from Military R&D Spending: The U.S. Experience Since World War II," Chapter 9 in *Strategic Defense and Western Alliance*, Sanford Lakoff and Randy Willoughby, eds. D.C. Heath and Co., Lexington, Mass.

Rouselot, R.S., and R.A. Schumacker. 1967. *General Electric Real Time Display*, NASA Report NAS9-3916. National Aeronautics and Space Administration, Washington, D.C.

Rowell, Amy. 1998. "Virtual Vehicles Set the Pace," *Computer Graphics World* 21(3):61-62.

R.R. Bowker Company. 1992. *The Software Encyclopedia 1992, Vol. 2.* R.R. Bowker Company, New Providence, N.J.

Salton, G. 1987. "Historical Note: The Past Thirty Years in Information Retrieval," *Journal of the American Society for Information Science* 38(5):375-380.

Seidel, Robert. 1996. "From Mars to Minerva: The Origins of Scientific Computing in the AEC Labs," *Physics Today* 49(10):33-39.

SEMATECH. 1991. *Annual Report.* SEMATECH, Austin, Tex.

Shannon, Claude E. 1938. "A Symbolic Analysis of Relay and Switching Circuits," *Transactions of the American Institute of Electrical Engineers* 57:1-11.

Shannon, Claude E. 1948. "A Mathematical Theory of Communication," *Bell System Technical Journal* 27:379-423, 623-656.

Shannon, Claude E. 1949. "Communication Theory of Secrecy Systems," *Bell System Technical Journal* 30:50-64.

Shannon, Claude E. 1950a. "Automatic Chess Player," *Scientific American* 182(2):48-51.

Shannon, Claude E. 1950b. "Programming a Computer for Playing Chess," *Philosophical Magazine* 41:256-275.

Shannon, Claude E. 1993. *Collected Papers*, N.J.A. Sloane and A.D. Wyner, eds. IEEE Press, New York.

Shannon, Claude E., and John McCarthy, eds. 1956. "Automata Studies," *Annals of Mathematics Studies*, No. 34. Princeton University Press, Princeton, N.J.

Shrobe, Howard. 1996. "The Innovative Applications of Artificial Intelligence Conference: Past and Future," *AI Magazine* 8(Winter):16.

Sichel, D.E. 1997. *The Computer Revolution: An Economic Perspective.* Brookings Institution Press, Washington, D.C.

Simon, Herbert A. 1965. *The Shape of Automation for Men and Management.* Harper & Row, New York.

Simon, Herbert A. 1995. "Artificial Intelligence: An Empirical Science," *Artificial Intelligence* 77(1):95-127.

Simon, Herbert A., and Allen Newell. 1958. "Heuristic Problem Solving: The Next Advance in Operations Research," *Operations Research* 6:7-8.

Simon, Herbert A., Allen Newell, and J.C. Shaw. 1958. *The Process of Creative Thinking,* Paper-1320. RAND Corporation, Santa Monica, Calif., September 16.

Smith, Bruce. 1966. *The RAND Corporation: Case Study of a Nonprofit Advisory Corporation.* Harvard University Press, Cambridge, Mass.

Smith, D.K., and R.C. Alexander. 1988. *Fumbling the Future.* William Morrow, New York.

SRI International. 1997. "The Internet," Chapter IV in *The Role of NSF's Support of Engineering in Enabling Technological Innovation.* SRI International, Arlington, Va., February 14. Available online at <http://unix.sri.com/policy/stp/technin/inter1.html>.

Stefik, Mark. 1985. "Strategic Computing at DARPA: Overview and Assessment," *Communications of the ACM* 28(7):690-704.

Stockham, Thomas G., Jr., and Martin E. Newell. 1975. "Sensory Information Processing and Symbolic Computation Research Proposal, 1 October 1975 through 30 September 1977," Research Proposal to DARPA. Available from National Archives Branch Depository, Suitland, Maryland, RG 330-78-0012, Box 3, folder "Utah A02477," p. 81. Cited in Norberg, Arthur L., and Judy E. O'Neill, 1996, *Transforming Computer Technology: Information Processing for the Pentagon, 1962-1986,* Johns Hopkins University Press, Baltimore, Md.

Stonebraker, M. 1976. "The Design and Implementation of Ingres," *ACM Transactions on Database Systems* 1(3):189-222.

Stonebraker, M. 1980. "Retrospection on a Database System," *ACM Transactions on Database Systems* 5(2):225-240.

Stonebraker, M., ed. 1994. *Readings in Database Systems.* Morgan Kaufmann, San Mateo, Calif.

Sutherland, Ivan E. 1968. "A Head-Mounted Three Dimensional Display," pp. 757-764 in *Proceedings of the Fall Joint Computer Conference.* AFIPS Press, Montvale, N.J.

Sutherland, Ivan E., and Carver Mead. 1977. "Microelectronics and Computer Science," *Scientific American* 237(3):210-219.

Sutherland, Ivan E., Carver A. Mead, and T.E. Carver. 1976. *Basic Limitations in Microcircuit Fabrication Technology,* RAND Corporation Report No. AD-AO35149, prepared under DARPA contract DAHC15-73-C-0181, ARPA Order 1891, Santa Monica, Calif., November.

Sutherland, Ivan, Robert F. Sproull, and Robert A. Schumacker. 1974. "A Characterization of Ten Hidden Surface Algorithms," *ACM Computer Surveys* 6(1):1-55.

System Development Corporation. 1964. *Proceedings of the Symposium on Development and Management of a Computer-centered Data Base.* System Development Corporation, Santa Monica, Calif. Cited in Olle, T.W., 1978, *The Codasyl Approach to Database Management,* John Wiley & Sons, New York.

Tanenbaum, A.S. 1988. *Computer Networks.* Prentice-Hall, Englewood Cliffs, N.J.

Taylor, Robert. 1989. Interview with William Aspray, Palo Alto, Calif., OH 154, Charles Babbage Institute Center for the History of Information Processing, University of Minnesota, Minneapolis, February 28.

Tomash, Irwin. 1973. Interview with Robina Mapstone, Woodland Hills, Calif., OH 53, Charles Babbage Institute Center for the History of Information Processing, University of Minnesota, Minneapolis, March 30.

Tomayko, James. 1985. "NASA's Manned Spacecraft Computers," *Annals of the History of Computing* 7(1):7-18.

Turing, A.M. 1936. "On Computable Numbers with an Application to the Entscheidungsproblem," *Proceedings of the London Mathematics Society* 2:230-265.

U.S. Congress. 1991. "New Developments in Computer Technology: Virtual Reality." Hearing before the Subcommittee on Science, Technology, and Space of the Senate Committee on Commerce, Science, and Transportation, 102nd Congress, First Session, May 8.

U.S. Department of Commerce. 1967. *Technological Innovation: Its Environment and Management*, report of the Panel on Invention and Innovation. U.S. Government Printing Office, Washington, D.C., January.

U.S. Department of Commerce. 1997. *America's New Deficit: The Shortage of Information Technology Workers.* U.S. Government Printing Office, Washington, D.C.

U.S. Department of Defense (DOD). 1996. DOD Directive 5000.1, Section D: Policy, Para 2: Acquiring Quality Products, item (f): Modeling and Simulation. DOD, Washington, D.C., March 15.

U.S. Department of Defense (DOD), Office of the Inspector General. 1997. *Requirements Planning for Development, Test, Evaluation, and Impact on Readiness of Training Simulators and Device*, Appendix D, Draft proposed audit report, Project No. 5AB-0070.00, January 10. Cited in Computer Science and Telecommunications Board, National Research Council, 1997, *Modeling and Simulation: Linking Entertainment and Defense*, National Academy Press, Washington D.C.

U.S. Department of Labor, Bureau of Labor Statistics. 1997. *Employment and Earnings*, Vol. 44, No. 1, Table B-12. U.S. Government Printing Office, Washington, D.C.

U.S. General Accounting Office (GAO). 1992. *Federal Research: SEMATECH's Technological Progress and Proposed R&D Program*, GAO/RCED-92-223BR. U.S. Government Printing Office, Washington, D.C., July.

Van Atta, Richard H., Sidney Reed, and Seymour J. Deitchman. 1991a. *DARPA Technical Accomplishments, Volume II: An Historical Review of Selected DARPA Projects*, IDA Paper P-2429. Institute for Defense Analyses, Alexandria, Va., April.

Van Atta, Richard H., Seymour J. Deitchman, and Sidney Reed. 1991b. *DARPA Technical Accomplishments, Volume III: An Overall Perspective and Assessment of the Technical Accomplishments of the Defense Advanced Research Projects Agency: 1958-1990*, IDA Paper P-2538. Institute for Defense Analyses, Alexandria, Va., July.

Van Dam, Andries, et al. 1991. "From Discipline in Crisis to Mature Science: Evolving Needs for Computing Research Infrastructure," report on an NSF workshop. National Science Foundation, Washington, D.C., July.

Vardi, M.Y., and P. Wolper. 1986. "An Automata-theoretic Approach to Automatic Program Verification," pp. 322-331 in *Proceedings of the Symposium on Logic in Computer Science.* IEEE Press, New York.

VLSI Research. 1992. As cited in the *Washington Post*, November 18, p. A7.

Warnock, John E. 1969. *A Hidden Surface Algorithm for Computer Generated Half-Tone Pictures*, Ph.D. dissertation, Department of Computer Science, University of Utah.

Watkins, Garry S. 1970. *A Real-Time Visible Surface Algorithm*, Ph.D. dissertation, Department of Computer Science, University of Utah.

Weaver, Warren. 1955. Diary of Warren Weaver, April 4, 1955. Available in the records of the Rockefeller Foundation, Rockefeller Archive Center, North Tarrytown, N.Y.

Weik, M.H. 1955. *A Survey of Domestic Electronic Digital Computing Systems.* Ballistics Research Laboratories, Aberdeen, Md.

West, C.H., and P. Zafiropulo. 1978. "Automated Validation of a Communications Protocol: The CCITT X.21 Recommendation," *IBM Journal of Research and Development* 22:60-71.

Wiederhold, Gio. 1984. "Databases," *IEEE Computer* 10(October):211-223.

Woodcock, Steven. 1997. Interview on the future of AI technology and the impact of multiplayer network-capable games, *Wall Street Journal Interactive Edition*, May 19.

Zakon, Robert H. 1998. *Hobbes' Internet Timeline, version 3.3.* Available online at <http://www.isoc.org/guest/zakon/Internet/history/HIT.html>.

Ziegler, Bart. 1997. "Lab Experiment: Gerstner Slashed R&D by $1 Billion; for IBM, It May Be a Good Thing—Latest Breakthrough Shows," *Wall Street Journal*, October 6, p. A1.

APPENDIX

Committee Biographies

THOMAS HUGHES (*chair*) is professor emeritus at the University of Pennsylvania and is currently Distinguished Visiting Professor at the Massachusetts Institute of Technology. He will be visiting professor at Stanford University and at the Royal Institute of Technology (Stockholm) in spring 1999. Professor Hughes is a member of the Royal Swedish Academy of Engineering Sciences, a Fellow of the American Academy of Arts and Sciences, and a member of Phi Beta Kappa. In 1985 he was awarded the Leonardo da Vinci Medal of the Society for the History of Technology. The Society for the Social Studies of Science awarded him the John Desmond Bernal Award in 1990. In 1990 he received the Kenan Enterprise Award. The Johns Hopkins University named him a member of the Society of Fellows in 1984. He has been a Fellow of the Wissenschaftskolleg (Institute of Advanced Study Berlin) and Distinguished Visiting Professor, New School for Social Research. His most recent book, *Rescuing Prometheus* (Pantheon Books, 1998) is about large technological systems. Previous publications include *Networks of Power: Electrification of Western Society, 1880-1930* and *Elmer Sperry: Inventor and Engineer*, both of which won the Dexter Prize for the outstanding book on the history of technology (in 1985 and 1972, respectively). With Agatha Hughes he edited *Lewis Mumford: Public Intellectual* (Oxford University Press, 1990). Dr. Hughes completed his graduate work in European history at the University of Virginia.

GWEN BELL is the founding president of The Computer Museum. She started the first and only computer museum in the world. Dr. Bell successfully applied for nonprofit status in 1981, moved to downtown Boston and opened a 42,000-square-foot facility in 1984, raised $3.3 million in capital and grew the operating budget from $30,000 to $1 million per year, and achieved a unique joint collecting agreement with the Smithsonian Institution's National Museum of American History. Before that, she was a social science editor for Pergamon Press where she was responsible for a 125-book product line. Dr. Bell was visiting associate professor, Graduate School of Design, Harvard University from 1972 to 1973. She was also associate professor of urban affairs, Graduate School of Public and International Affairs, University of Pittsburgh. Her published books are *Strategies for Human Settlements* (University Press of Hutchinson & Ross: Stroudsburg, Pennsylvania) and *Human Identity in the Urban Environment* with J. Tyrwhitt (A Pelican Original, London and New York). Dr. Bell was a United Nations consultant for Indonesia, The Philippines, and Brazil from 1970 to 1977. She received her Ph.D. in geography from Clark University, Worcester, Massachusetts, in 1967, her M.C.R.P. in city and regional planning from Harvard University in 1959, and her B.S. from the University of Wisconsin at Madison.

ERICH BLOCH is a Distinguished Fellow with the Counsel on Competitiveness. He was previously the director of the National Science Foundation (1984-1990) and a corporate vice-president for technical personnel development at IBM, which he joined in 1952 after receiving a B.S. degree in electrical engineering from the University of Buffalo. He is the recipient of many honorary degrees and the National Medal of Technology for his part in the development of the IBM/System 360 computer, which "revolutionized the computer industry." Mr. Bloch has received the Institute of Electrical and Electronics Engineers (IEEE) Computer Pioneer Award, the IEEE Founders Medal, and the National Academy of Engineering's Bueche Award. He is a member of the National Academy of Engineering, Sweden's Academy of Engineering Sciences, and the Japan Academy of Engineering, a Fellow of the IEEE, a member of its Computer Society, and a Fellow of the American Association for the Advancement of Science.

ROBERT BRESSLER is chief scientist of networking for Sun Microsystems, Inc. His responsibilities include charting the future directions for networking products and advanced development in networking for Sun as well as working across all the Sun companies to guide the direction of networking technologies. Prior to joining Sun in 1994, Mr. Bressler spent 4 years at Network Equipment Technologies (N.E.T.) as senior vice-president, technology and corporate development, and chief technical officer. His responsibilities included long-term strategic planning and overall product architecture for N.E.T. and ADAPTIVE, as well as the investment strategy for R&D spending, and advanced R&D activities. Before joining N.E.T. in 1990, Mr. Bressler spent 4 years at 3Com Corporation. His most recent assignment at 3Com was as chief technical officer and vice-president, corporate development. His responsibilities included overall product strategy for 3Com, and, in particular, the creation, with Microsoft, of the OS/2 LAN Manager. Prior to joining 3Com in 1986, Mr. Bressler spent more than 13 years with Bolt, Beranek, and Newman, Inc. (BBN), in Cambridge, Massachusetts, where he held a variety of senior management positions, most recently senior vice-president of development and engineering for BBN Communications. At BBN, Mr. Bressler played a key role in the management and development of packet switching for data communications including the ARPANET and the evolution of protocols including TCP/IP, X.25, satellite-based communications, and data communications security. Mr. Bressler holds both an MSEE and a BSEE from the Massachusetts Institute of Technology. His thesis topic was in the area of distributed computing, the research for which was all done on the ARPANET.

PAUL DAVID is an economist and economic historian who has held the William Robertson Coe Professorship of American Economic History at Stanford University since 1978. He was educated at Harvard University and the University of Cambridge, and joined the Stanford Economics Department in 1961. The evolution and diffusion of technological systems and the role of technological and organizational innovation in long-term economic growth have been focal points in Dr. David's research and teaching, which has included such themes as the importance of the systems approach to understanding technological change, the economic significance of network externalities and technical standards in system development, and the "path-dependent," historical character of these processes. A frequent contributor to books and scholarly journals, Dr. David currently co-edits *Economics of Innovation and New Technology* and serves on the editorial boards of *Computers, Standards and Interfaces*, the *Journal of Industrial and Corporate Change*, and other journals. He has been a consultant to the National Research Council, the Library of Congress, the World Bank, the Organisation for Economic Cooperation and Development, and other national and international bodies. Dr. David is a Fellow of the American Academy of Arts and Sciences and a Fellow of the International Econometric Society. In May of 1993 he was elected to a senior research fellowship in economics at All Souls College, Oxford.

MARVIN DENICOFF graduated from Temple University in 1949 with a degree in liberal arts. He did graduate work in literature and linguistics at Temple University and Mexico City College. Mr. Denicoff joined the Navy Department in 1951, and was among the early civil service trainees in the emerging fields of computer science and operations research. Beginning in 1954, he was assigned to George Washington University as liaison for research in logistics and computation. During a 6-year period with George Washington University, he wrote or co-wrote more than 20 scientific papers in the topic areas of inventory control, value theory, failure analysis, and business data processing. In 1960, Mr. Denicoff took a research management position with the Office of Naval Research (ONR) and 2 years later became director of the Information Sciences Program. In this capacity, he directed, until his retirement in August 1983, a multimillion-dollar-per-year basic research grant program in such fields as artificial intelligence, robotics, computer graphics, man-machine systems, computer architecture, and software. Mr. Denicoff has served as ex-officio member of the Computer Science Board of the National Research Council and has been a participant, leader, or advisor to such government groups as the Department of Defense (DOD) Tri-Service Software Research Committee, the Science Advisory Board on Supercomputers, and the United States Information Agency Program on Artificial Intelligence. Mr. Denicoff has been honored for his government service with a Meritorious Service Award; he is one of the few individuals who have been given two Distinguished Civilian Service Awards. In 1983, he was given a special award by the American Association for Artificial Intelligence for continuing contributions to that field of research. Mr. Denicoff was a co-founder, in 1983, of Thinking Machines Corporation and served with that firm as a vice-president and board member until his retirement in 1996. He has had an affiliation with the Massachusetts Institute of Technology's Media Lab in the capacity of principal research associate. In addition to his long career in computer science, Mr. Denicoff is a short-story writer and playwright. His stories have been published in various literary magazines and anthologies.

DAVID HOUNSHELL is Luce Professor of Technology and Social Change at Carnegie Mellon University, where he studies innovation in both its technological and its organizational dimensions. Since 1982, he has addressed the rise of industrial research and development in the United States and the problems of managing scientific and technical research in organizations. He is also studying the Cold War and its influence on the pursuit of science, technology, and enterprise in the United States, and this work has led to one of his current projects, a history of the RAND Corporation of Santa Monica, California, from its creation in 1948 to the end of the Cold War. Another current project is the development of a sequel to his first book, which will bring his study of the development of American manufacturing technology to the end of the 20th century. His long-term writing project is a book tentatively titled *The Wealth of a Nation: The Dynamics of Science, Technology, and Business in the United States, 1775-1990*. A shorter-term project is his editorial work on a massive diary kept by the late Crawford H. Greenewalt in his role as liaison between the University of Chicago's Metallurgical Laboratory and the DuPont Company during the Manhattan Project (the atomic bomb project); this diary will be published by the American Philosophical Society. Hounshell received the 1978 Browder J. Thompson Memorial Prize Award of the IEEE, the 1987 Dexter Prize in the history of technology, the 1992 Thomas Newcomen Award in business history, and the 1992 Williamson Medal from the Business History Conference.

AMOS JOEL is retired after a 43-year career at Lucent Bell Laboratories. He is a pioneer in the design, development, and evaluation of electronic switching and information processing systems. He has lectured and written extensively in the United States and abroad on switching principles and history. Mr. Joel received a B.S. (1940) and an M.S. (1942) from the Massachusetts Institute of Technology. He is a life Fellow of the IEEE and a member of the National Academy of Engineering, the Association for Computing Machinery, the American Association for the Advancement of Science, and the American Academy of Arts and Sciences. Mr. Joel has won numerous awards, including the IEEE Medal of Honor (1992) and Bell Medal (1972), the International Telecommunications Union (ITU) Centenary Award (1983), the Columbian Genoa Prize (1984), the Kyoto Prize (1989), and the U.S. National Medal of Technology (1993).

TIMOTHY LENOIR is professor and co-chair of Stanford University's program on the history of science. Dr. Lenoir received a B.A. (1970) from Saint Mary's College, Morage, California. He also received a Ph.D. in the history and philosophy of science from Indiana University in 1974. He has received numerous honors and awards, including a NATO Postdoctoral Fellowship in Science (1975-1976), an NSF Research Grant (1978-1980), and the Provost's Research Fund Award, Stanford University (1994). Among his many publications are *The Strategy of Life: Teleology and Mechanics in Nineteenth Century German Biology* (D. Reidel, Dordrecht and Boston, 1982), *Politik im Tempel der Wissenschaft: Forschung und Machtausubung im deutschen Kaiserreich* (Campus Verlag, Frankfurt/Main, 1992), *Instituting Science: The Cultural Production of Scientific Disciplines* (Stanford University Press, 1997), and *Inscribing Science: Scientific Texts and the Materiality of Communication* (Stanford University Press, 1998).

M. DOUGLAS McILROY, retired from Bell Laboratories, is an adjunct professor of computer science at Dartmouth College. His research interests focus on computer programming and systems, especially programming languages and text processing, graphics algorithms, searching and sorting, and computer security. He received a B.E.P. (1954) from Cornell University and a Ph.D. (mathematics, 1959) from the Massachusetts Institute of Technology. He is a Fellow of the American Association for the Advancement of Science.

EMERSON W. PUGH is the author or co-author of a college physics text and four books on the history of IBM and the information processing industry. His most recent book is *Building IBM: Shaping an Industry and Its Technology* (MIT Press, 1995). After receiving his Ph.D. in physics from the Carnegie Institute of Technology in 1956, Dr. Pugh worked for IBM for 35 years in a variety of capacities, including research scientist, product development manager, and corporate executive. He is chairman of the IEEE History Committee, a director of the IEEE Foundation, a trustee of the Charles Babbage Foundation, and a trustee of the Samuel F.B. Morse Historic Site. Dr. Pugh is a Fellow of the IEEE, the American Physical Society, and the American Association for the Advancement of Science, and he served as president of the IEEE in 1989.

CHARLES L. SEITZ is president of Myricom, Inc., a start-up company involved in research, development, production, and sales of high-speed computers and local-area networks. During the 16 years before founding Myricom, he was a professor of computer science at the California Institute of Technology (Caltech), where his research and teaching were in the areas of very large scale integrated circuit (VLSI) design, computer architecture and programming, and concurrent computation. He earned S.B. (1965), S.M. (1967), and Ph.D. (1971) degrees from the Massachusetts Institute of Technology, where he was also an instructor and the recipient of the Goodwin Medal for "conspicuously effective teaching." He was a consultant and member of the technical staff of the Evans & Sutherland Computer Corporation during its initial years (1968-1972), an assistant professor of computer science at the University of Utah (1970-1972), and a consultant and leader of several research and development projects for Burroughs Corporation (1971-1978). His research in VLSI and concurrent computing at Caltech, including the development of the Cosmic Cube multicomputer, was selected by *Science Digest* as one of the top 100 innovations in 1985. Dr. Seitz was elected to the National Academy of Engineering in 1992 for "pioneering contributions to the design of asynchronous and concurrent computer systems."

CHARLES THACKER is director of advanced systems for Microsoft Corporation. He was previously a senior corporate consultant engineer at Digital Equipment Corporation's Systems Research Center. During his 13 years at Digital, Mr. Thacker led the development of Firefly (the first multiprocessor workstation), the Alpha Demonstration Unit, the first Alpha system, and the AN1 and AN2 networks, precursors of Digital's Gigaswitch/ATM products. Before joining Digital, he spent 13 years at the Xerox Palo Alto Research Center, where he was responsible for the development of a number of experimental computer systems including Alto, the first personal workstation. He is a co-inventor of the Ethernet local area network and holds over 20 patents in computer architecture and networking. Mr. Thacker is a Fellow of the Association for Computing Machinery and a member of the National Academy of Engineering.